**THE UNBEATABLE SQUIRREL GIRL VOL. 2: SQUIRREL YOU KNOW IT'S TRUE.** Contains material originally published in magazine form as THE UNBEATABLE SQUIRREL GIRL #5-8, GLX-MAS SPECIAL #1, THE THING #8 and AGE OF HEROES #3. Second printing 2018. ISBN 978-0-7851-9703-4. Published by MARVEL WORLDWIDE, INC., a subsidiary of MARVEL ENTERTAINMENT, LLC. OFFICE OF PUBLICATION: 135 West 50th Street, New York, NY 10020. Copyright © 2015 MARVEL No similarity between any of the names, characters, persons, and/or institutions in this magazine with those of any living or dead person or institution is intended, and any such similarity which may exist is purely coincidental. **Printed in Canada.** DAN BUCKLEY, President, Marvel Entertainment; JOHN NEE, Publisher; JOE QUESADA, Chief Creative Officer; TOM BREVOORT, SVP of Publishing; DAVID BOGART, SVP of Business Affairs & Operations, Publishing & Partnership; DAVID GABRIEL, SVP of Sales & Marketing, Publishing; JEFF YOUNGQUIST, VP of Production & Special Projects; DAN CARR, Executive Director of Publishing Technology; ALEX MORALES, Director of Publishing Operations; SUSAN CRESPI, Production Manager; STAN LEE, Chairman Emeritus. For information regarding advertising in Marvel Comics or on Marvel.com, please contact Vit DeBellis, Custom Solutions & Integrated Advertising Manager, at vdebellis@marvel.com. For Marvel subscription inquiries, please call 888-511-5480. **Manufactured between 2/14/2018 and 2/27/2018 by SOLISCO PRINTERS, SCOTT, QC, CANADA.**

1 0 9 8 7 6 5 4 3 2

P9-CEN-342

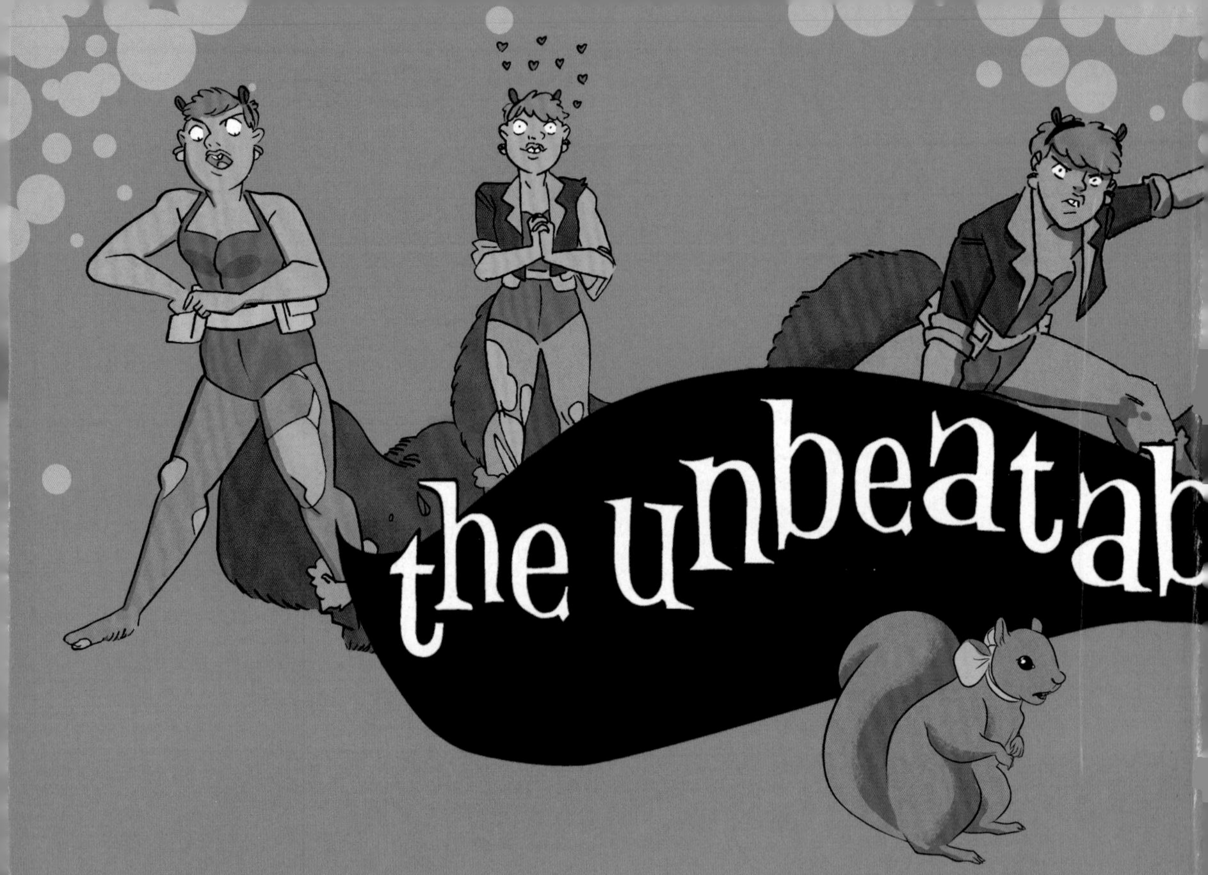
the unbeatab

***GLX-Mas Special #1***
“EGGNOG, TOILET PAPER AND PEACE ON EARTH”

WRITER: **DAN SLOTT**
ARTIST: **MATT HALEY**
LETTERER: **DAVE LANPHEAR**
COVER ART: **PAUL PELLETIER, RICK MAGYAR & WIL QUINTANA**
ASSISTANT EDITORS: **ANDY SCHMIDT, MOLLY LAZER & AUBREY SITTERSON**
EDITOR: **TOM BREVOORT**

***The Thing #8***
“LAST HAND”

WRITER: **DAN SLOTT**
ARTIST: **KIERON DWYER**
COLOR ARTIST: **LAURA VILLARI**
LETTERER: **DAVE LANPHEAR**
COVER ART: **ANDREA DI VITO & LAURA VILLARI**
ASSISTANT EDITORS: **ANDY SCHMIDT, MOLLY LAZER & AUBREY SITTERSON**
EDITOR: **TOM BREVOORT**

***Age of Heroes #3***
“NUTS TO THIS”

WRITER: **DAN SLOTT**
ARTIST: **TY TEMPLETON**
COLOR ARTIST: **JORGE MAESE**
LETTERER: **DAVE LANPHEAR**
COVER ART: **YANICK PAQUETTE, MICHEL LACOMBE & NATHAN FAIRBAIRN**
EDITORS: **LAUREN SANKOVITCH & TOM BREVOORT**

COLLECTION EDITOR: **JENNIFER GRÜNWALD**
ASSISTANT EDITOR: **CAITLIN O’CONNELL**
ASSOCIATE MANAGING EDITOR: **KATERI WOODY**
EDITOR, SPECIAL PROJECTS: **MARK D. BEAZLEY**
VP PRODUCTION & SPECIAL PROJECTS: **JEFF YOUNGQUIST**
SVP PRINT, SALES & MARKETING: **DAVID GABRIEL**
BOOK DESIGNER: **JAY BOWEN**

EDITOR IN CHIEF: **C.B. CEBULSKI**
CHIEF CREATIVE OFFICER: **JOE QUESADA**
PRESIDENT: **DAN BUCKLEY**
EXECUTIVE PRODUCER: **ALAN FINE**

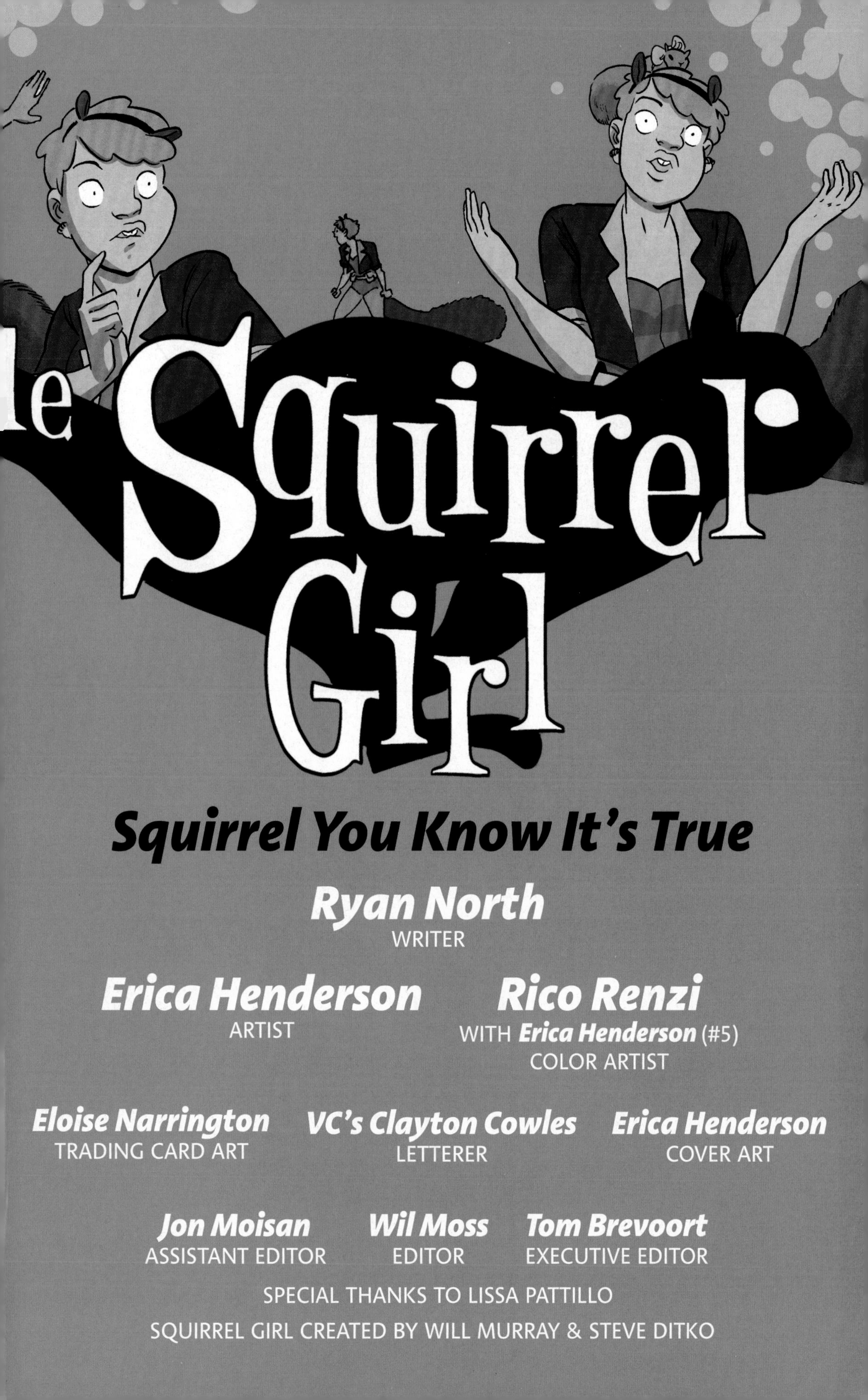
Squirrel Girl

# Squirrel You Know It's True


**Ryan North**
WRITER

**Erica Henderson**
ARTIST

**Rico Renzi**
WITH **Erica Henderson** (#5)
COLOR ARTIST

**Eloise Narrington**
TRADING CARD ART

**VC's Clayton Cowles**
LETTERER

**Erica Henderson**
COVER ART

**Jon Moisan**
ASSISTANT EDITOR

**Wil Moss**
EDITOR

**Tom Brevoort**
EXECUTIVE EDITOR


SPECIAL THANKS TO LISSA PATTILLO

SQUIRREL GIRL CREATED BY WILL MURRAY & STEVE DITKO

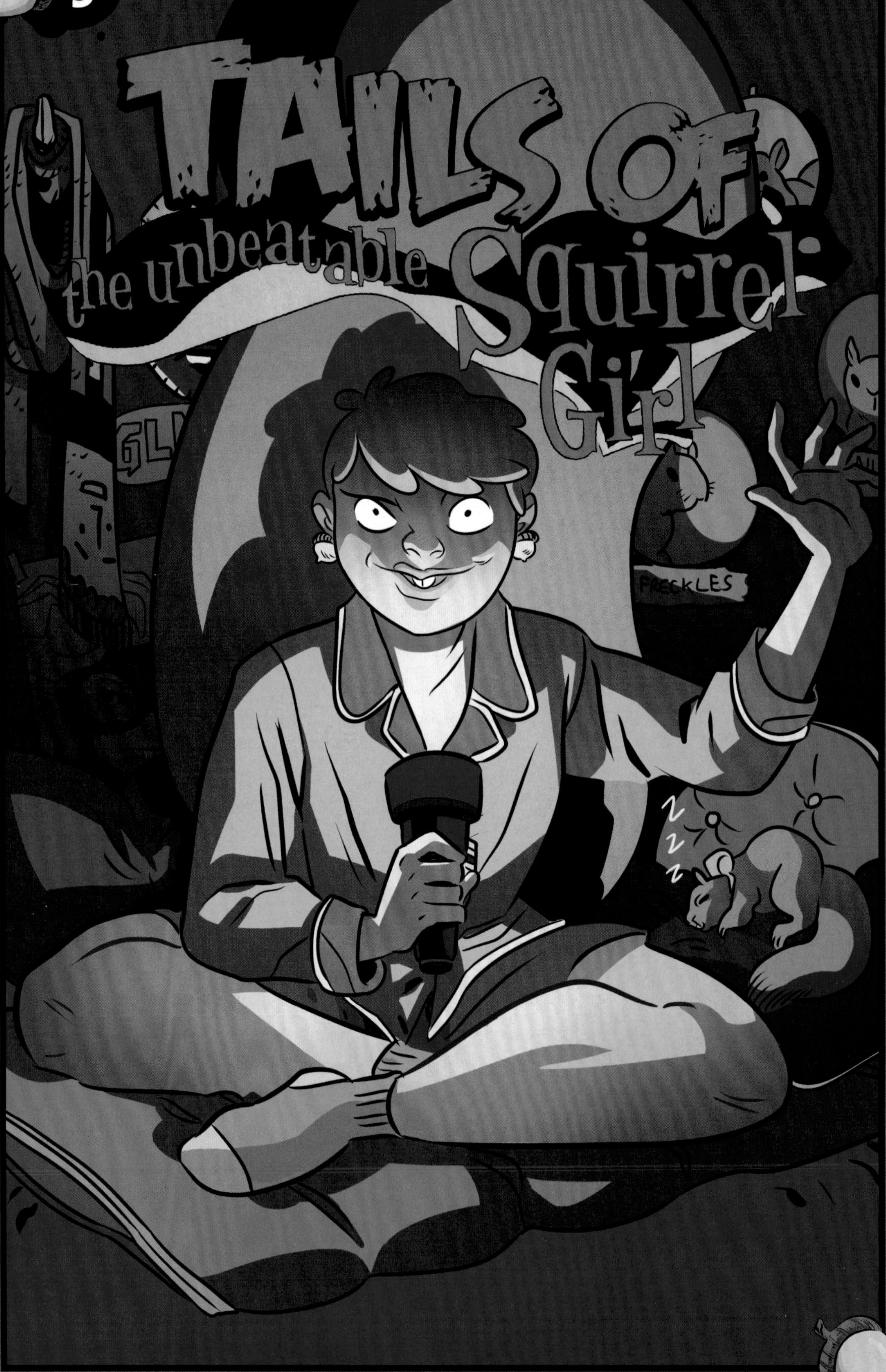
TAILS OF
the unbeatable Squirrel Girl
FRECKLES
Z
Z
Z

Doreen Green isn't just a first-year computer science student: she secretly also has all the powers of both squirrel and girl! She uses her amazing abilities to fight crime **and** be as awesome as possible. You know her as...The Unbeatable Squirrel Girl! Let's catch up with what she's been up to until now, with...

# Squirrel Girl *in a nutshell*

**search!**

#dinosaurs

#basslass

#clones

#acronyms

#nuthorde

#TIPPPPPPPY!!

**Squirrel Girl!** @unbeatablesg
@xGALACTUSx hey dude thanks for not eating the planet after all!!

**GALACTUS** @xGALACTUSx
@unbeatablesg NO PROBLEM THAT PLANET OF NUTS YOU FOUND WAS WAY BETTER ANYWAY

**Deadpool** @pooltothedead
@unbeatablesg @xGALACTUSx Wait, what? You guys weren't joking about that?

**Deadpool** @pooltothedead
@unbeatablesg @xGALACTUSx Galactus ACTUALLY came to Earth?? Yesterday? The ACTUAL GALACTUS was HERE??

**Deadpool** @pooltothedead
@unbeatablesg @xGALACTUSx dang man I spent the whole day at home watching tv in my underpants

**Deadpool** @pooltothedead
@unbeatablesg @xGALACTUSx CALL ME NEXT TIME!!

**Tony Stark** @starkmantony ✓
A bunch of my Iron Man suit parts showed up in NYC with moon dust on them. That's actually extremely valuable, so thanks @unbeatablesg.

**Tippy-Toe** @yoitstippytoe
@starkmantony CHITT CHUK CHITTT?

**Tony Stark** @starkmantony ✓
@yoitstippytoe I can't understand you. None of my translation algorithms can understand you. Probably because you are a literal squirrel.

**Tippy-Toe** @yoitstippytoe
@starkmantony CHUKKA.... CHITT CHUK CHITTT?

**Tony Stark** @starkmantony ✓
@unbeatablesg Little help?

**Squirrel Girl!** @unbeatablesg
@starkmantony she's asking you if you figured out that the dust came from the new moon restaurant

**Tony Stark** @starkmantony ✓
@unbeatablesg @yoitstippytoe What new moon restaurant?

**Tippy-Toe** @yoitstippytoe
@starkmantony CHUTT CHUK CHUKK CHITTY CHIT

**Squirrel Girl!** @unbeatablesg
@starkmantony She says "The one that just opened up! The food's good, but it doesn't have much of an ATMOSPHERE"

**Squirrel Girl!** @unbeatablesg
@starkmantony hahaha, that's pretty good actually!! good work @yoitstippytoe

**Tony Stark** @starkmantony ✓
@unbeatablesg @yoitstippytoe You guys know I'm the head of a major corporation, right?

**Tony Stark** @starkmantony ✓
@unbeatablesg @yoitstippytoe I shouldn't even be hanging out here as it is

**Nancy W.** @sewwiththeflo
I bet being covered from head to toe in a living squirrel suit doesn't smell as bad as you think it would.

**Nancy W.** @sewwiththeflo
IMPORTANT UPDATE:

**Nancy W.** @sewwiththeflo
So it turns out being covered head to toe in a living squirrel suit doesn't smell as GOOD as you think it would either

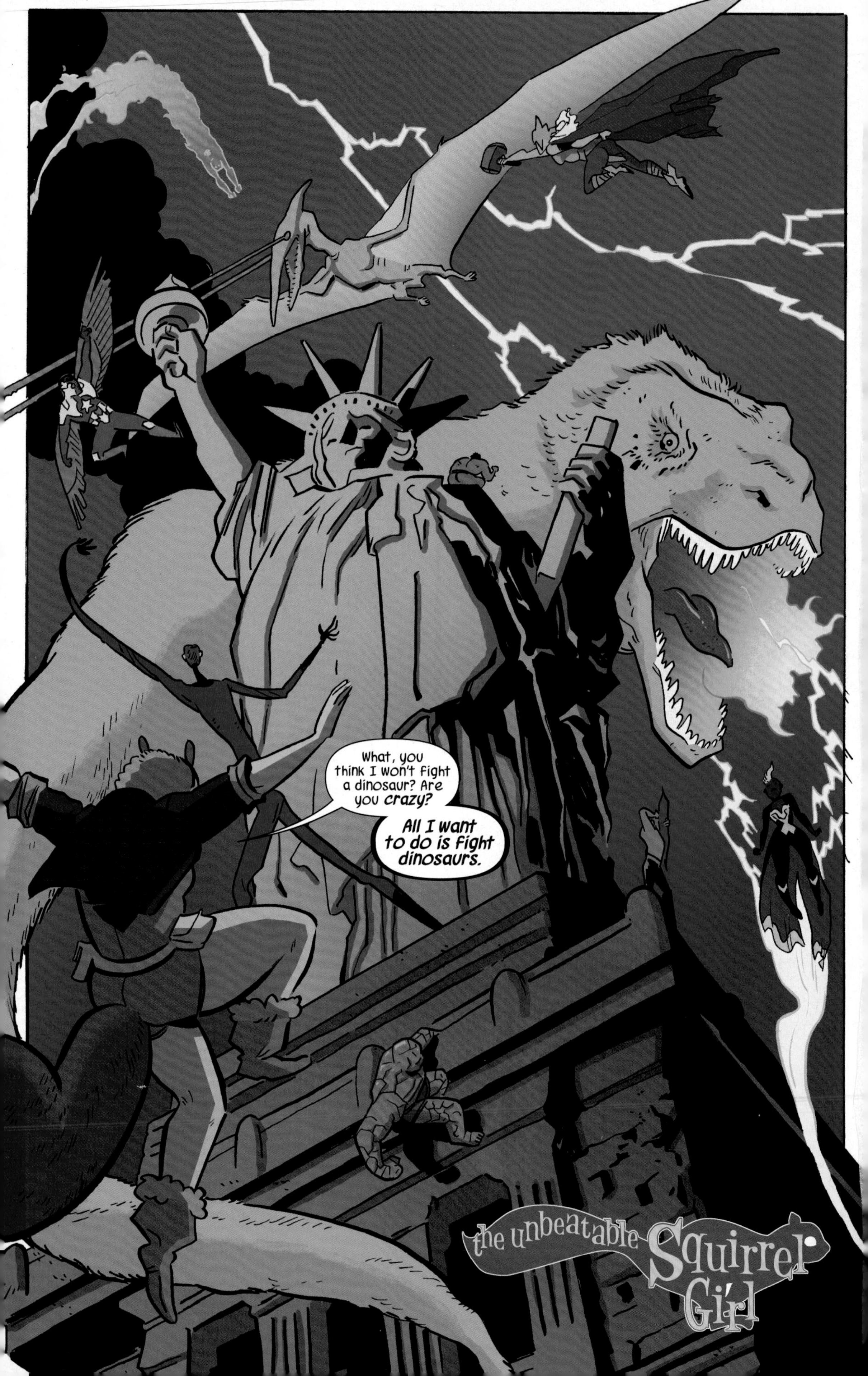
What, you think I won't fight a dinosaur? Are you crazy?
All I want to do is fight dinosaurs.
the unbeatable Squirrel Girl

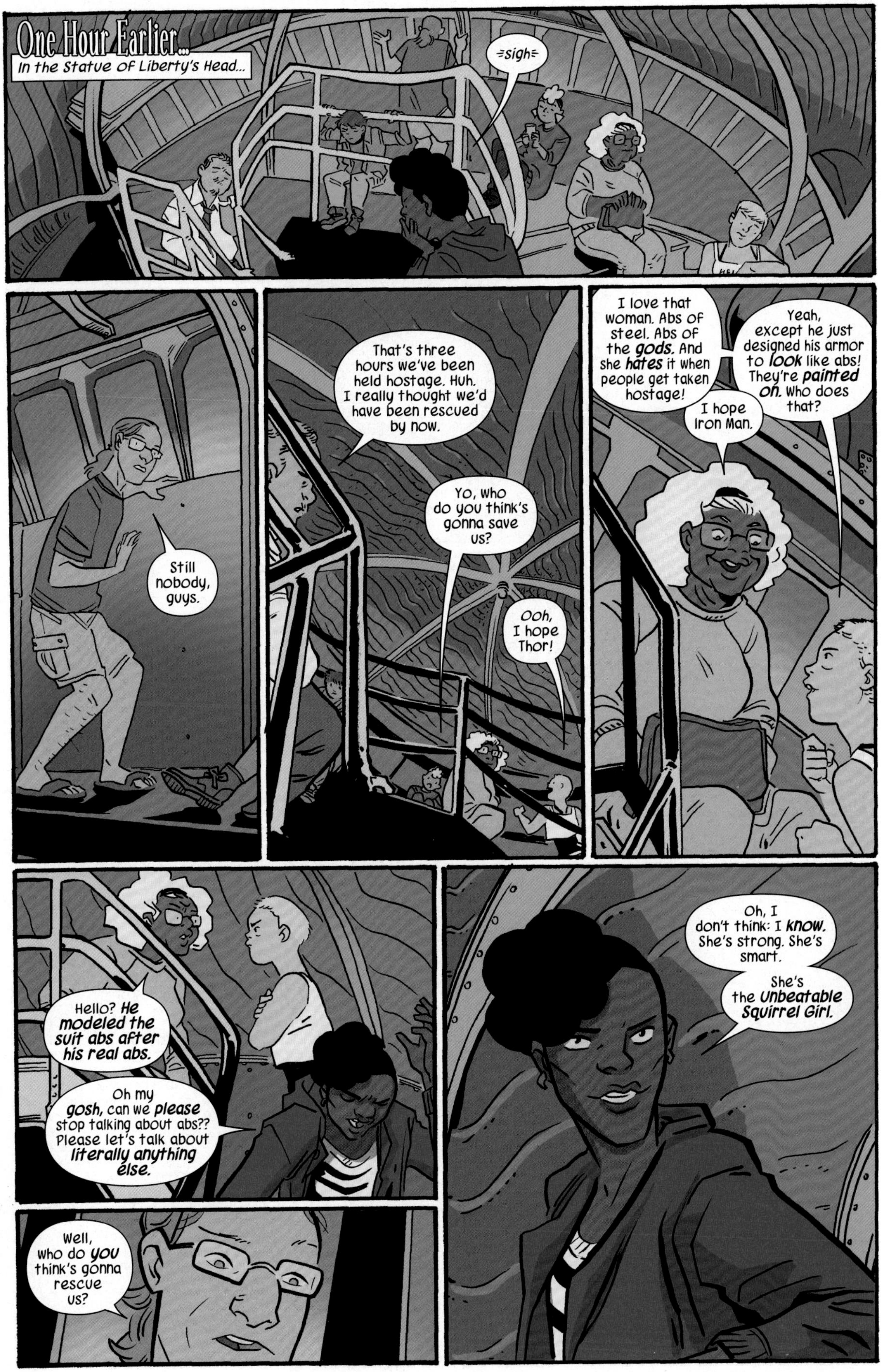
One Hour Earlier...
In the Statue of Liberty's Head...
=sigh=
Still nobody, guys.
That's three hours we've been held hostage. Huh. I really thought we'd have been rescued by now.
Yo, who do you think's gonna save us?
Ooh, I hope Thor!
I hope Iron Man.
I love that woman. Abs of steel. Abs of the gods. And she hates it when people get taken hostage!
Yeah, except he just designed his armor to look like abs! They're painted on. Who does that?
Hello? He modeled the suit abs after his real abs.
Oh my gosh, can we please stop talking about abs?? Please let's talk about literally anything else.
Well, who do you think's gonna rescue us?
Oh, I don't think: I know. She's strong. She's smart.
She's the Unbeatable Squirrel Girl.

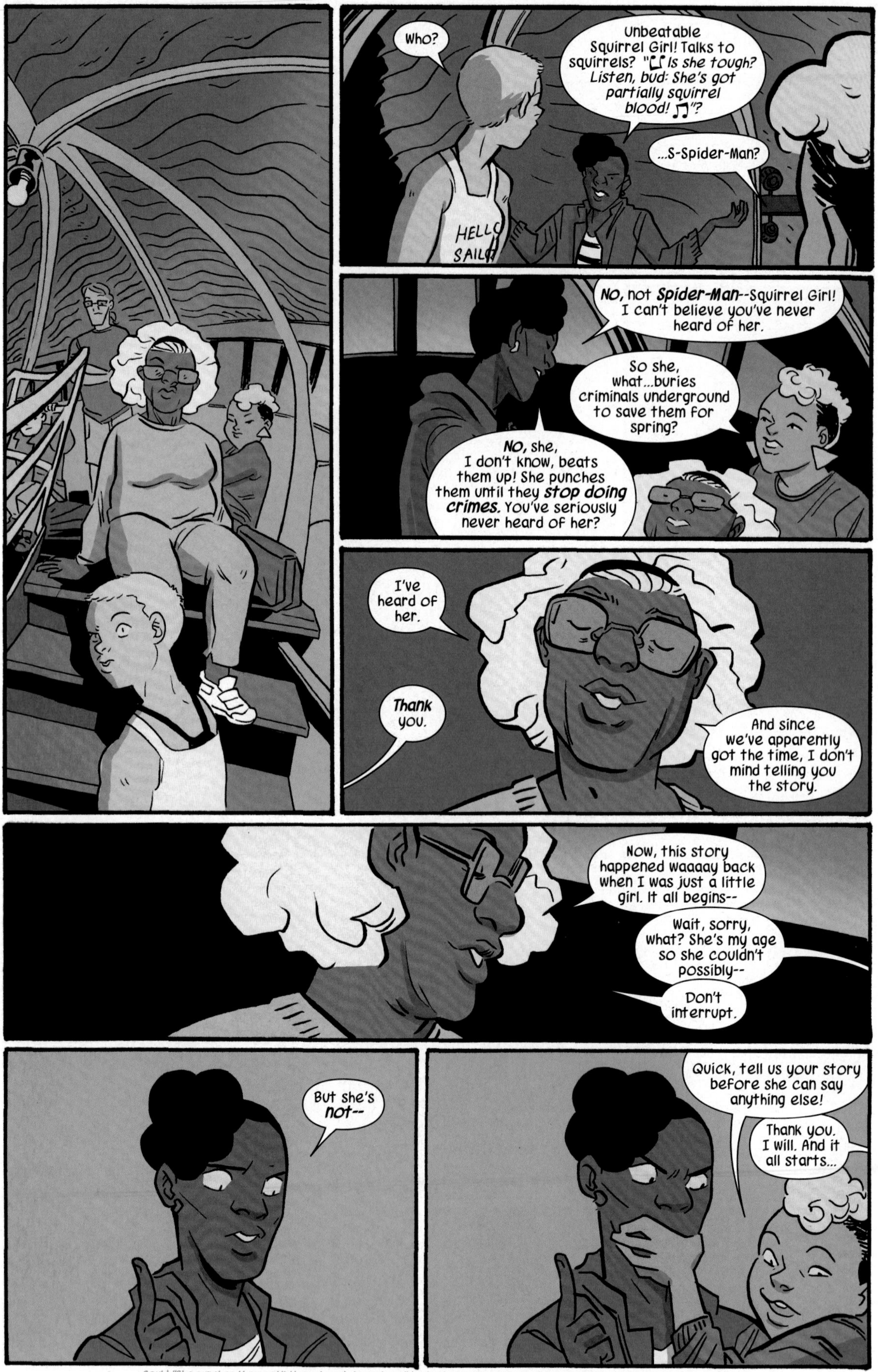
Who?
Unbeatable Squirrel Girl! Talks to squirrels? "♫ Is she tough? Listen, bud: She's got partially squirrel blood! ♫"?
...S-Spider-Man?
HELLO SAILOR
NO, not Spider-Man--Squirrel Girl! I can't believe you've never heard of her.
So she, what...buries criminals underground to save them for spring?
NO, she, I don't know, beats them up! She punches them until they stop doing crimes. You've seriously never heard of her?
I've heard of her.
Thank you.
And since we've apparently got the time, I don't mind telling you the story.
Now, this story happened waaaay back when I was just a little girl. It all begins--
Wait, sorry, what? She's my age so she couldn't possibly--
Don't interrupt.
But she's not--
Quick, tell us your story before she can say anything else!
Thank you. I will. And it all starts...

Could "She punches them until they stop doing crimes" be basically the perfect description of every super hero ever? This author who just now wrote that sentence says: yes!

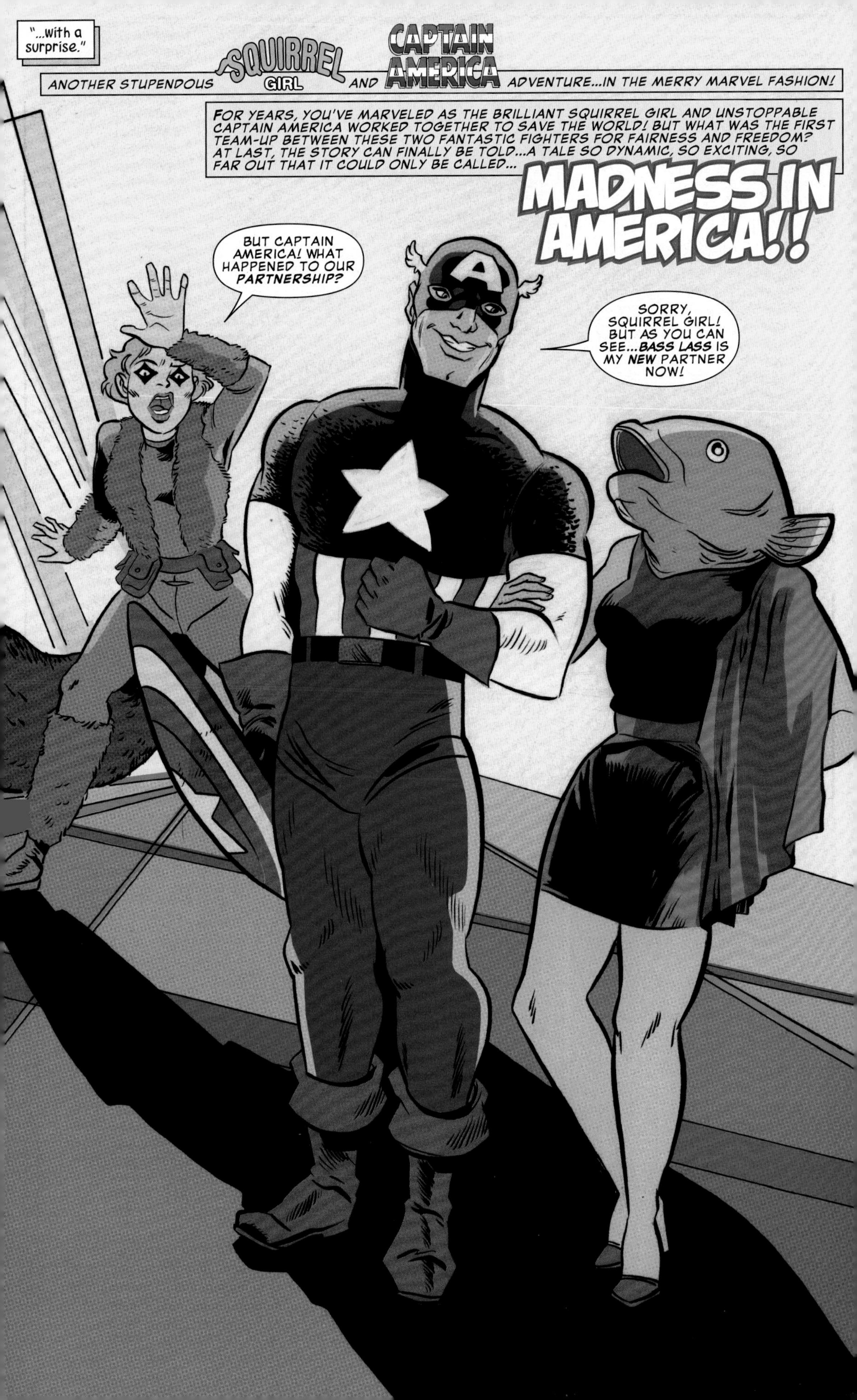
"...with a surprise."
ANOTHER STUPENDOUS SQUIRREL GIRL AND CAPTAIN AMERICA ADVENTURE...IN THE MERRY MARVEL FASHION!
FOR YEARS, YOU'VE MARVELED AS THE BRILLIANT SQUIRREL GIRL AND UNSTOPPABLE CAPTAIN AMERICA WORKED TOGETHER TO SAVE THE WORLD! BUT WHAT WAS THE FIRST TEAM-UP BETWEEN THESE TWO FANTASTIC FIGHTERS FOR FAIRNESS AND FREEDOM? AT LAST, THE STORY CAN FINALLY BE TOLD...A TALE SO DYNAMIC, SO EXCITING, SO FAR OUT THAT IT COULD ONLY BE CALLED...
MADNESS IN AMERICA!!
BUT CAPTAIN AMERICA! WHAT HAPPENED TO OUR PARTNERSHIP?
SORRY, SQUIRREL GIRL! BUT AS YOU CAN SEE...BASS LASS IS MY NEW PARTNER NOW!

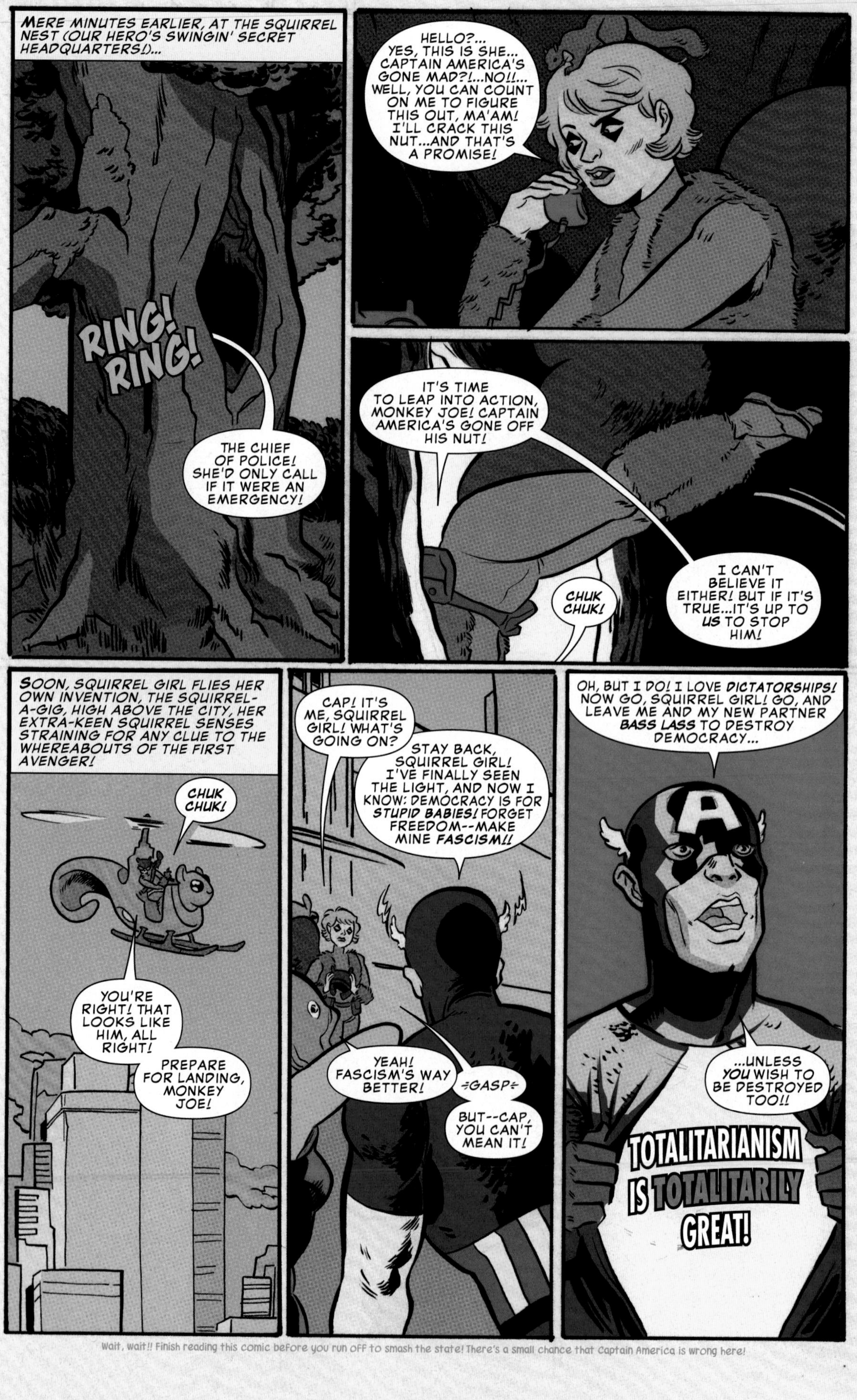
MERE MINUTES EARLIER, AT THE SQUIRREL NEST (OUR HERO'S SWINGIN' SECRET HEADQUARTERS!)...
RING! RING!
THE CHIEF OF POLICE! SHE'D ONLY CALL IF IT WERE AN EMERGENCY!
HELLO?... YES, THIS IS SHE... CAPTAIN AMERICA'S GONE MAD?!...NO!!... WELL, YOU CAN COUNT ON ME TO FIGURE THIS OUT, MA'AM! I'LL CRACK THIS NUT...AND THAT'S A PROMISE!
IT'S TIME TO LEAP INTO ACTION, MONKEY JOE! CAPTAIN AMERICA'S GONE OFF HIS NUT!
CHUK CHUK!
I CAN'T BELIEVE IT EITHER! BUT IF IT'S TRUE...IT'S UP TO US TO STOP HIM!
SOON, SQUIRREL GIRL FLIES HER OWN INVENTION, THE SQUIRREL-A-GIG, HIGH ABOVE THE CITY, HER EXTRA-KEEN SQUIRREL SENSES STRAINING FOR ANY CLUE TO THE WHEREABOUTS OF THE FIRST AVENGER!
CHUK CHUK!
YOU'RE RIGHT! THAT LOOKS LIKE HIM, ALL RIGHT!
PREPARE FOR LANDING, MONKEY JOE!
CAP! IT'S ME, SQUIRREL GIRL! WHAT'S GOING ON?
STAY BACK, SQUIRREL GIRL! I'VE FINALLY SEEN THE LIGHT, AND NOW I KNOW: DEMOCRACY IS FOR STUPID BABIES! FORGET FREEDOM--MAKE MINE FASCISM!!
YEAH! FASCISM'S WAY BETTER!
÷GASP÷
BUT--CAP, YOU CAN'T MEAN IT!
OH, BUT I DO! I LOVE DICTATORSHIPS! NOW GO, SQUIRREL GIRL! GO, AND LEAVE ME AND MY NEW PARTNER BASS LASS TO DESTROY DEMOCRACY...
...UNLESS YOU WISH TO BE DESTROYED TOO!!
TOTALITARIANISM IS TOTALITARILY GREAT!

Wait, wait!! Finish reading this comic before you run off to smash the state! There's a small chance that Captain America is wrong here!

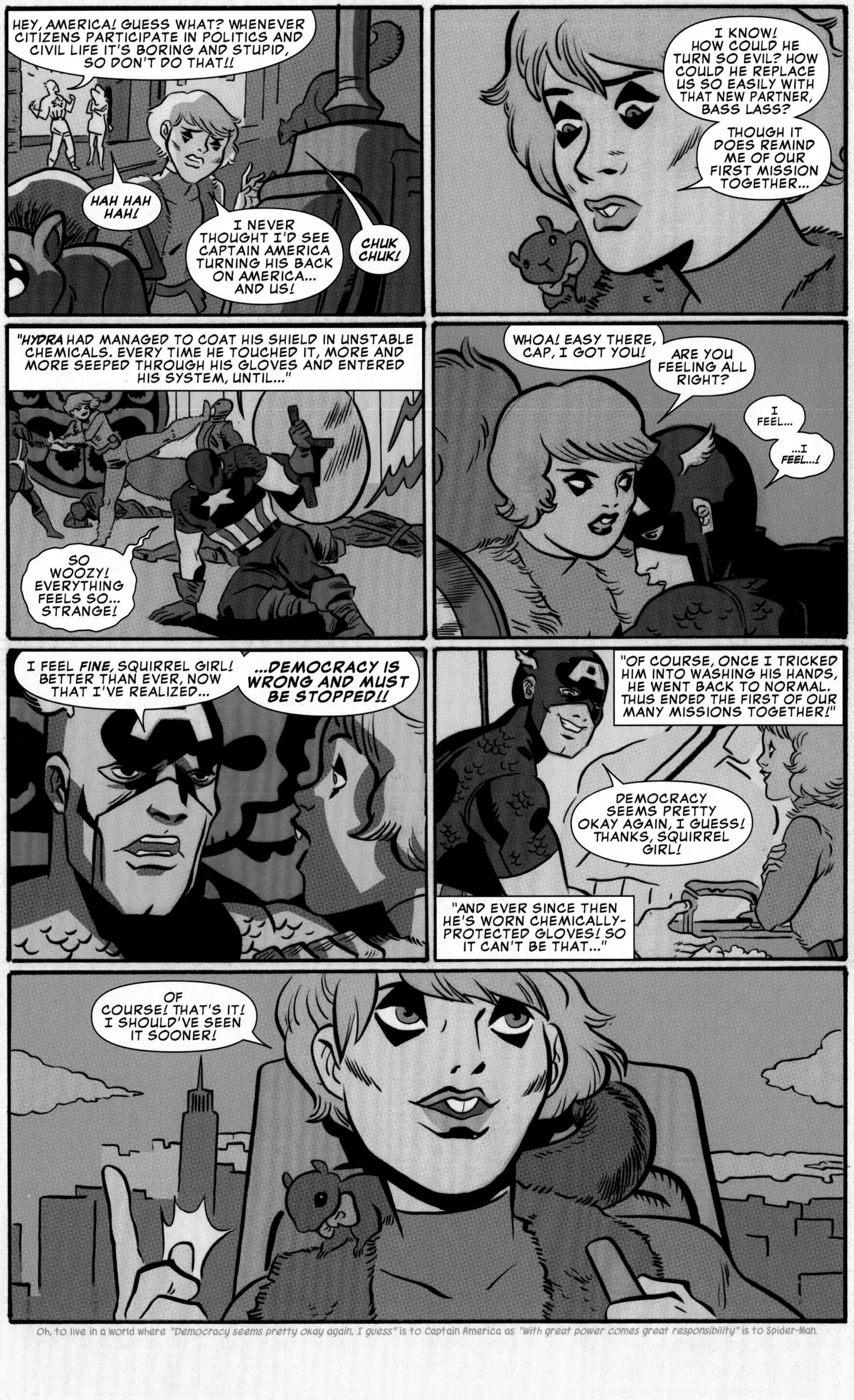
HEY, AMERICA! GUESS WHAT? WHENEVER CITIZENS PARTICIPATE IN POLITICS AND CIVIL LIFE IT'S BORING AND STUPID, SO DON'T DO THAT!!
HAH HAH HAH!
I NEVER THOUGHT I'D SEE CAPTAIN AMERICA TURNING HIS BACK ON AMERICA... AND US!
CHUK CHUK!
I KNOW! HOW COULD HE TURN SO EVIL? HOW COULD HE REPLACE US SO EASILY WITH THAT NEW PARTNER, BASS LASS?
THOUGH IT DOES REMIND ME OF OUR FIRST MISSION TOGETHER...
"HYDRA HAD MANAGED TO COAT HIS SHIELD IN UNSTABLE CHEMICALS. EVERY TIME HE TOUCHED IT, MORE AND MORE SEEPED THROUGH HIS GLOVES AND ENTERED HIS SYSTEM, UNTIL..."
SO WOOZY! EVERYTHING FEELS SO... STRANGE!
WHOA! EASY THERE, CAP, I GOT YOU!
ARE YOU FEELING ALL RIGHT?
I FEEL...
...I FEEL...!
I FEEL FINE, SQUIRREL GIRL! BETTER THAN EVER, NOW THAT I'VE REALIZED...
...DEMOCRACY IS WRONG AND MUST BE STOPPED!!
"OF COURSE, ONCE I TRICKED HIM INTO WASHING HIS HANDS, HE WENT BACK TO NORMAL. THUS ENDED THE FIRST OF OUR MANY MISSIONS TOGETHER!"
DEMOCRACY SEEMS PRETTY OKAY AGAIN, I GUESS! THANKS, SQUIRREL GIRL!
"AND EVER SINCE THEN HE'S WORN CHEMICALLY-PROTECTED GLOVES! SO IT CAN'T BE THAT..."
OF COURSE! THAT'S IT! I SHOULD'VE SEEN IT SOONER!

Oh, to live in a world where *"Democracy seems pretty okay again, I guess"* is to Captain America as *"With great power comes great responsibility"* is to Spider-Man.

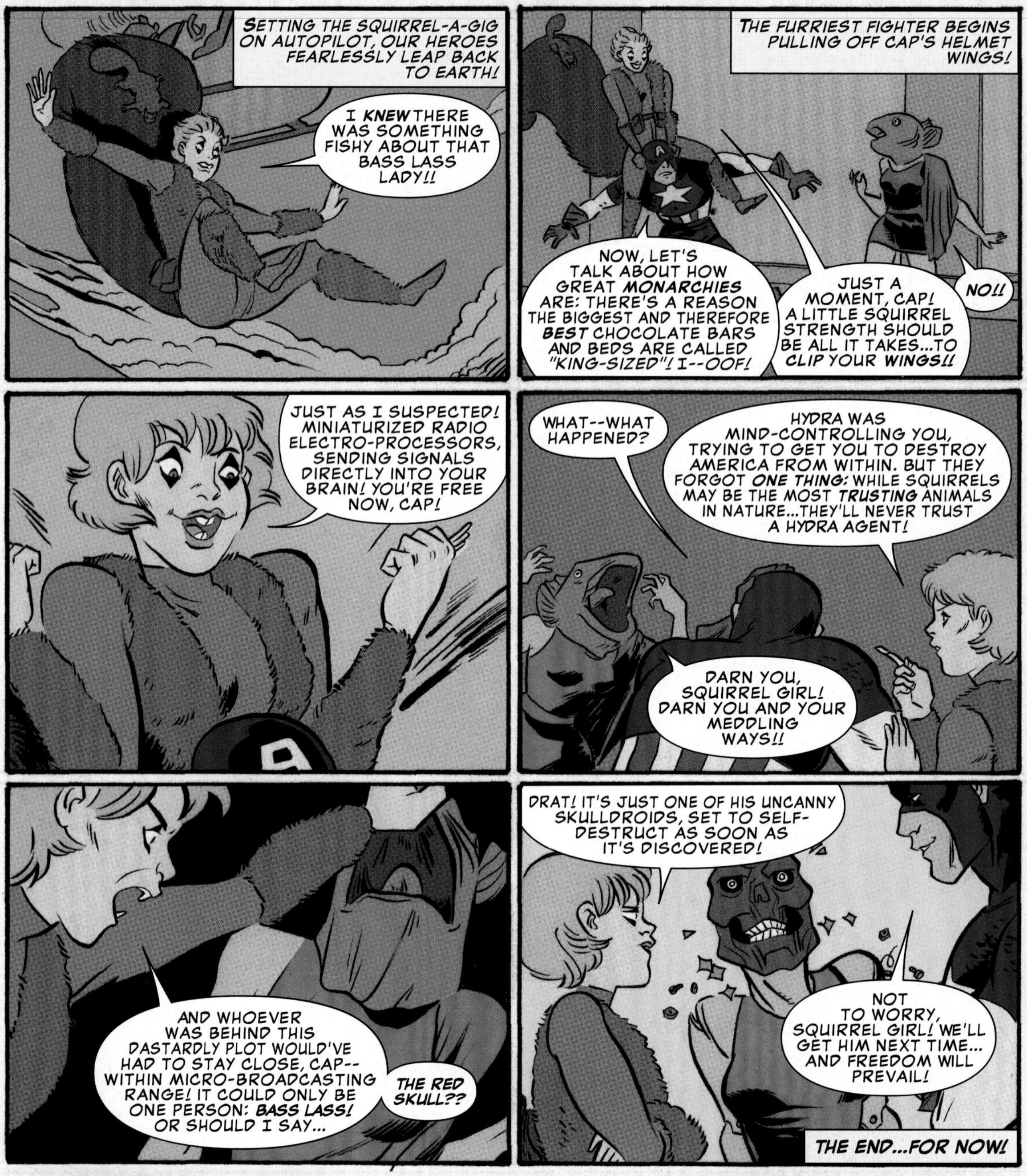
SETTING THE SQUIRREL-A-GIG ON AUTOPILOT, OUR HEROES FEARLESSLY LEAP BACK TO EARTH!
I KNEW THERE WAS SOMETHING FISHY ABOUT THAT BASS LASS LADY!!
THE FURRIEST FIGHTER BEGINS PULLING OFF CAP'S HELMET WINGS!
NOW, LET'S TALK ABOUT HOW GREAT MONARCHIES ARE: THERE'S A REASON THE BIGGEST AND THEREFORE BEST CHOCOLATE BARS AND BEDS ARE CALLED "KING-SIZED"! I--OOF!
JUST A MOMENT, CAP! A LITTLE SQUIRREL STRENGTH SHOULD BE ALL IT TAKES...TO CLIP YOUR WINGS!!
NO!!
JUST AS I SUSPECTED! MINIATURIZED RADIO ELECTRO-PROCESSORS, SENDING SIGNALS DIRECTLY INTO YOUR BRAIN! YOU'RE FREE NOW, CAP!
WHAT--WHAT HAPPENED?
HYDRA WAS MIND-CONTROLLING YOU, TRYING TO GET YOU TO DESTROY AMERICA FROM WITHIN. BUT THEY FORGOT ONE THING: WHILE SQUIRRELS MAY BE THE MOST TRUSTING ANIMALS IN NATURE...THEY'LL NEVER TRUST A HYDRA AGENT!
DARN YOU, SQUIRREL GIRL! DARN YOU AND YOUR MEDDLING WAYS!!
AND WHOEVER WAS BEHIND THIS DASTARDLY PLOT WOULD'VE HAD TO STAY CLOSE, CAP--WITHIN MICRO-BROADCASTING RANGE! IT COULD ONLY BE ONE PERSON: BASS LASS! OR SHOULD I SAY...
THE RED SKULL??
DRAT! IT'S JUST ONE OF HIS UNCANNY SKULLDROIDS, SET TO SELF-DESTRUCT AS SOON AS IT'S DISCOVERED!
NOT TO WORRY, SQUIRREL GIRL! WE'LL GET HIM NEXT TIME... AND FREEDOM WILL PREVAIL!
THE END...FOR NOW!

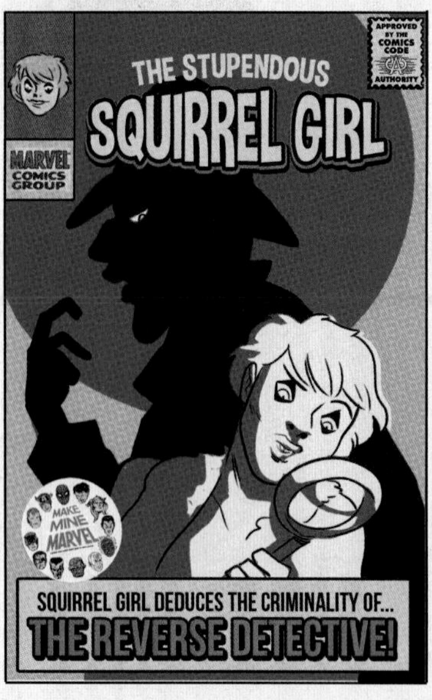
THE STUPENDOUS
SQUIRREL GIRL
APPROVED BY THE COMICS CODE AUTHORITY
MARVEL COMICS GROUP
MAKE MINE MARVEL
SQUIRREL GIRL DEDUCES THE CRIMINALITY OF...
THE REVERSE DETECTIVE!

NEXT MONTH...

MORE AMAZING ADVENTURES WITH YOUR FAVORITE FANTASTIC HEROES!

In that comic, Captain America says "Stand down! That's an order, Corporal." and then Corporal USA is all "Um yeah so the thing is, I think it's pretty clear we're both operating outside the traditional military chain of command here??"

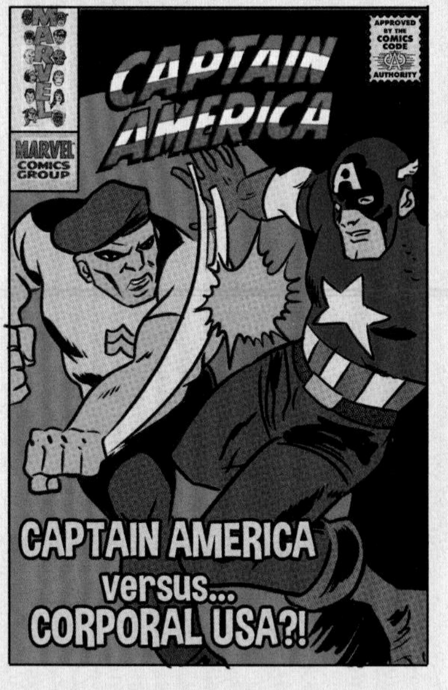
CAPTAIN AMERICA
APPROVED BY THE COMICS CODE AUTHORITY
MARVEL COMICS GROUP
CAPTAIN AMERICA
versus...
CORPORAL USA?!

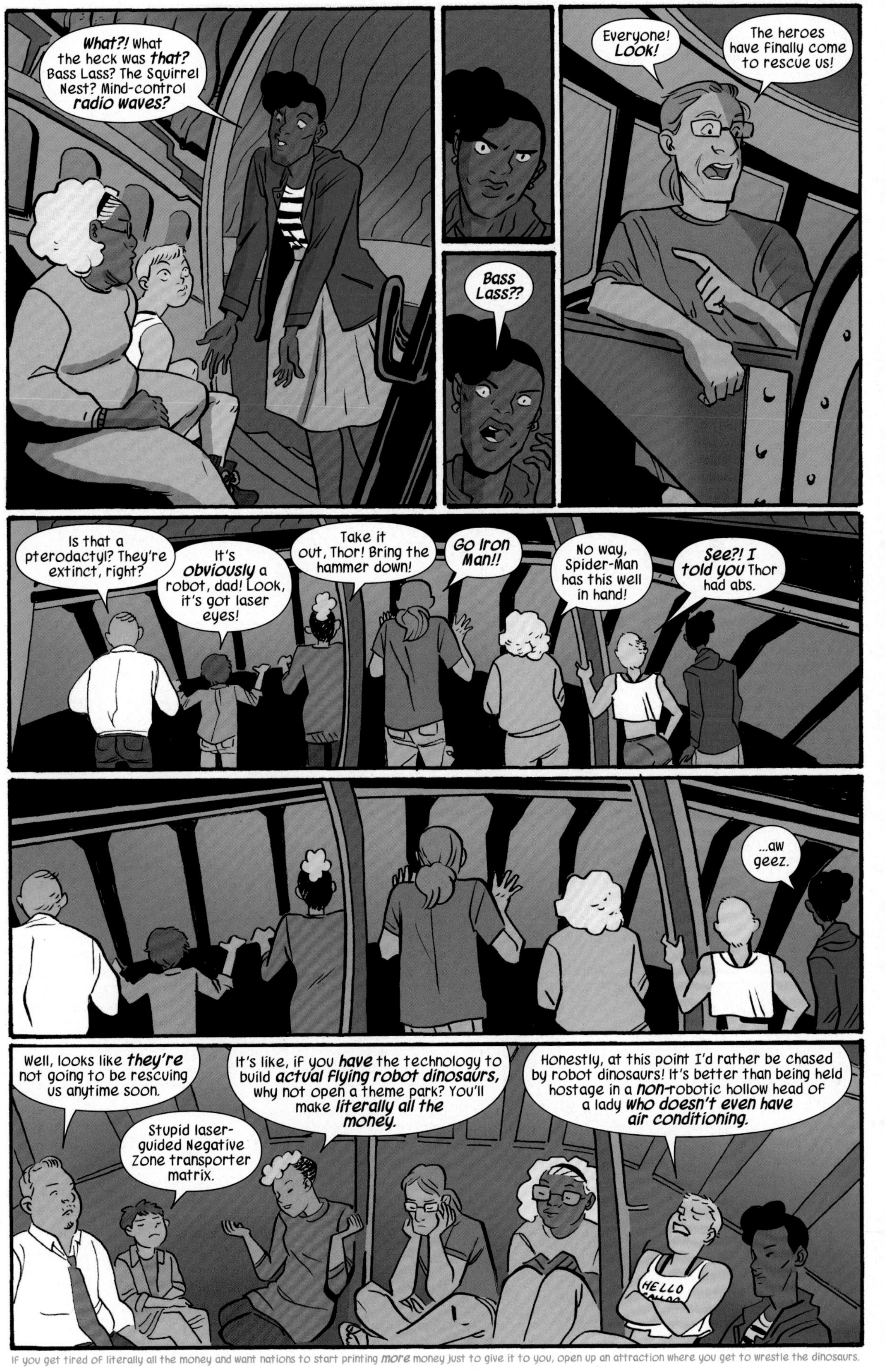

What?! What the heck was that? Bass Lass? The Squirrel Nest? Mind-control radio waves?
Bass Lass??
Everyone! Look!
The heroes have finally come to rescue us!
Is that a pterodactyl? They're extinct, right?
It's obviously a robot, dad! Look, it's got laser eyes!
Take it out, Thor! Bring the hammer down!
Go Iron Man!!
No way, Spider-Man has this well in hand!
See?! I told you Thor had abs.
...aw geez.
Well, looks like they're not going to be rescuing us anytime soon.
Stupid laser-guided Negative Zone transporter matrix.
It's like, if you have the technology to build actual flying robot dinosaurs, why not open a theme park? You'll make literally all the money.
Honestly, at this point I'd rather be chased by robot dinosaurs! It's better than being held hostage in a non-robotic hollow head of a lady who doesn't even have air conditioning.
HELLO


If you get tired of literally all the money and want nations to start printing *more* money just to give it to you, open up an attraction where you get to wrestle the dinosaurs.

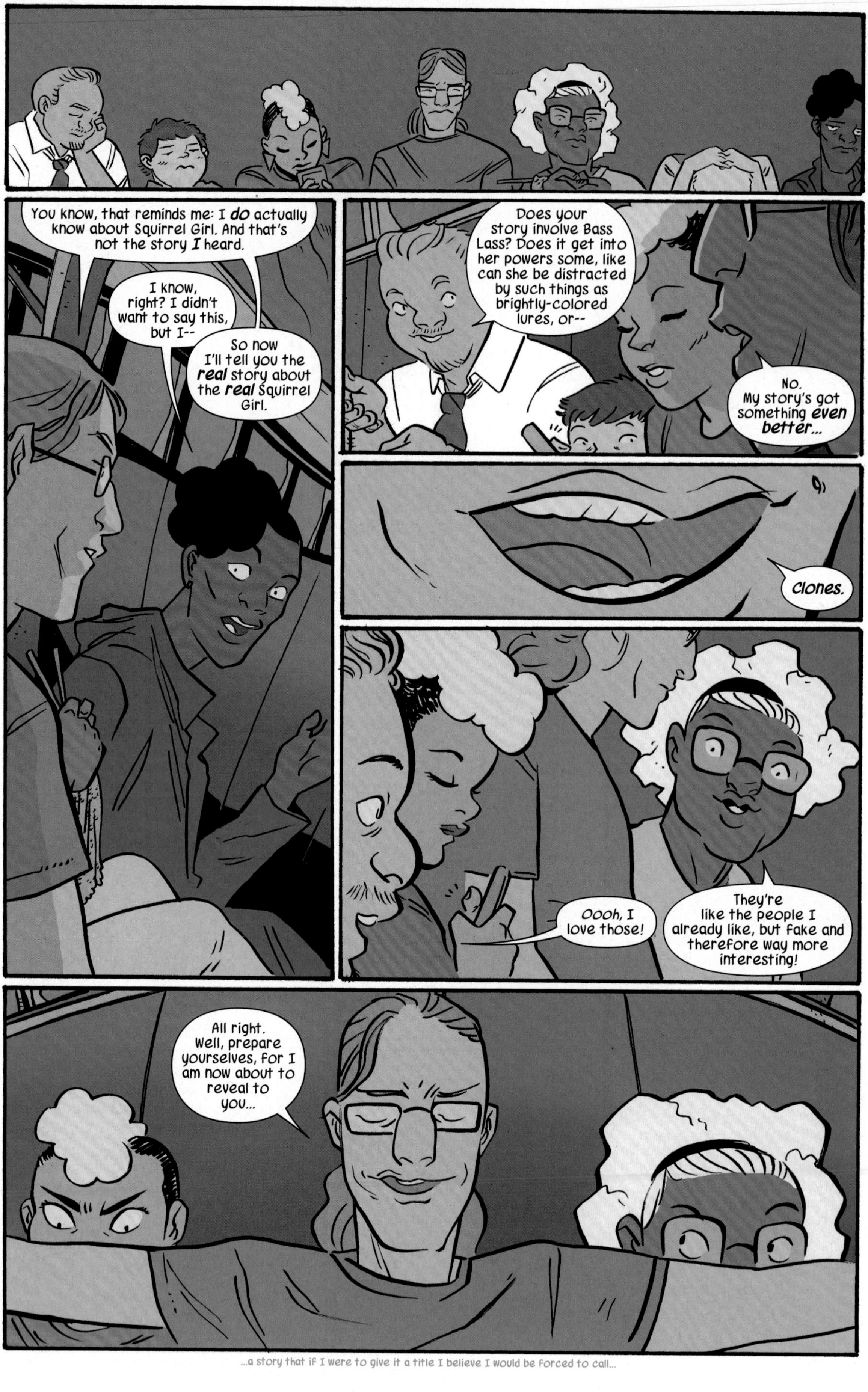

You know, that reminds me: I do actually know about Squirrel Girl. And that's not the story I heard.
I know, right? I didn't want to say this, but I--
So now I'll tell you the real story about the real Squirrel Girl.
Does your story involve Bass Lass? Does it get into her powers some, like can she be distracted by such things as brightly-colored lures, or--
No. My story's got something even better...
Clones.
They're like the people I already like, but fake and therefore way more interesting!
Oooh, I love those!
All right. Well, prepare yourselves, for I am now about to reveal to you...


...a story that if I were to give it a title I believe I would be forced to call...

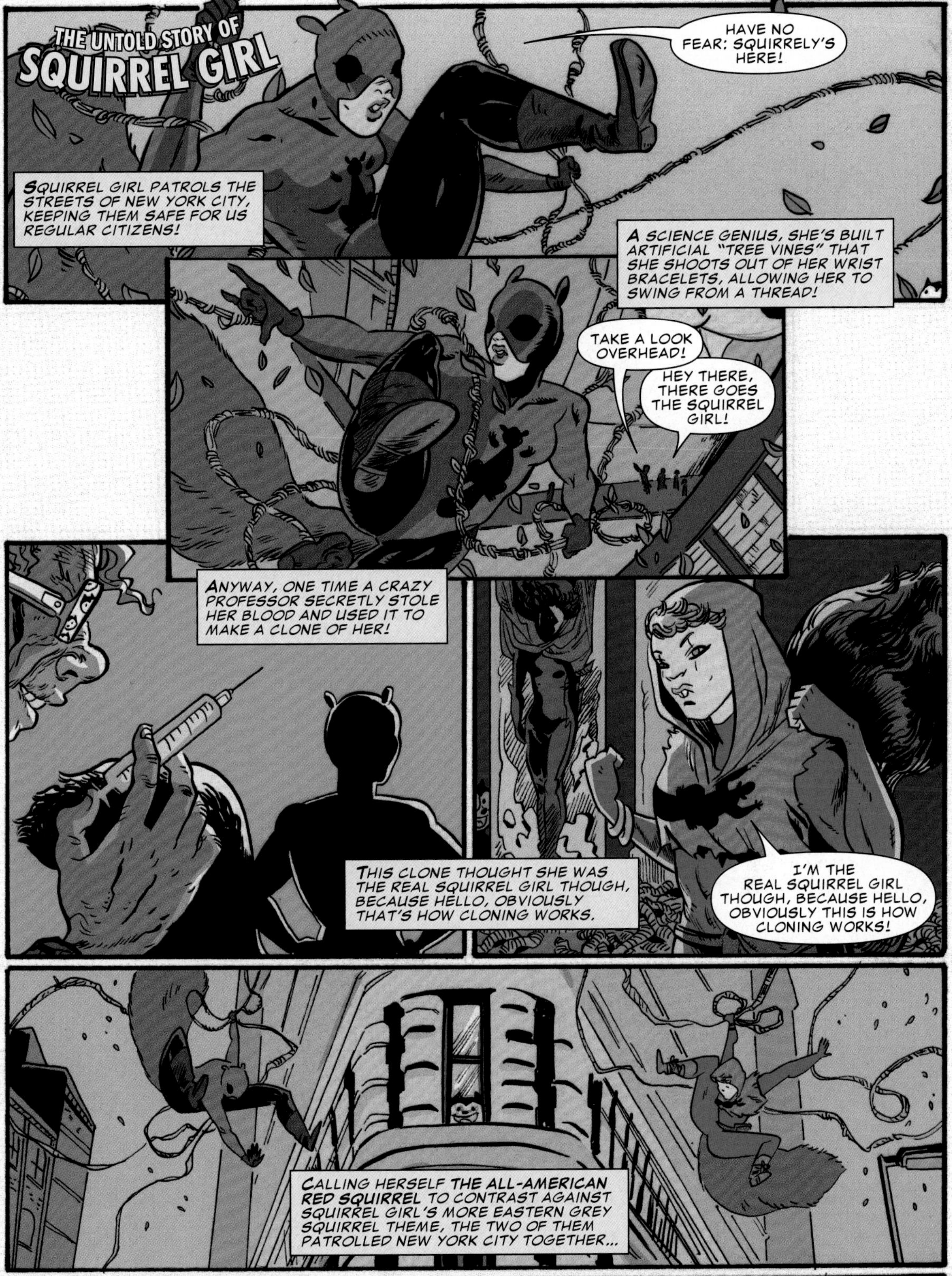
THE UNTOLD STORY OF SQUIRREL GIRL
HAVE NO FEAR: SQUIRRELY'S HERE!
SQUIRREL GIRL PATROLS THE STREETS OF NEW YORK CITY, KEEPING THEM SAFE FOR US REGULAR CITIZENS!
A SCIENCE GENIUS, SHE'S BUILT ARTIFICIAL "TREE VINES" THAT SHE SHOOTS OUT OF HER WRIST BRACELETS, ALLOWING HER TO SWING FROM A THREAD!
TAKE A LOOK OVERHEAD!
HEY THERE, THERE GOES THE SQUIRREL GIRL!
ANYWAY, ONE TIME A CRAZY PROFESSOR SECRETLY STOLE HER BLOOD AND USED IT TO MAKE A CLONE OF HER!
THIS CLONE THOUGHT SHE WAS THE REAL SQUIRREL GIRL THOUGH, BECAUSE HELLO, OBVIOUSLY THAT'S HOW CLONING WORKS.
I'M THE REAL SQUIRREL GIRL THOUGH, BECAUSE HELLO, OBVIOUSLY THIS IS HOW CLONING WORKS!
CALLING HERSELF THE ALL-AMERICAN RED SQUIRREL TO CONTRAST AGAINST SQUIRREL GIRL'S MORE EASTERN GREY SQUIRREL THEME, THE TWO OF THEM PATROLLED NEW YORK CITY TOGETHER...
...AND EVEN CAME TO BLOWS!!
HEY!
HEY YOURSELF!
OUCH!
OUCH YOURSELF!!
HENDO 2015

Hey, this reminds me: with great power doesn't come great responsibility! With great power *actually* comes great joules per second, or "watts," the integral of which over time measures the work performed. Librarians: please go ahead and file this comic in the "WOW! SCIENCE FACTS" section of the library.

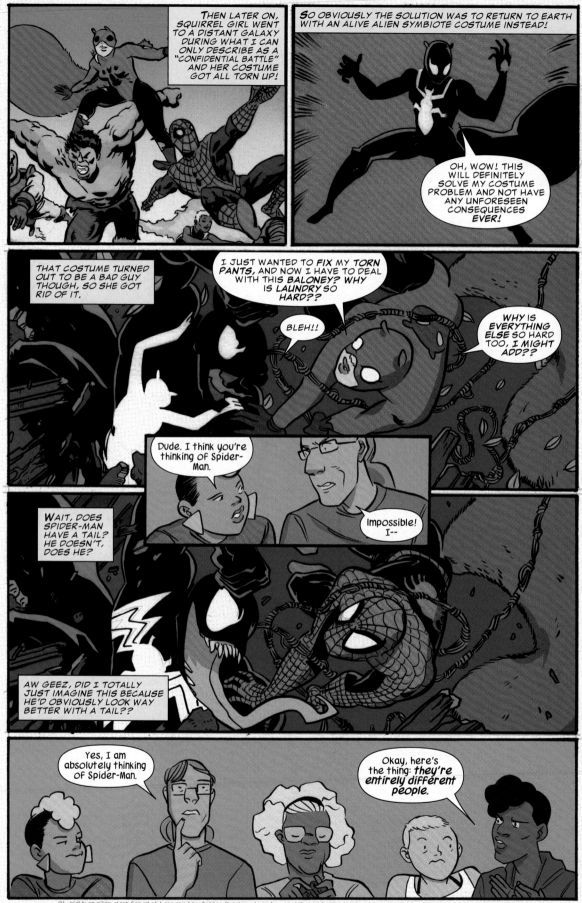

THEN LATER ON, SQUIRREL GIRL WENT TO A DISTANT GALAXY DURING WHAT I CAN ONLY DESCRIBE AS A "CONFIDENTIAL BATTLE" AND HER COSTUME GOT ALL TORN UP!

SO OBVIOUSLY THE SOLUTION WAS TO RETURN TO EARTH WITH AN ALIVE ALIEN SYMBIOTE COSTUME INSTEAD!

OH, WOW! THIS WILL DEFINITELY SOLVE MY COSTUME PROBLEM AND NOT HAVE ANY UNFORESEEN CONSEQUENCES EVER!

THAT COSTUME TURNED OUT TO BE A BAD GUY THOUGH, SO SHE GOT RID OF IT.

I JUST WANTED TO FIX MY TORN PANTS, AND NOW I HAVE TO DEAL WITH THIS BALONEY? WHY IS LAUNDRY SO HARD??

BLEH!!

WHY IS EVERYTHING ELSE SO HARD TOO, I MIGHT ADD??

Dude. I think you're thinking of Spider-Man.

Impossible! I--

WAIT, DOES SPIDER-MAN HAVE A TAIL? HE DOESN'T, DOES HE?

AW GEEZ, DID I TOTALLY JUST IMAGINE THIS BECAUSE HE'D OBVIOUSLY LOOK WAY BETTER WITH A TAIL??

Yes, I am absolutely thinking of Spider-Man.

Okay, here's the thing: they're entirely different people.

Oh, right: spoiler alert for what happened to Spider-Man two decades ago! If you don't want to know what Spider-Man was doing two decades ago, please forget this page riiiight...now. Perfect!

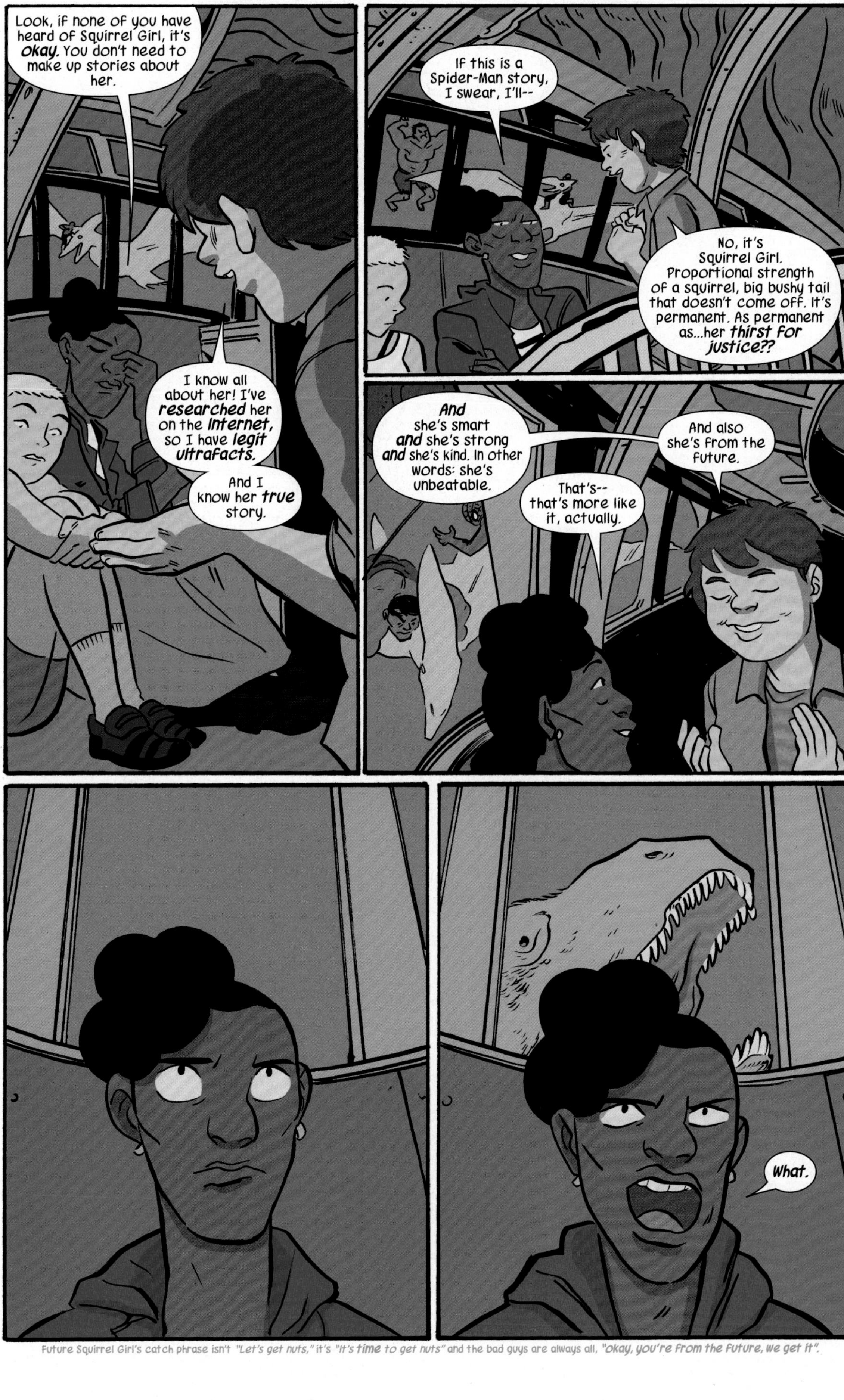
Look, if none of you have heard of Squirrel Girl, it's *okay.* You don't need to make up stories about her.
I know all about her! I've ***researched*** her on the ***Internet,*** so I have ***legit ultrafacts.***
And I know her ***true*** story.
If this is a Spider-Man story, I swear, I'll--
No, it's Squirrel Girl. Proportional strength of a squirrel, big bushy tail that doesn't come off. It's permanent. As permanent as...her ***thirst for justice??***
***And*** she's smart ***and*** she's strong ***and*** she's kind. In other words: she's unbeatable.
And also she's from the future.
That's-- that's more like it, actually.
***What.***

Future Squirrel Girl's catch phrase isn't *"Let's get nuts,"* it's *"It's* **time** *to get nuts"* and the bad guys are always all, *"Okay, you're from the future, we get it".*

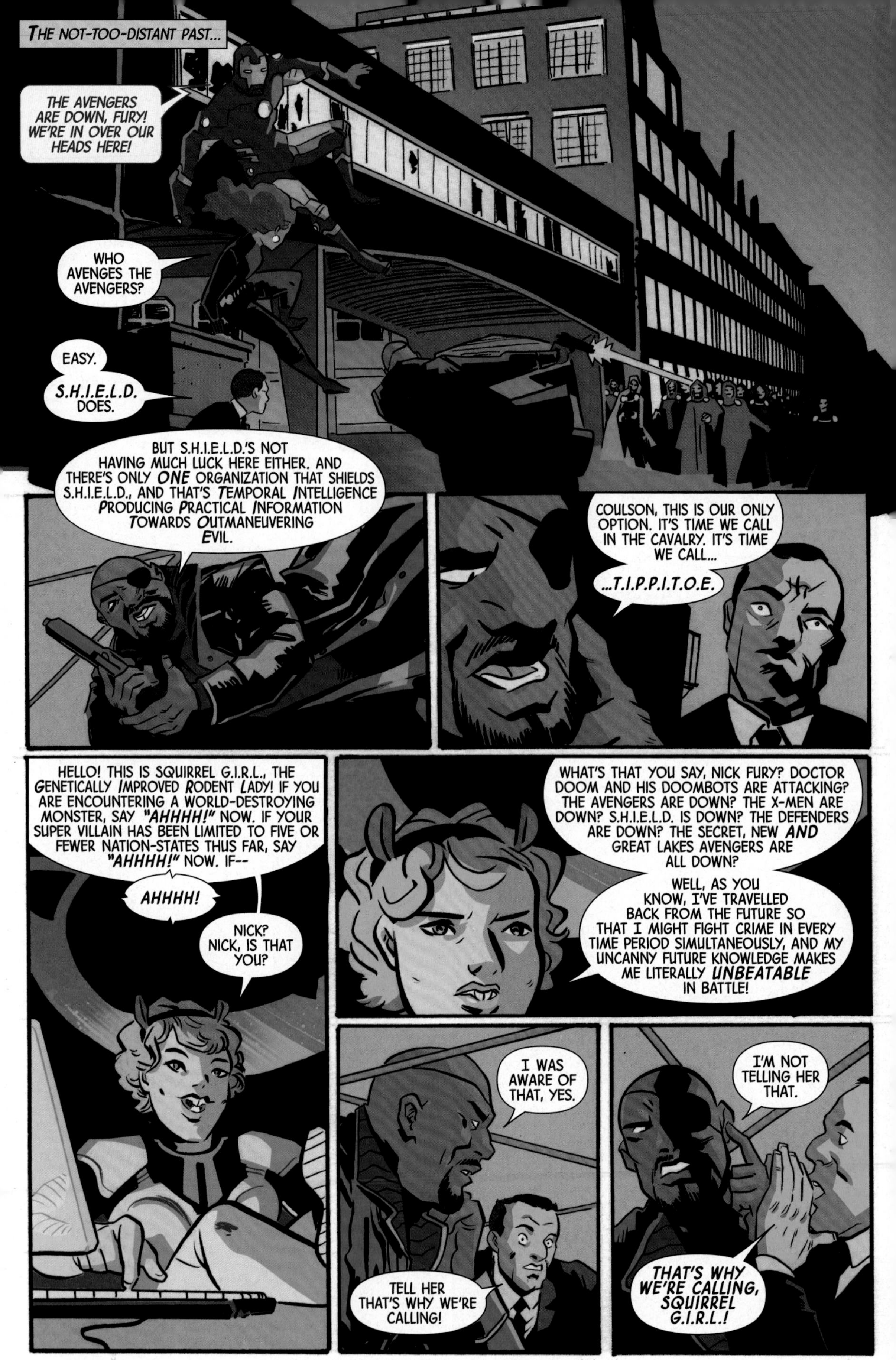
THE NOT-TOO-DISTANT PAST...
THE AVENGERS ARE DOWN, FURY! WE'RE IN OVER OUR HEADS HERE!
WHO AVENGES THE AVENGERS?
EASY.
S.H.I.E.L.D. DOES.
BUT S.H.I.E.L.D.'S NOT HAVING MUCH LUCK HERE EITHER. AND THERE'S ONLY ONE ORGANIZATION THAT SHIELDS S.H.I.E.L.D., AND THAT'S TEMPORAL INTELLIGENCE PRODUCING PRACTICAL INFORMATION TOWARDS OUTMANEUVERING EVIL.
COULSON, THIS IS OUR ONLY OPTION. IT'S TIME WE CALL IN THE CAVALRY. IT'S TIME WE CALL...
...T.I.P.P.I.T.O.E.
HELLO! THIS IS SQUIRREL G.I.R.L., THE GENETICALLY IMPROVED RODENT LADY! IF YOU ARE ENCOUNTERING A WORLD-DESTROYING MONSTER, SAY "AHHHH!" NOW. IF YOUR SUPER VILLAIN HAS BEEN LIMITED TO FIVE OR FEWER NATION-STATES THUS FAR, SAY "AHHHH!" NOW. IF--
AHHHH!
NICK? NICK, IS THAT YOU?
WHAT'S THAT YOU SAY, NICK FURY? DOCTOR DOOM AND HIS DOOMBOTS ARE ATTACKING? THE AVENGERS ARE DOWN? THE X-MEN ARE DOWN? S.H.I.E.L.D. IS DOWN? THE DEFENDERS ARE DOWN? THE SECRET, NEW AND GREAT LAKES AVENGERS ARE ALL DOWN?
WELL, AS YOU KNOW, I'VE TRAVELLED BACK FROM THE FUTURE SO THAT I MIGHT FIGHT CRIME IN EVERY TIME PERIOD SIMULTANEOUSLY, AND MY UNCANNY FUTURE KNOWLEDGE MAKES ME LITERALLY UNBEATABLE IN BATTLE!
I WAS AWARE OF THAT, YES.
TELL HER THAT'S WHY WE'RE CALLING!
I'M NOT TELLING HER THAT.
THAT'S WHY WE'RE CALLING, SQUIRREL G.I.R.L.!

Q: Who secret avenges the Secret Avengers? A: It's a secret. *Obviously.*

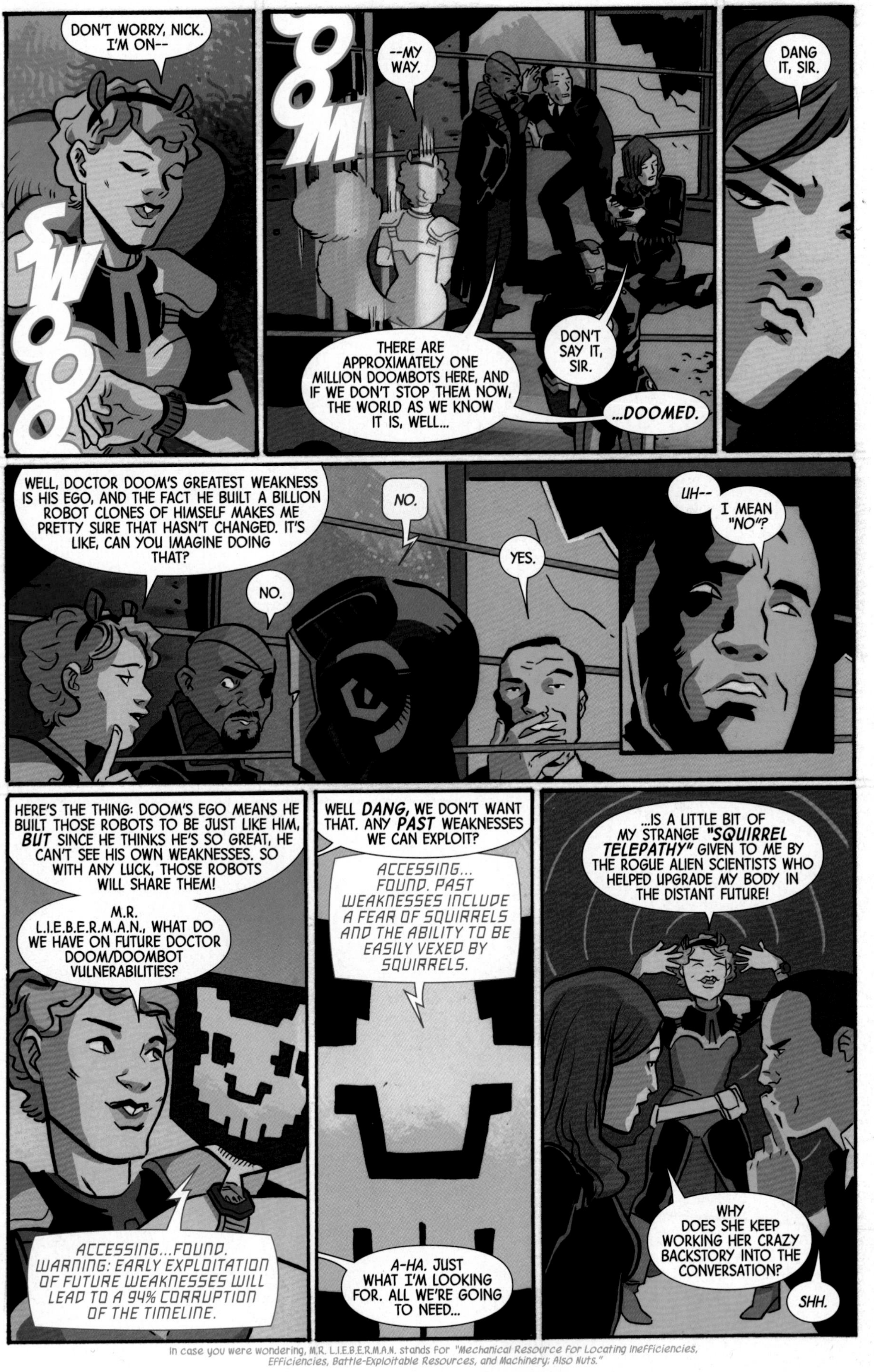
DON'T WORRY, NICK. I'M ON--
SWOOOOOM
--MY WAY.
THERE ARE APPROXIMATELY ONE MILLION DOOMBOTS HERE, AND IF WE DON'T STOP THEM NOW, THE WORLD AS WE KNOW IT IS, WELL...
DON'T SAY IT, SIR.
...DOOMED.
DANG IT, SIR.
WELL, DOCTOR DOOM'S GREATEST WEAKNESS IS HIS EGO, AND THE FACT HE BUILT A BILLION ROBOT CLONES OF HIMSELF MAKES ME PRETTY SURE THAT HASN'T CHANGED. IT'S LIKE, CAN YOU IMAGINE DOING THAT?
NO.
NO.
YES.
UH--
I MEAN "NO"?
HERE'S THE THING: DOOM'S EGO MEANS HE BUILT THOSE ROBOTS TO BE JUST LIKE HIM, BUT SINCE HE THINKS HE'S SO GREAT, HE CAN'T SEE HIS OWN WEAKNESSES. SO WITH ANY LUCK, THOSE ROBOTS WILL SHARE THEM!
M.R. L.I.E.B.E.R.M.A.N., WHAT DO WE HAVE ON FUTURE DOCTOR DOOM/DOOMBOT VULNERABILITIES?
ACCESSING...FOUND. WARNING: EARLY EXPLOITATION OF FUTURE WEAKNESSES WILL LEAD TO A 94% CORRUPTION OF THE TIMELINE.
WELL DANG, WE DON'T WANT THAT. ANY PAST WEAKNESSES WE CAN EXPLOIT?
ACCESSING... FOUND. PAST WEAKNESSES INCLUDE A FEAR OF SQUIRRELS AND THE ABILITY TO BE EASILY VEXED BY SQUIRRELS.
A-HA. JUST WHAT I'M LOOKING FOR. ALL WE'RE GOING TO NEED...
...IS A LITTLE BIT OF MY STRANGE "SQUIRREL TELEPATHY" GIVEN TO ME BY THE ROGUE ALIEN SCIENTISTS WHO HELPED UPGRADE MY BODY IN THE DISTANT FUTURE!
WHY DOES SHE KEEP WORKING HER CRAZY BACKSTORY INTO THE CONVERSATION?
SHH.

In case you were wondering, M.R. L.I.E.B.E.R.M.A.N. stands for *"Mechanical Resource for Locating Inefficiencies, Efficiencies, Battle-Exploitable Resources, and Machinery; Also Nuts."*

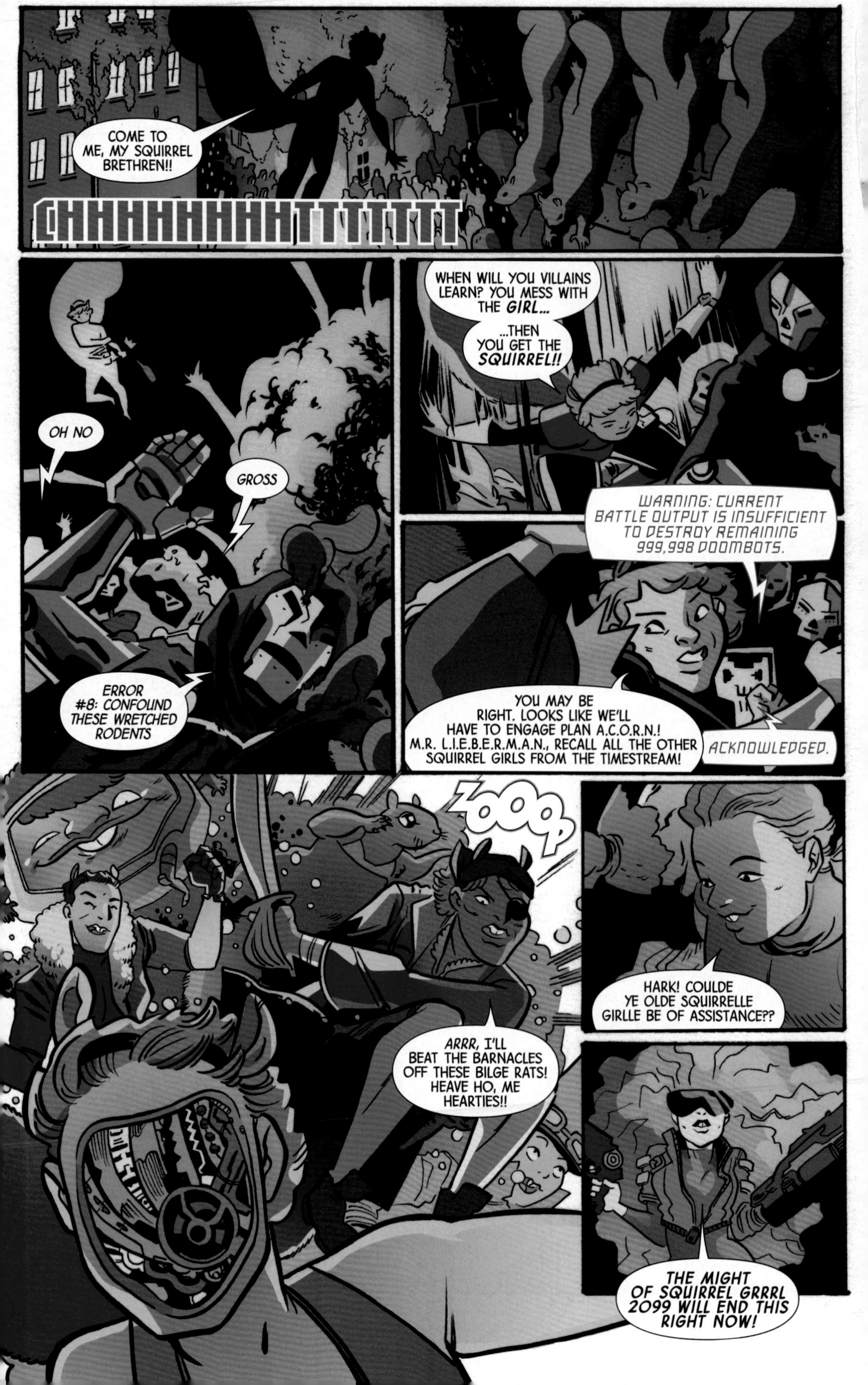
COME TO ME, MY SQUIRREL BRETHREN!!
CHHHHHHHHTTTTTTT
OH NO
GROSS
ERROR #8: CONFOUND THESE WRETCHED RODENTS
WHEN WILL YOU VILLAINS LEARN? YOU MESS WITH THE GIRL...
...THEN YOU GET THE SQUIRREL!!
WARNING: CURRENT BATTLE OUTPUT IS INSUFFICIENT TO DESTROY REMAINING 999,998 DOOMBOTS.
YOU MAY BE RIGHT. LOOKS LIKE WE'LL HAVE TO ENGAGE PLAN A.C.O.R.N.! M.R. L.I.E.B.E.R.M.A.N., RECALL ALL THE OTHER SQUIRREL GIRLS FROM THE TIMESTREAM!
ACKNOWLEDGED.
ZOOOP
ARRR, I'LL BEAT THE BARNACLES OFF THESE BILGE RATS! HEAVE HO, ME HEARTIES!!
HARK! COULDE YE OLDE SQUIRRELLE GIRLLE BE OF ASSISTANCE??
THE MIGHT OF SQUIRREL GRRRL 2099 WILL END THIS RIGHT NOW!

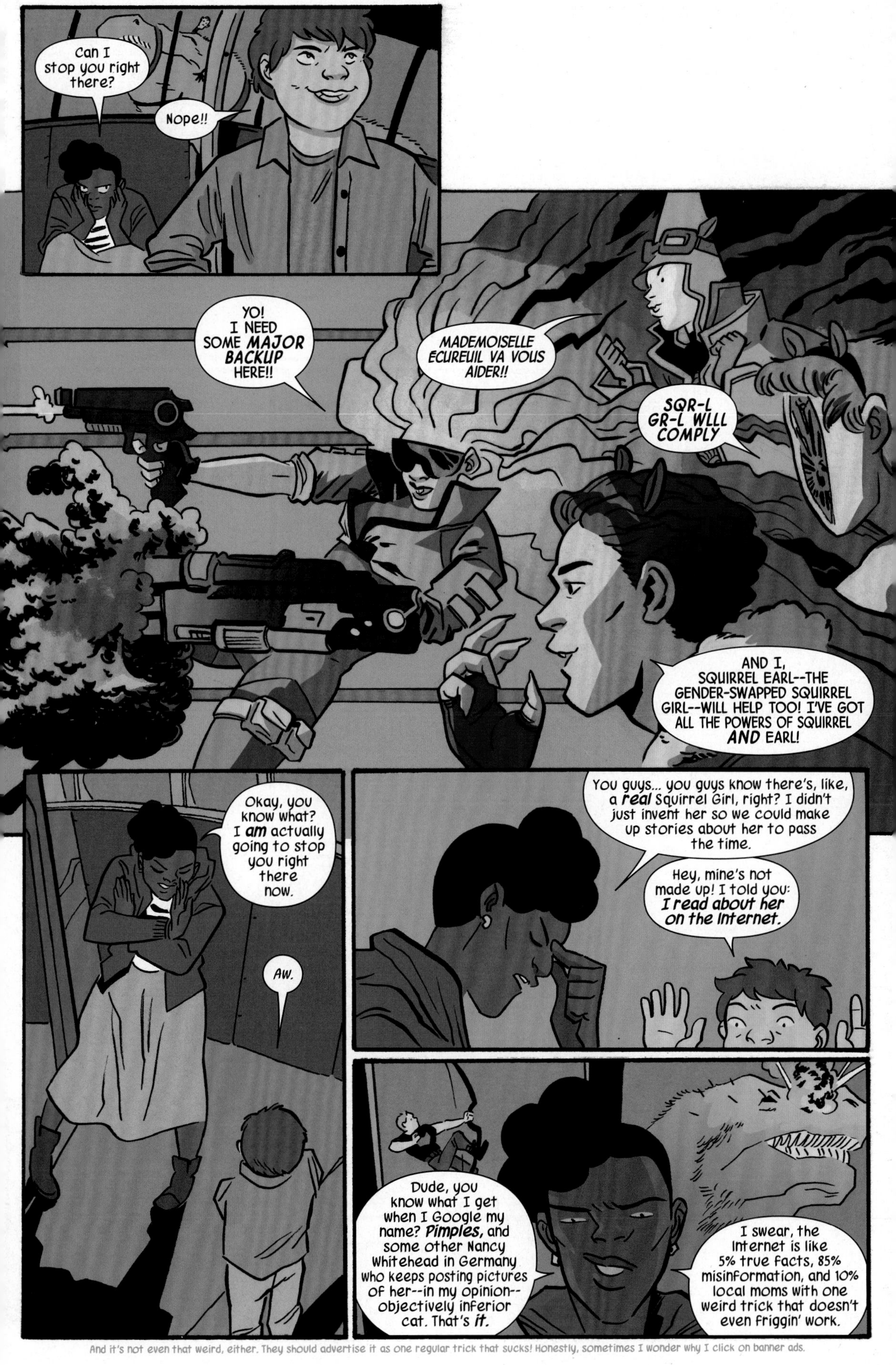
Can I stop you right there?
Nope!!
YO! I NEED SOME MAJOR BACKUP HERE!!
MADEMOISELLE ECUREUIL VA VOUS AIDER!!
SQR-L GR-L WLLL COMPLY
AND I, SQUIRREL EARL--THE GENDER-SWAPPED SQUIRREL GIRL--WILL HELP TOO! I'VE GOT ALL THE POWERS OF SQUIRREL AND EARL!
Okay, you know what? I am actually going to stop you right there now.
AW.
You guys... you guys know there's, like, a real Squirrel Girl, right? I didn't just invent her so we could make up stories about her to pass the time.
Hey, mine's not made up! I told you: I read about her on the Internet.
Dude, you know what I get when I Google my name? Pimples, and some other Nancy Whitehead in Germany who keeps posting pictures of her--in my opinion--objectively inferior cat. That's it.
I swear, the Internet is like 5% true facts, 85% misinformation, and 10% local moms with one weird trick that doesn't even friggin' work.

And it's not even that weird, either. They should advertise it as one regular trick that sucks! Honestly, sometimes I wonder why I click on banner ads.

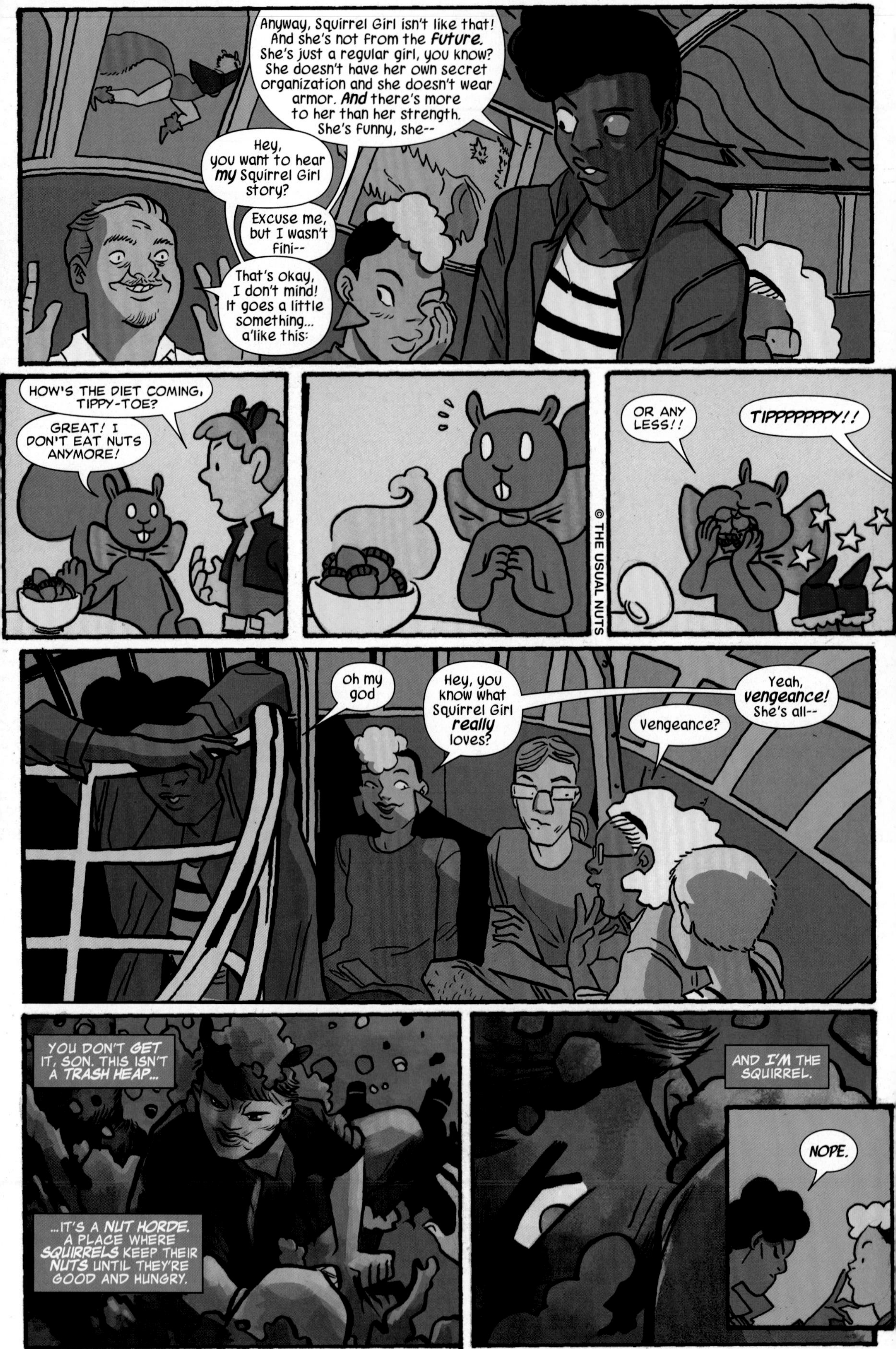
Anyway, Squirrel Girl isn't like that! And she's not from the *future.* She's just a regular girl, you know? She doesn't have her own secret organization and she doesn't wear armor. *And* there's more to her than her strength. She's funny, she--
Hey, you want to hear *my* Squirrel Girl story?
Excuse me, but I wasn't fini--
That's okay, I don't mind! It goes a little something... a'like this:
HOW'S THE DIET COMING, TIPPY-TOE?
GREAT! I DON'T EAT NUTS ANYMORE!
© THE USUAL NUTS
OR ANY LESS!!
TIPPPPPPPY!!
Oh my god
Hey, you know what Squirrel Girl *really* loves?
Vengeance?
Yeah, *vengeance!* She's all--
YOU DON'T *GET* IT, SON. THIS ISN'T A *TRASH HEAP...*
...IT'S A *NUT HORDE.* A PLACE WHERE *SQUIRRELS* KEEP THEIR *NUTS* UNTIL THEY'RE GOOD AND HUNGRY.
AND *I'M* THE SQUIRREL.
NOPE.

I've got squirrels. Lots of squirrels. Sometimes I count them just to make myself feel crazy.

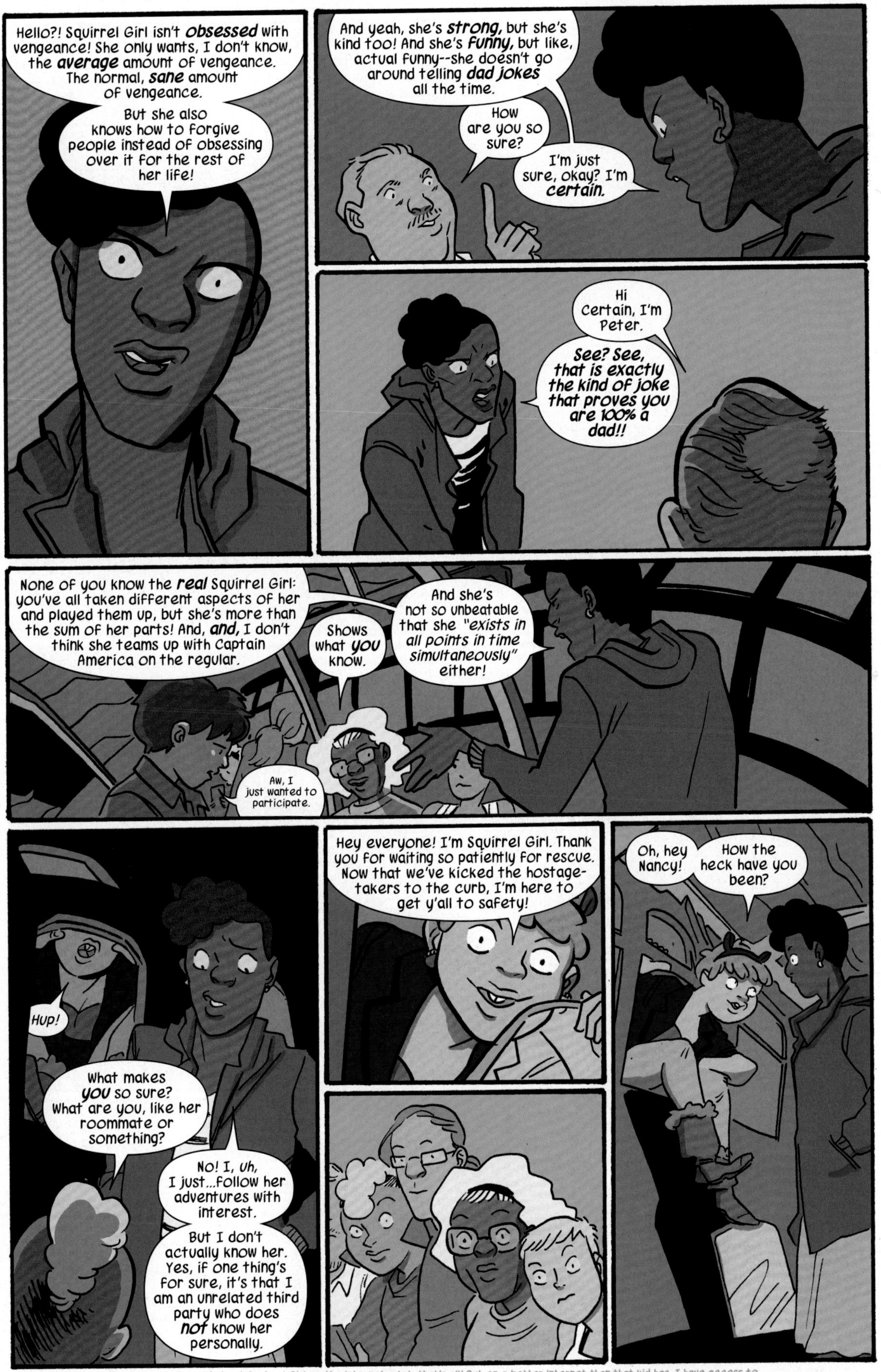
Hello?! Squirrel Girl isn't obsessed with vengeance! She only wants, I don't know, the average amount of vengeance. The normal, sane amount of vengeance.
But she also knows how to forgive people instead of obsessing over it for the rest of her life!
And yeah, she's strong, but she's kind too! And she's funny, but like, actual funny--she doesn't go around telling dad jokes all the time.
How are you so sure?
I'm just sure, okay? I'm certain.
Hi Certain, I'm Peter.
See? See, that is exactly the kind of joke that proves you are 100% a dad!!
None of you know the real Squirrel Girl: you've all taken different aspects of her and played them up, but she's more than the sum of her parts! And, and, I don't think she teams up with Captain America on the regular.
Shows what you know.
And she's not so unbeatable that she "exists in all points in time simultaneously" either!
Aw, I just wanted to participate.
Hup!
What makes you so sure? What are you, like her roommate or something?
No! I, uh, I just...follow her adventures with interest.
But I don't actually know her. Yes, if one thing's for sure, it's that I am an unrelated third party who does not know her personally.
Hey everyone! I'm Squirrel Girl. Thank you for waiting so patiently for rescue. Now that we've kicked the hostage-takers to the curb, I'm here to get y'all to safety!
Oh, hey Nancy!
How the heck have you been?

I, uh, I just...read about Squirrel Girl on the Internet a lot, that's all! But on a better Internet than that kid has. I have access to Internet 2: Internet Platinum Supreme. Yeah: invite only. You've probably never heard of it.

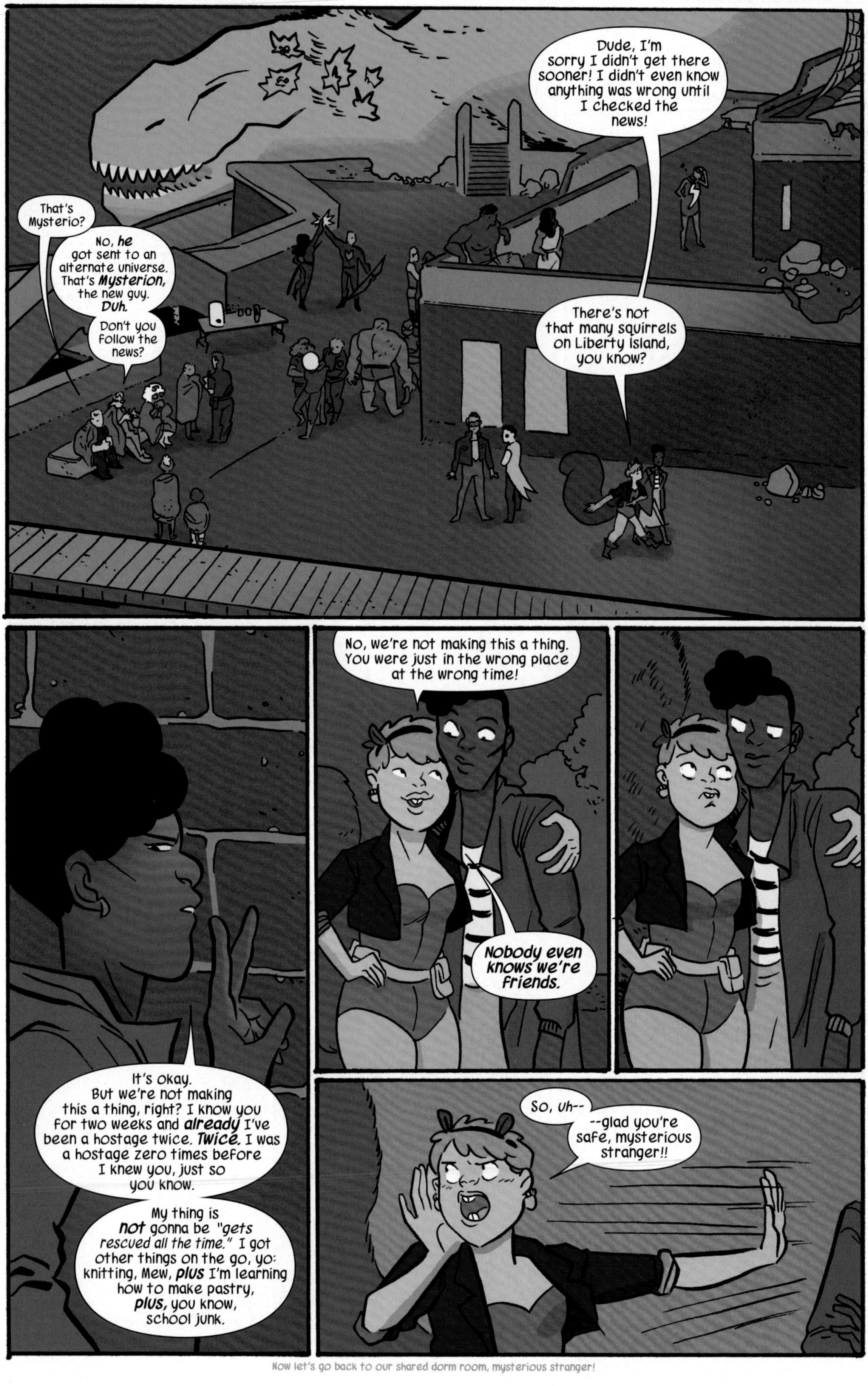
That's Mysterio?
No, he got sent to an alternate universe. That's Mysterion, the new guy. Duh.
Don't you follow the news?
Dude, I'm sorry I didn't get there sooner! I didn't even know anything was wrong until I checked the news!
There's not that many squirrels on Liberty Island, you know?
It's okay. But we're not making this a thing, right? I know you for two weeks and already I've been a hostage twice. Twice. I was a hostage zero times before I knew you, just so you know.
My thing is not gonna be "gets rescued all the time." I got other things on the go, yo: knitting, Mew, plus I'm learning how to make pastry, plus, you know, school junk.
No, we're not making this a thing. You were just in the wrong place at the wrong time!
Nobody even knows we're friends.
So, uh--
--glad you're safe, mysterious stranger!!

Now let's go back to our shared dorm room, mysterious stranger!

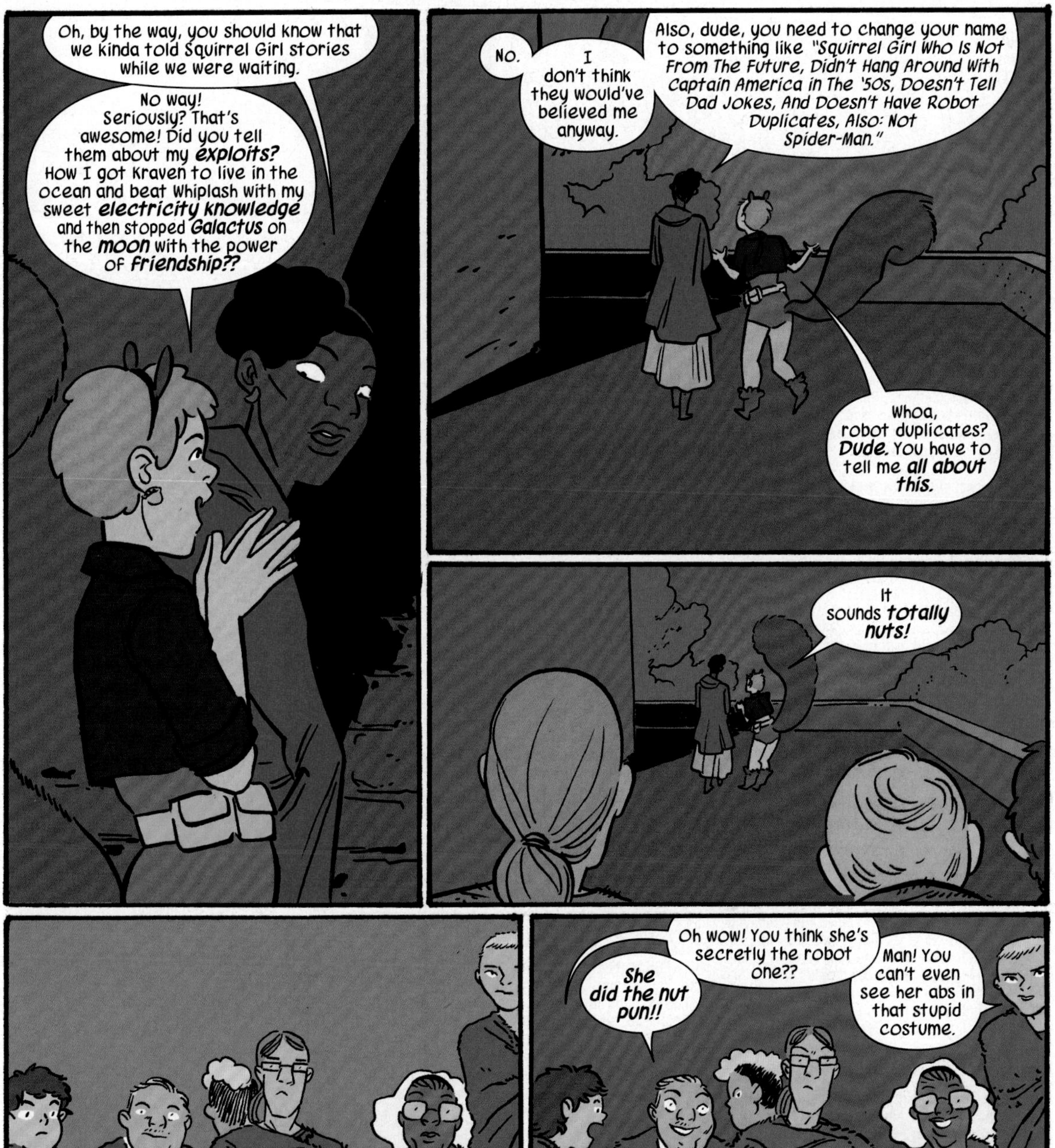
Oh, by the way, you should know that we kinda told Squirrel Girl stories while we were waiting.
No way! Seriously? That's awesome! Did you tell them about my *exploits?* How I got Kraven to live in the ocean and beat Whiplash with my sweet *electricity knowledge* and then stopped *Galactus* on the *moon* with the power of *friendship??*
No.
I don't think they would've believed me anyway.
Also, dude, you need to change your name to something like *"Squirrel Girl Who Is Not From The Future, Didn't Hang Around With Captain America in The '50s, Doesn't Tell Dad Jokes, And Doesn't Have Robot Duplicates, Also: Not Spider-Man."*
Whoa, robot duplicates? *Dude.* You have to tell me *all about this.*
It sounds *totally nuts!*
Oh wow! You think she's secretly the robot one??
*She did the nut pun!!*
Man! You can't even see her abs in that stupid costume.
The End!

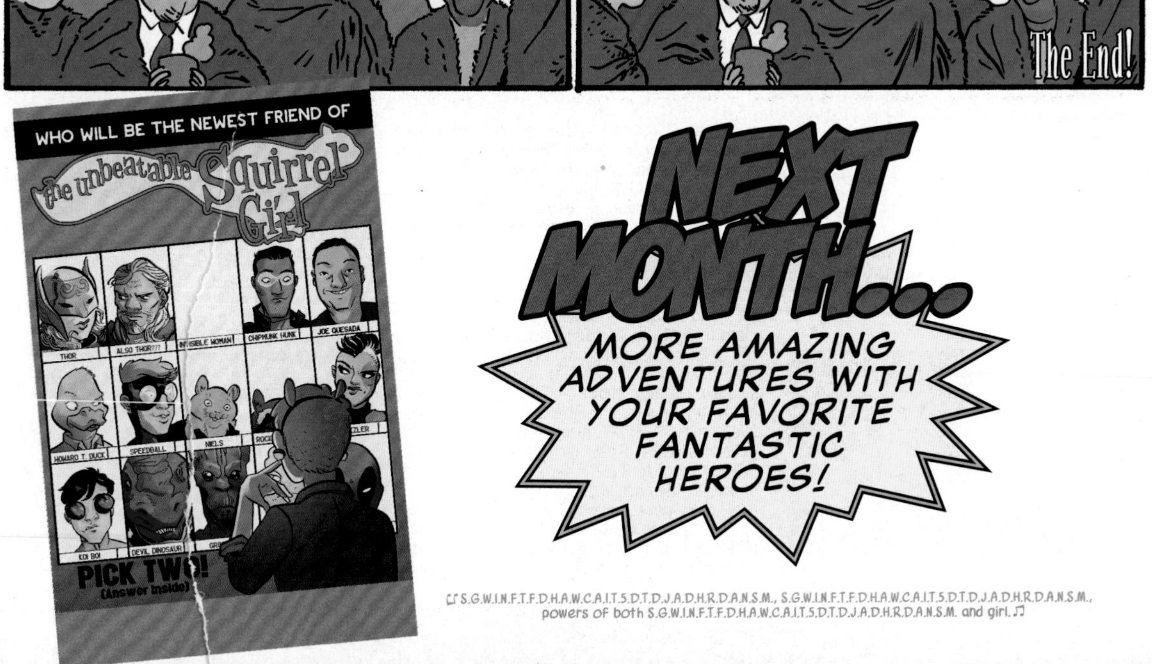
WHO WILL BE THE NEWEST FRIEND OF
the unbeatable Squirrel Girl
THOR
ALSO THOR???
INVISIBLE WOMAN
CHIPMUNK HUNK
JOE QUESADA
HOWARD T. DUCK
SPEEDBALL
NIELS
KOI BOI
DEVIL DINOSAUR
PICK TWO!
(Answer Inside)

# NEXT MONTH...

MORE AMAZING ADVENTURES WITH YOUR FAVORITE FANTASTIC HEROES!

♫ S.G.W.I.N.F.T.F.D.H.A.W.C.A.I.T.5.D.T.D.J.A.D.H.R.D.A.N.S.M., S.G.W.I.N.F.T.F.D.H.A.W.C.A.I.T.5.D.T.D.J.A.D.H.R.D.A.N.S.M., powers of both S.G.W.I.N.F.T.F.D.H.A.W.C.A.I.T.5.D.T.D.J.A.D.H.R.D.A.N.S.M. and girl. ♫

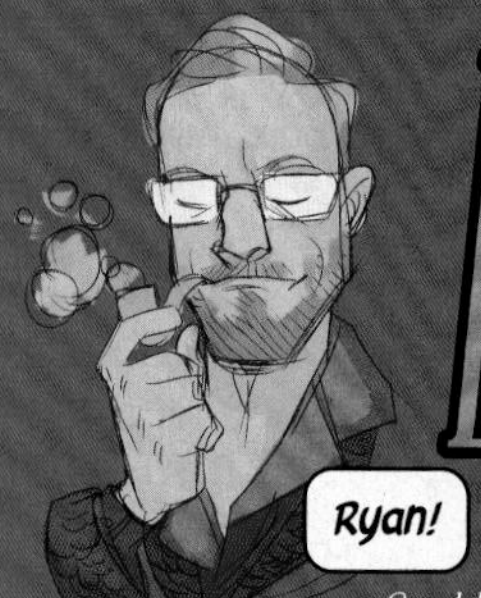
Ryan!

# Letters From Nuts

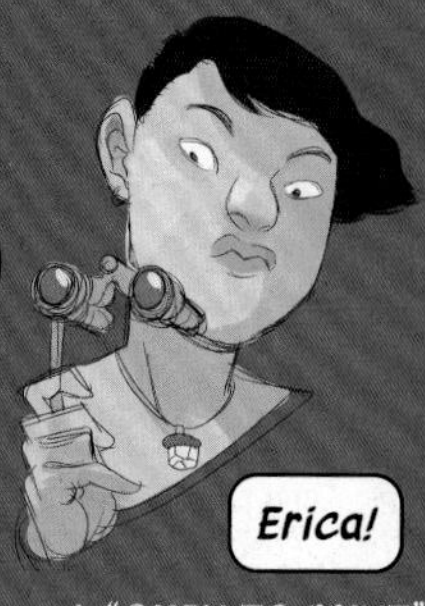
Erica!

*Send letters to mheroes@marvel.com or 135 W 50th St, 7th Floor, New York, NY 10020 (Please mark "OKAY TO PRINT")*

**Hope everyone enjoyed this issue! Our sincerest thanks/apologies to John Romita Sr., Jack Kirby, George Roussos, Dick Sprang, Edmond Hamilton, Todd McFarlane, Greg Wright, Mike Zeck, Christie Scheele, Chris Samnee, Matthew Wilson, Chris Giarrusso, Frank Miller and Lynn Varley for providing inspiration for the various "Squirrel Girl tails." Now on to your letters!**

Congratulations on a tremendous first three issues of THE UNBEATABLE SQUIRREL GIRL! I am beyond pleased to see this comic and constantly amazed at how good it is. Like other commentators, I have largely abandoned other titles by the two big boys because everything out there seems bloated, grim, derivative, and tiresome. But Squirrel Girl has breathed new life into my pull list at my Friendly Local Comic Shop and I am exhausting the patience of my friends by telling them over and over again how they need to buy this book. Extra copies are being set aside as birthday and Christmas gifts. All I need now is an updated Heroclix figure so I can bring SG to tabletop gaming, a way to locate (and afford) all the wonderful alternate covers, and a Tippy-Toe bath toy. (To keep the Submariner from getting up to anything naughty.)

Excellent work, please continue until ALL evil has been vanquished from EVERY multiverse!

Best regards,<br>Kevin Hendryx<br>Austin, TX<br>WWSGD

**RYAN: Thanks! Though as we have now had FOUR issues (well, now FIVE) since you wrote your letter, hopefully the next letter you write us won't be "the first three were great but then WHOAH, WHAT HAPPENED??" (please do not write this letter). And my favorite thing to say (well, about comics) is that it's a medium, not a genre, and that there's room enough for all sorts of stories here. So let's tell all sorts of stories!**

**p.s.: WWSGD? CLEARLY she would eat nuts and/or kick butts.**

**ERICA: AH! Such kind words! It warms my heart. I love having a diversity of stories to pick from and I think we're starting to get more of that at the forefront now. My own comic collection spans titles from Uncle Scrooge to Sky Doll. But honestly we're not trying to do something different, we're just doing something that we'd want to read ourselves.**

I absolutely adore Squirrel Girl. She is my favorite super hero of all time in the history of ever. I recommend this comic to everybody I know who is into comics. And I'm really thankful my brother showed me this book. I find her a very relatable character and I love the humor in the comics. I also appreciate that she isn't like any other comic book character I've come across and the comic is something anybody can enjoy. Keep up the amazing work you guys are doing! Also when decorating Easter eggs this year I made Doreen Green/ Squirrel Girl and Tippy Toe themed Easter eggs so I've attached a picture for you guys.

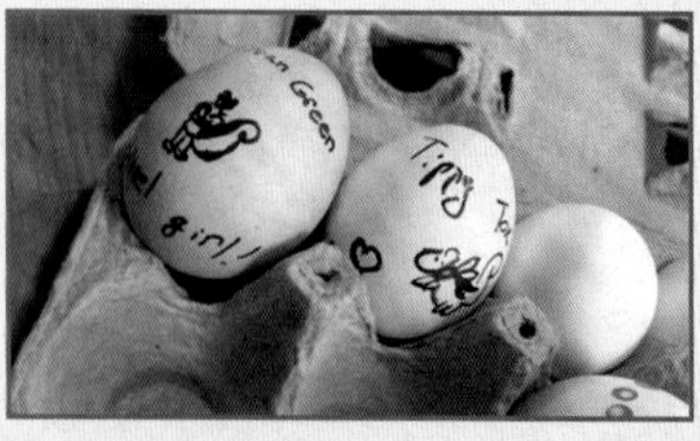

Susie S.

**RYAN: Awesome! I love when people hear about comics by someone sharing their issue, because I feel like comics live when they're shared around and not stuffed in a bag and put into a box. Thank you for the kind words, and thank your brother for me too! And those eggs are off the HOOK.**

Dear purveyors of fine squirrel literature,

I've never written into a comic before, I don't even read comics very often, but after arriving at the store too early... and then too late, I finally got copies of Squirrel Girl and felt like I had to thank you!

I followed Squirrel Girl during her time in the GLA, and I am ecstatic to see her headlining her own title. I've never really felt a strong connection to any heroes in the past, but I can really relate to Squirrel Girl, she just feels down to earth. On top of the excellent writing and characterization, the art is just adorable. Congratulations on a great release, I don't even have any questions (unless you can suggest a good one), I just wanted to say thanks for getting me interested in comics for the first time in years.

Thanks,<br>Robert 'MrAptronym'

**RYAN: Thanks, Robert! And let me suggest a question for you: "How come Doreen hasn't met any flying squirrels yet?" And the answer is that, until LITERALLY YESTERDAY when Erica proved me wrong, I thought that there weren't any in North America. I saw some flying squirrels at a zoo when I was a kid and I guess I assumed all zoo animals were from far away? Anyway, turns out they DO live on at least the same continent that Doreen lives on, so I'm a big dummy but at least I'm slightly smarter now, and we'll hopefully see some in the comic sooner rather than later.**

**ERICA: The 44 varieties of flying squirrel live in North America, Europe, and Asia, but there's like one kind in America and one that spans from Finland to Japan and then the other 42 are all in Asia. So, really Asia is still has the best flying-squirrel-to-continent ratio. Oh, wait, the original question wasn't about flying squirrels. I'm glad you like our take on Doreen, being a long time Squirrel Girl fan!**

Dear Ryan & Erica,

What's with all this talk of Chipmunk Hunk? Are you teasing us with a prospective Woodland Avengers? I could definitely get behind that series.

Keep up the good work,<br>Mitch

**RYAN: I wasn't planning the Woodland Avengers, but now that you mention it it's all I can think about, so let's say... DEFINITELY YES, THAT IS EXACTLY WHAT IS GOING TO HAPPEN.**

**ERICA: I thought we weren't supposed to talk about the Yosemite Avengers until after Secret Wars.**

Dear Ryan & Erica,

Thank you for teaming up an empowered girl with the world's most charismatic microfauna. You have made a lot of female squirrel biologists very happy. (By "a lot," I mean proportionally... sadly, we aren't that numerous.) I especially appreciate Doreen's sensible footwear choice and her blind optimism about the coolness of squirrels. Please keep making this comic FOREVER. Also, if you can swing it, please introduce a paleontologist who is woefully dull compared to Squirrel Girl. For an added touch of realism. My boyfriend studies theropods, and I'm sure I don't have to say who's the bigger hit at parties.

Lastly, please enjoy this portrait of me with some of my squirrel friends. I would have also included a photo of my pre-Unbeatable Squirrel Girl costume, but the furry one-piece bathing suit is, erm, a little alarming.

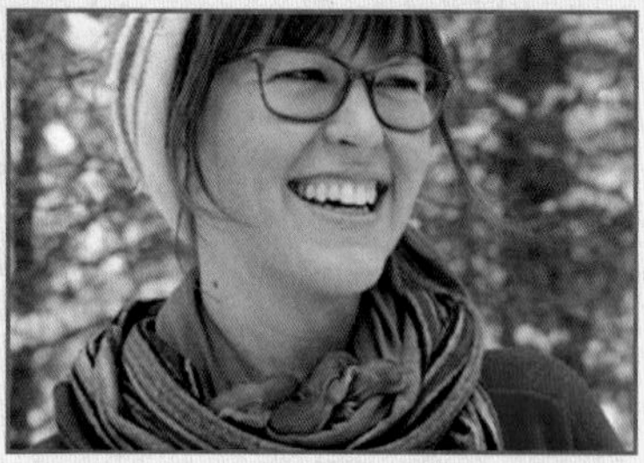

Sincerely,<br>Amanda

**RYAN: Amanda! I didn't even NOTICE the squirrels at first because they match your whole ensemble so well! I had never considered using baby squirrels as a fashion accessory until now but clearly I was not dreaming big enough. That is an amazing picture. I love it.**

**As someone who was always big into theropods from my Dinosaur Comics strip and who is now big into squirrels for obvious reasons, I feel like I can't decide who is cooler between you and your boyfriend! Probably you're both tied for first? But in any case I feel like you and your boyfriend and I could share some pretty friggin' scintillating conversation at cool parties, so please attend some cool parties soon and invite me, THANKS IN ADVANCE.**

**ERICA: I think I know who the winner is, because I'm pretty sure small mammals made it past the KT extinction. Amanda, I am 100% jealous of your woodland creature friends. So many of us watched Sleeping Beauty (and should totally watch it again because of that Eyvind Earle art) and said, "yes, when I grow up, I'm going to have a woodland posse" but we gave up and moved onto other, lesser endeavors. I salute you.**

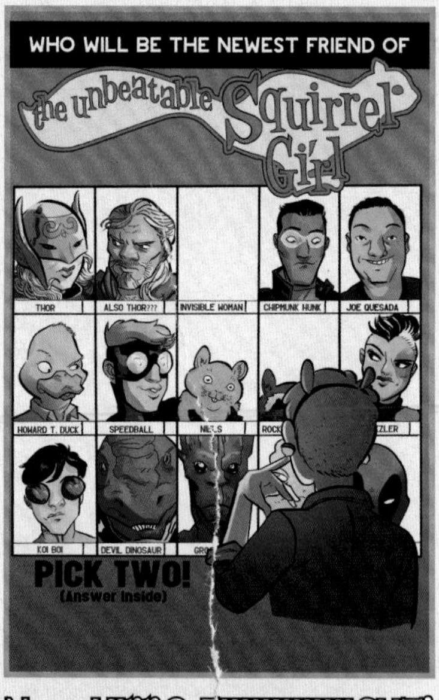
WHO WILL BE THE NEWEST FRIEND OF
the unbeatable Squirrel Girl
THOR
ALSO THOR???
INVISIBLE WOMAN
CHIPMUNK HUNK
JOE QUESADA
HOWARD T. DUCK
SPEEDBALL
KOI BOI
DEVIL DINOSAUR
PICK TWO!
(Answer inside)

**Next: HIPPO FIIIIIIIIIIGHT!**

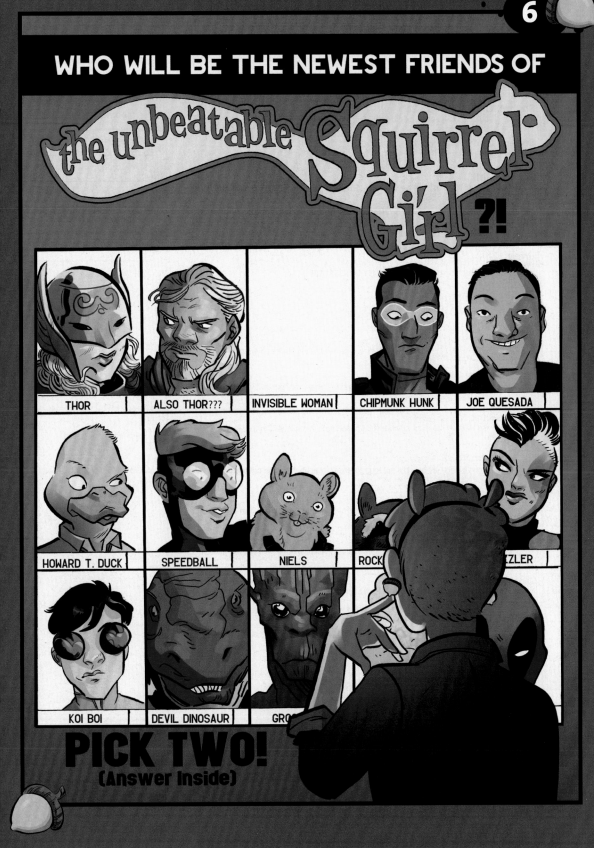

*Doreen Green isn't just a first-year computer science student: she secretly also has all the powers of both squirrel and girl! She uses her amazing abilities to fight crime **and** be as awesome as possible. You know her as...**The Unbeatable Squirrel Girl!** Let's catch up with what she's been up to until now, with...*

# Squirrel Girl in a nutshell

**Squirrel Girl!** @unbeatablesg
RT if you helped defeat Mysterion and his ROBOT DINOSAURS and saved the statue of liberty!!

**Squirrel Girl!** @unbeatablesg
RT @unbeatablesg: RT if you helped defeat Mysterion and his ROBOT DINOSAURS and saved the statue of liberty!!

**Squirrel Girl!** @unbeatablesg
Yes I did just retweet myself

**Squirrel Girl!** @unbeatablesg
PROBABLY because I totally just helped defeat Mysterion and his ROBOT DINOSAURS and saved the STATUE OF LIBERTY??

**Squirrel Girl!** @unbeatablesg
@HULKYSMASHY hey thanks for the RT!

**HULK** @HULKYSMASHY
@unbeatablesg HULK SMASH PUNY DINOSAUR!!

**Squirrel Girl!** @unbeatablesg
@HULKYSMASHY haha we sure did!!

**HULK** @HULKYSMASHY
@unbeatablesg HULK GLAD WHEN SOCIOLOGICAL PROBLEMS CAN BE SOLVED BY SMASHING

**Squirrel Girl!** @unbeatablesg
@HULKYSMASHY yeah it's always nice when things work out that way actually

**CampusBank** @campusbank
Good news! We've fixed the giant squirrel-suit-shaped hole in our wall. CampusBank: We've Got Class Too™.

**Squirrel Girl!** @unbeatablesg
@campusbank okay but let's not forget the only reason that hole is there is because i saved all the hostages

**CampusBank** @campusbank
We think you'll be INTERESTed in our new savings account fee schedules. CampusBank: We've Got Class Too™.

**Squirrel Girl!** @unbeatablesg
@campusbank cool pun bro but can we at least acknowledge how i saved all the hostages

**CampusBank** @campusbank
We can't take all the CREDIT for our new student charge card plans. CampusBank: We've Got Class Too™.

**Squirrel Girl!** @unbeatablesg
@campusbank sometimes i wonder why i follow so many #brands on social media

**Squirrel Girl!** @unbeatablesg
Okay everyone, HONESTLY, tell me this wall doesn't look WAY BETTER with a hole:

REC

**search!**

#hippothehippo

#imwithskrull

#liontomeetyou

#squirrelgirl

#kicksbuttseatsnuts

Oh that poor narrator

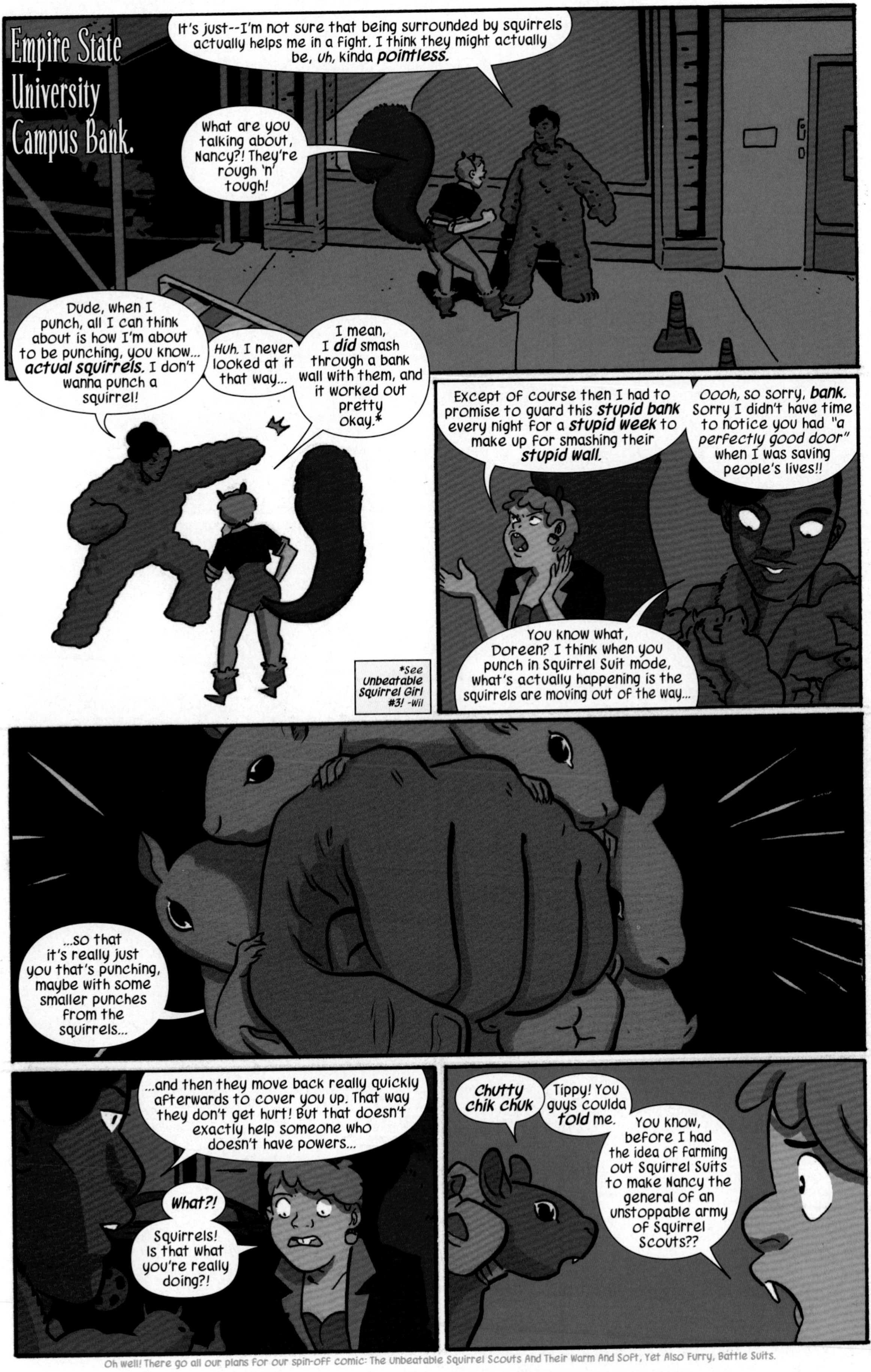
Empire State University Campus Bank.
It's just--I'm not sure that being surrounded by squirrels actually helps me in a fight. I think they might actually be, uh, kinda pointless.
What are you talking about, Nancy?! They're rough 'n' tough!
Dude, when I punch, all I can think about is how I'm about to be punching, you know... actual squirrels. I don't wanna punch a squirrel!
Huh. I never looked at it that way...
I mean, I did smash through a bank wall with them, and it worked out pretty okay.*
*See Unbeatable Squirrel Girl #3! -Wil
Except of course then I had to promise to guard this stupid bank every night for a stupid week to make up for smashing their stupid wall.
Oooh, so sorry, bank. Sorry I didn't have time to notice you had "a perfectly good door" when I was saving people's lives!!
You know what, Doreen? I think when you punch in Squirrel Suit mode, what's actually happening is the squirrels are moving out of the way...
...so that it's really just you that's punching, maybe with some smaller punches from the squirrels...
...and then they move back really quickly afterwards to cover you up. That way they don't get hurt! But that doesn't exactly help someone who doesn't have powers...
What?!
Squirrels! Is that what you're really doing?!
Chutty chik chuk
Tippy! You guys coulda told me.
You know, before I had the idea of farming out Squirrel Suits to make Nancy the general of an unstoppable army of Squirrel Scouts??

Oh well! There go all our plans for our spin-off comic: The Unbeatable Squirrel Scouts And Their Warm And Soft, Yet Also Furry, Battle Suits.

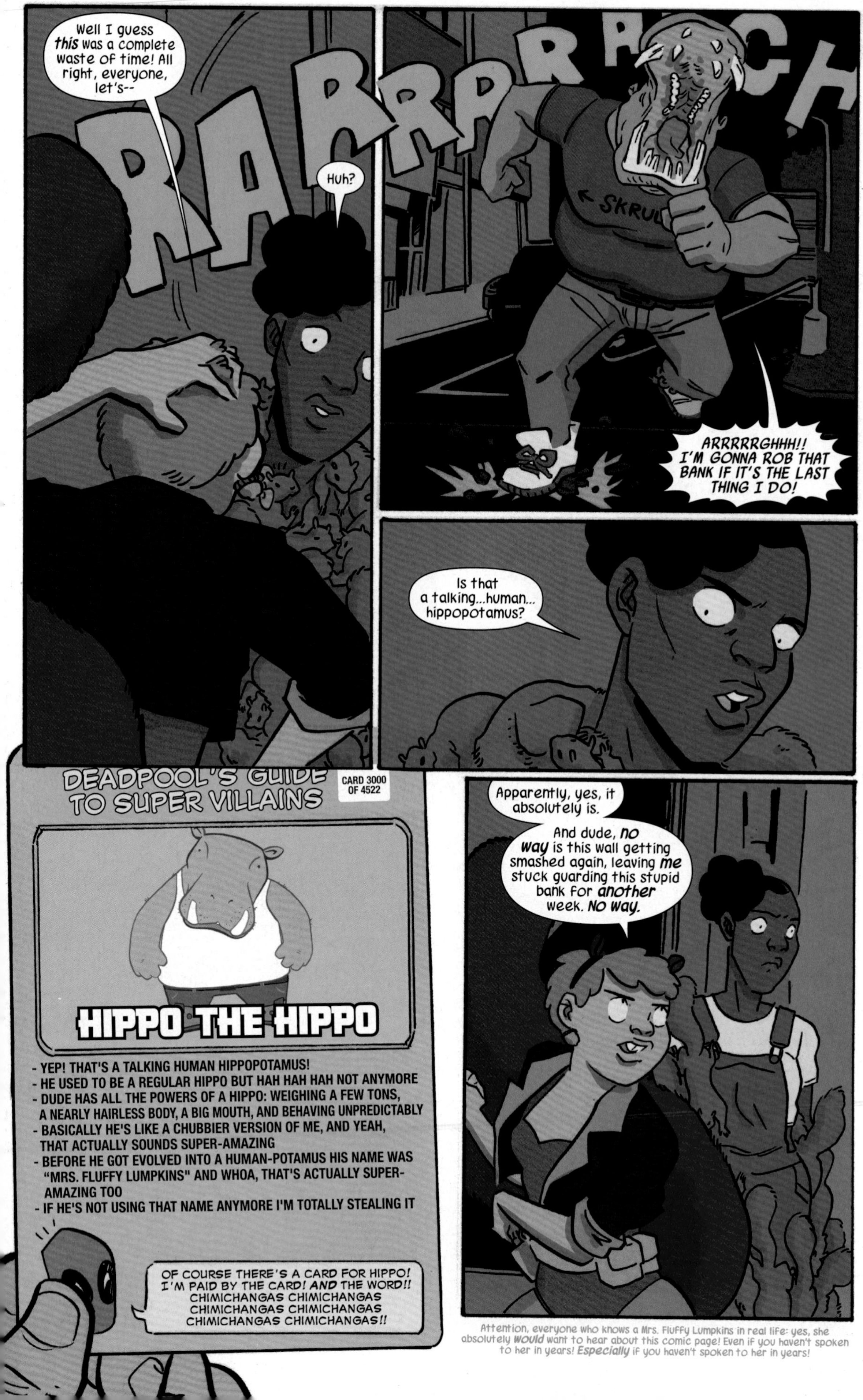

Well I guess this was a complete waste of time! All right, everyone, let's--
RARRRRRAGH
Huh?
ARRRRRGHHH!! I'M GONNA ROB THAT BANK IF IT'S THE LAST THING I DO!
SKRUL
Is that a talking...human... hippopotamus?
DEADPOOL'S GUIDE TO SUPER VILLAINS
CARD 3000 OF 4522
HIPPO THE HIPPO
- YEP! THAT'S A TALKING HUMAN HIPPOPOTAMUS!
- HE USED TO BE A REGULAR HIPPO BUT HAH HAH HAH NOT ANYMORE
- DUDE HAS ALL THE POWERS OF A HIPPO: WEIGHING A FEW TONS, A NEARLY HAIRLESS BODY, A BIG MOUTH, AND BEHAVING UNPREDICTABLY
- BASICALLY HE'S LIKE A CHUBBIER VERSION OF ME, AND YEAH, THAT ACTUALLY SOUNDS SUPER-AMAZING
- BEFORE HE GOT EVOLVED INTO A HUMAN-POTAMUS HIS NAME WAS "MRS. FLUFFY LUMPKINS" AND WHOA, THAT'S ACTUALLY SUPER-AMAZING TOO
- IF HE'S NOT USING THAT NAME ANYMORE I'M TOTALLY STEALING IT
OF COURSE THERE'S A CARD FOR HIPPO! I'M PAID BY THE CARD! AND THE WORD!! CHIMICHANGAS CHIMICHANGAS CHIMICHANGAS CHIMICHANGAS CHIMICHANGAS CHIMICHANGAS!!
Apparently, yes, it absolutely is.
And dude, no way is this wall getting smashed again, leaving me stuck guarding this stupid bank for another week. No way.

Attention, everyone who knows a Mrs. Fluffy Lumpkins in real life: yes, she absolutely *would* want to hear about this comic page! Even if you haven't spoken to her in years! *Especially* if you haven't spoken to her in years!

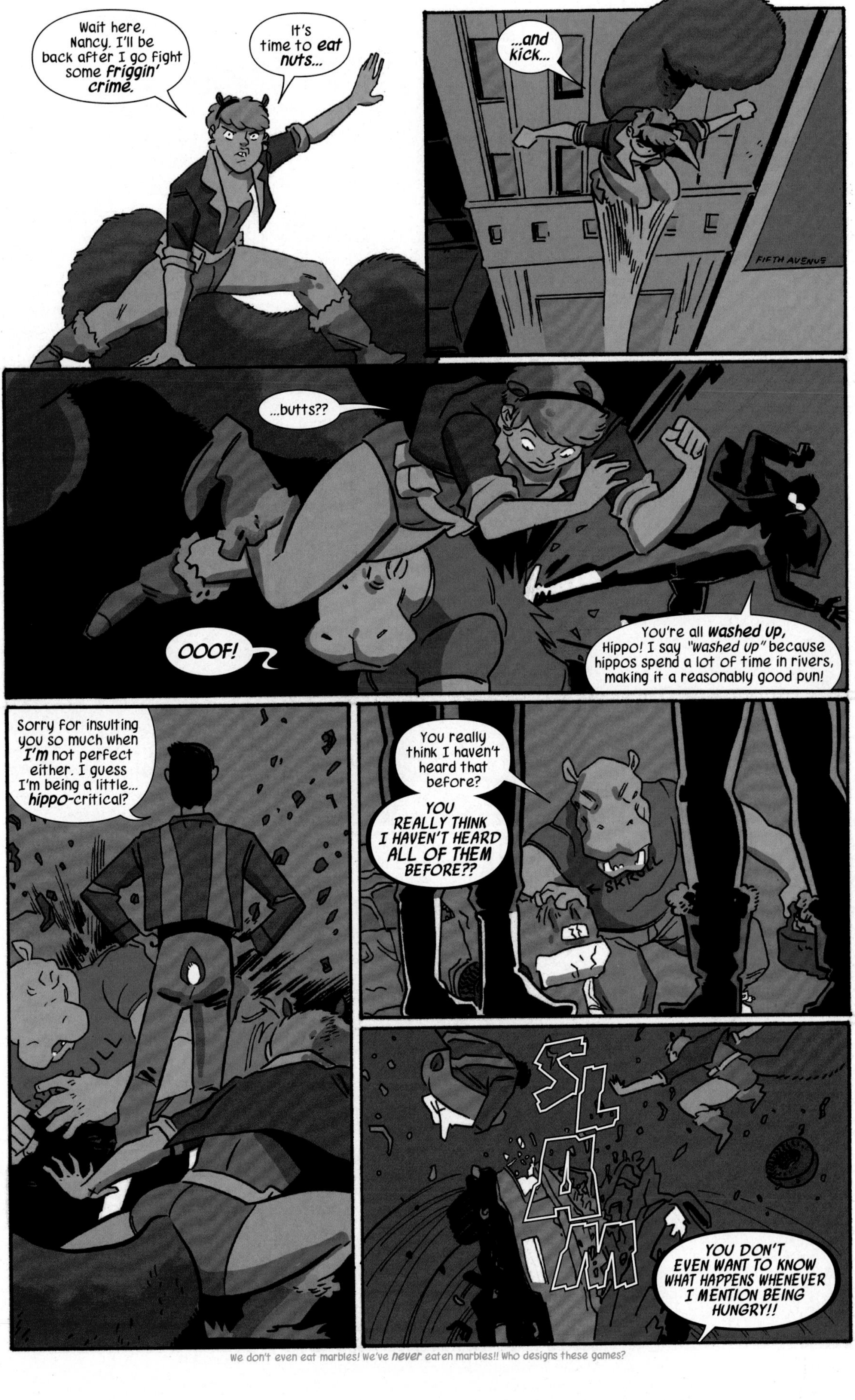
Wait here, Nancy. I'll be back after I go fight some friggin' crime.
It's time to eat nuts...
...and kick...
FIFTH AVENUE
...butts??
OOOF!
You're all washed up, Hippo! I say "washed up" because hippos spend a lot of time in rivers, making it a reasonably good pun!
Sorry for insulting you so much when I'm not perfect either. I guess I'm being a little... hippo-critical?
You really think I haven't heard that before?
YOU REALLY THINK I HAVEN'T HEARD ALL OF THEM BEFORE??
SLAM
YOU DON'T EVEN WANT TO KNOW WHAT HAPPENS WHENEVER I MENTION BEING HUNGRY!!

We don't even eat marbles! We've *never* eaten marbles!! Who designs these games?

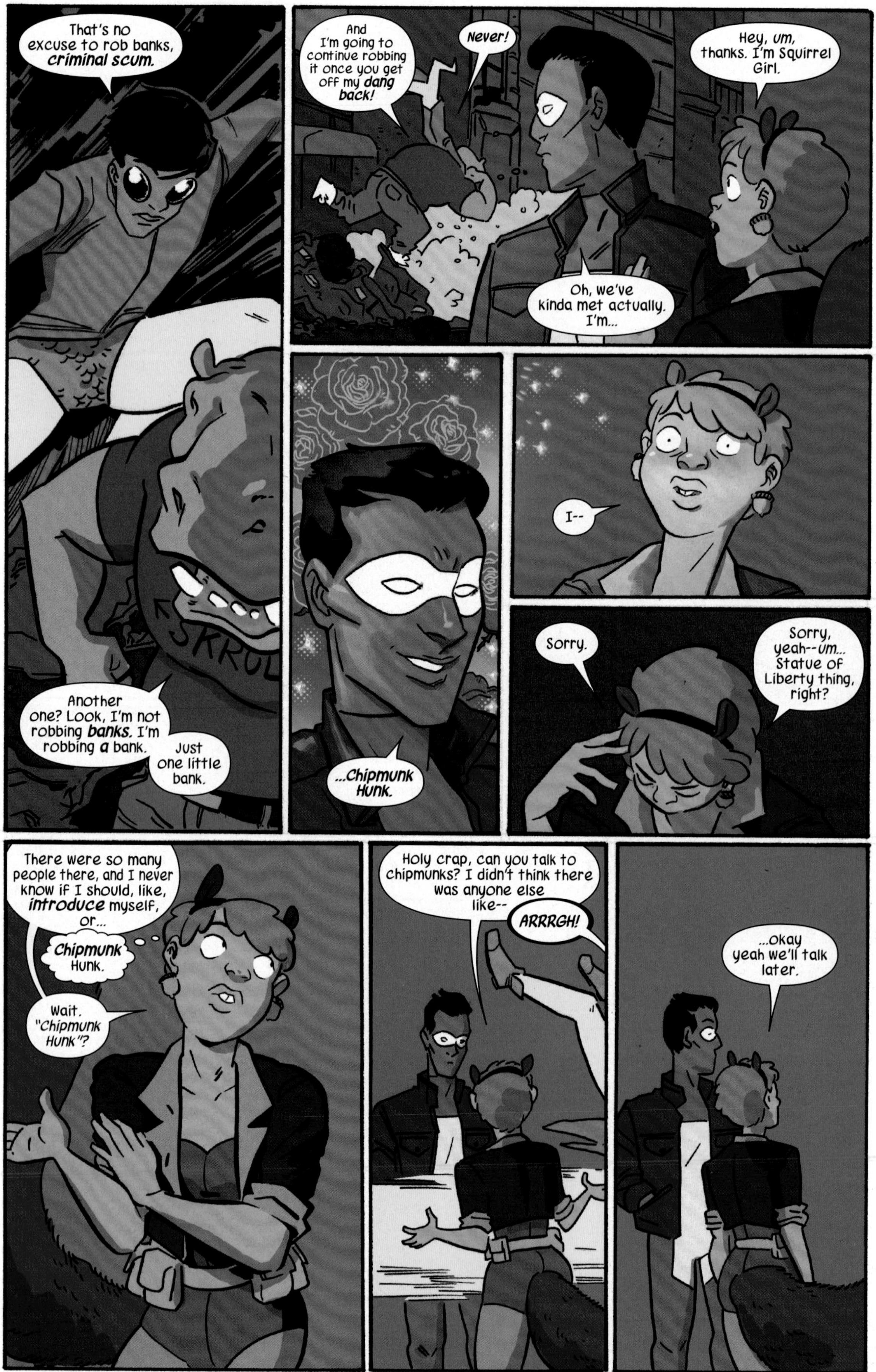
That's no excuse to rob banks, criminal scum.
Another one? Look, I'm not robbing banks. I'm robbing a bank.
Just one little bank.
And I'm going to continue robbing it once you get off my dang back!
Never!
Hey, um, thanks. I'm Squirrel Girl.
Oh, we've kinda met actually. I'm...
...Chipmunk Hunk.
I--
Sorry.
Sorry, yeah--um... Statue of Liberty thing, right?
There were so many people there, and I never know if I should, like, introduce myself, or...
Chipmunk Hunk.
Wait. "Chipmunk Hunk"?
Holy crap, can you talk to chipmunks? I didn't think there was anyone else like--
ARRRGH!
...okay yeah we'll talk later.

Plus a lot of the other heroes don't really talk as much as I do. I dunno. I don't want to make it weird for them, but then I worry it's weird to *not* introduce myself, you know?

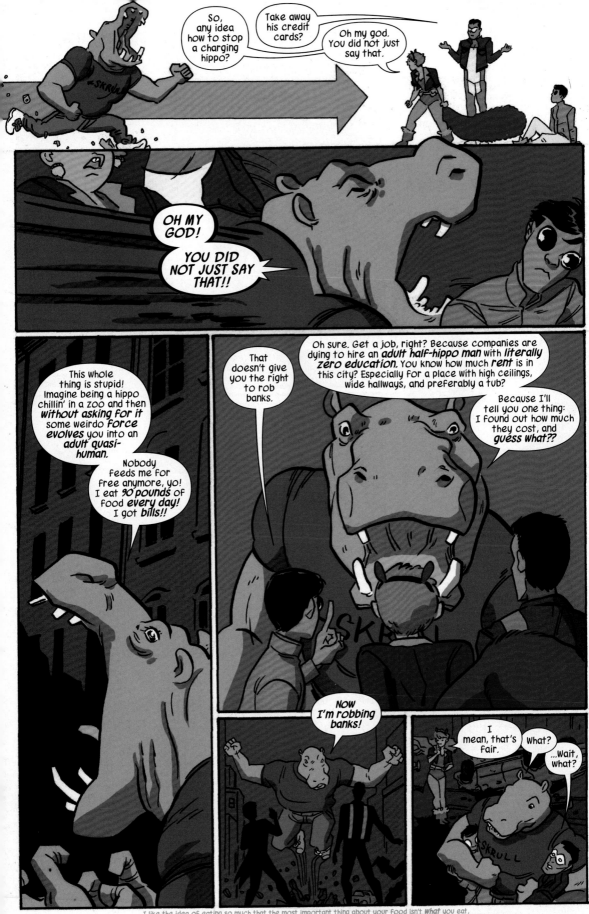

So, any idea how to stop a charging hippo?

Take away his credit cards?

Oh my god. You did not just say that.

OH MY GOD!

YOU DID NOT JUST SAY THAT!!

This whole thing is stupid! Imagine being a hippo chillin' in a zoo and then *without asking for it* some weirdo *force evolves* you into an *adult quasi-human.*

Nobody feeds me for free anymore, yo! I eat *90 pounds* of food *every day!* I got *bills!!*

That doesn't give you the right to rob banks.

Oh sure. Get a job, right? Because companies are dying to hire an *adult half-hippo man* with *literally zero education.* You know how much *rent* is in this city? Especially for a place with high ceilings, wide hallways, and preferably a tub?

Because I'll tell you one thing: I found out how much they cost, and *guess what??*

NOW I'm robbing banks!

I mean, that's fair.

What?

...Wait, what?

I like the idea of eating so much that the most important thing about your food isn't *what* you eat, but rather just the number of pounds it weighs. I--I really like eating, you guys.

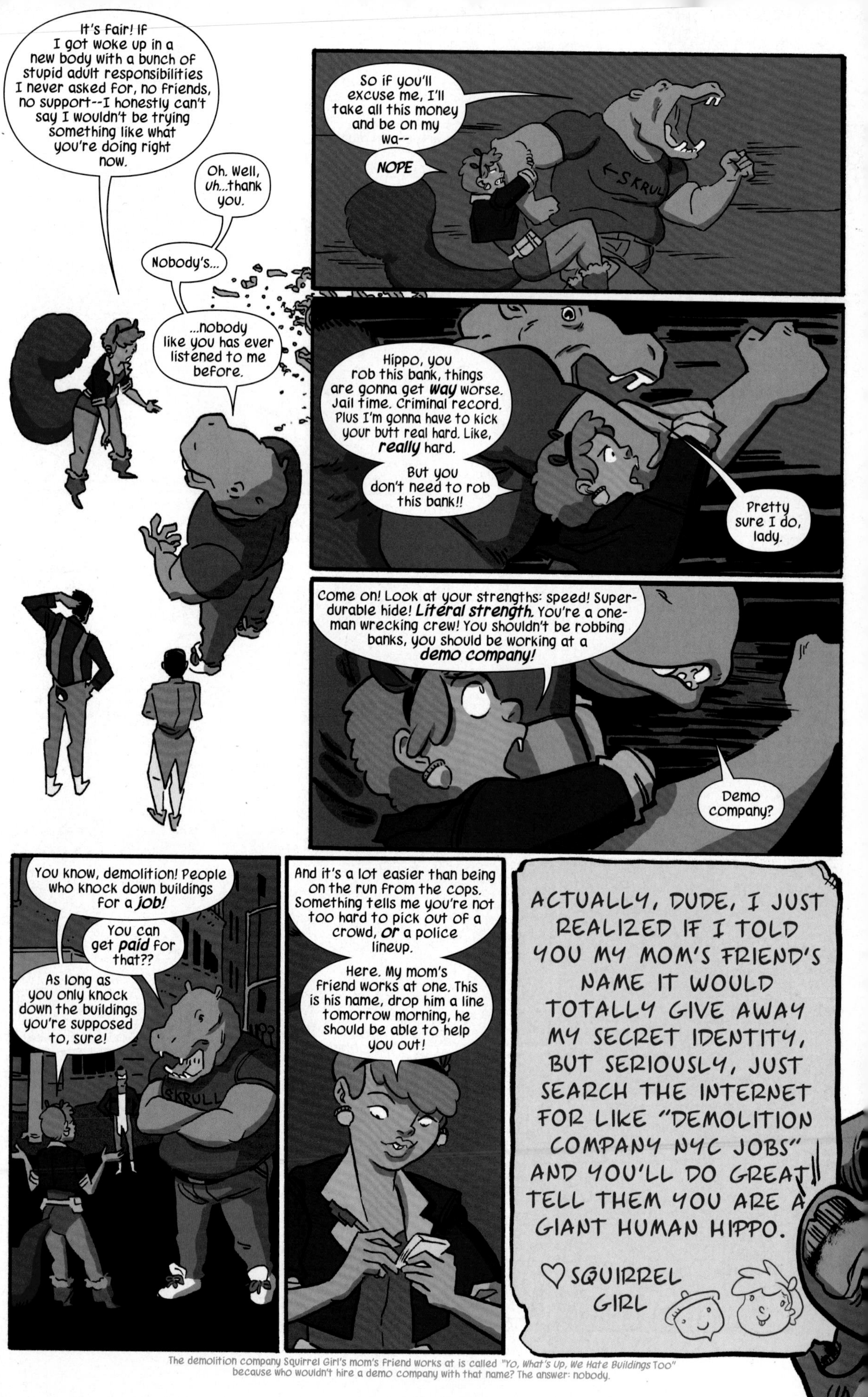
It's fair! If I got woke up in a new body with a bunch of stupid adult responsibilities I never asked for, no friends, no support--I honestly can't say I wouldn't be trying something like what you're doing right now.
Oh. Well, uh...thank you.
Nobody's...
...nobody like you has ever listened to me before.
So if you'll excuse me, I'll take all this money and be on my wa--
NOPE
SKRUL
Hippo, you rob this bank, things are gonna get *way* worse. Jail time. Criminal record. Plus I'm gonna have to kick your butt real hard. Like, *really* hard.
But you don't need to rob this bank!!
Pretty sure I do, lady.
Come on! Look at your strengths: speed! Super-durable hide! *Literal strength.* You're a one-man wrecking crew! You shouldn't be robbing banks, you should be working at a *demo company!*
Demo company?
You know, demolition! People who knock down buildings for a *job!*
You can get *paid* for that??
As long as you only knock down the buildings you're supposed to, sure!
SKRULL
And it's a lot easier than being on the run from the cops. Something tells me you're not too hard to pick out of a crowd, *or* a police lineup.
Here. My mom's friend works at one. This is his name, drop him a line tomorrow morning, he should be able to help you out!
ACTUALLY, DUDE, I JUST REALIZED IF I TOLD YOU MY MOM'S FRIEND'S NAME IT WOULD TOTALLY GIVE AWAY MY SECRET IDENTITY, BUT SERIOUSLY, JUST SEARCH THE INTERNET FOR LIKE "DEMOLITION COMPANY NYC JOBS" AND YOU'LL DO GREAT. TELL THEM YOU ARE A GIANT HUMAN HIPPO.
♡ SQUIRREL GIRL

The demolition company Squirrel Girl's mom's friend works at is called *"Yo, What's Up, We Hate Buildings Too"* because who wouldn't hire a demo company with that name? The answer: nobody.

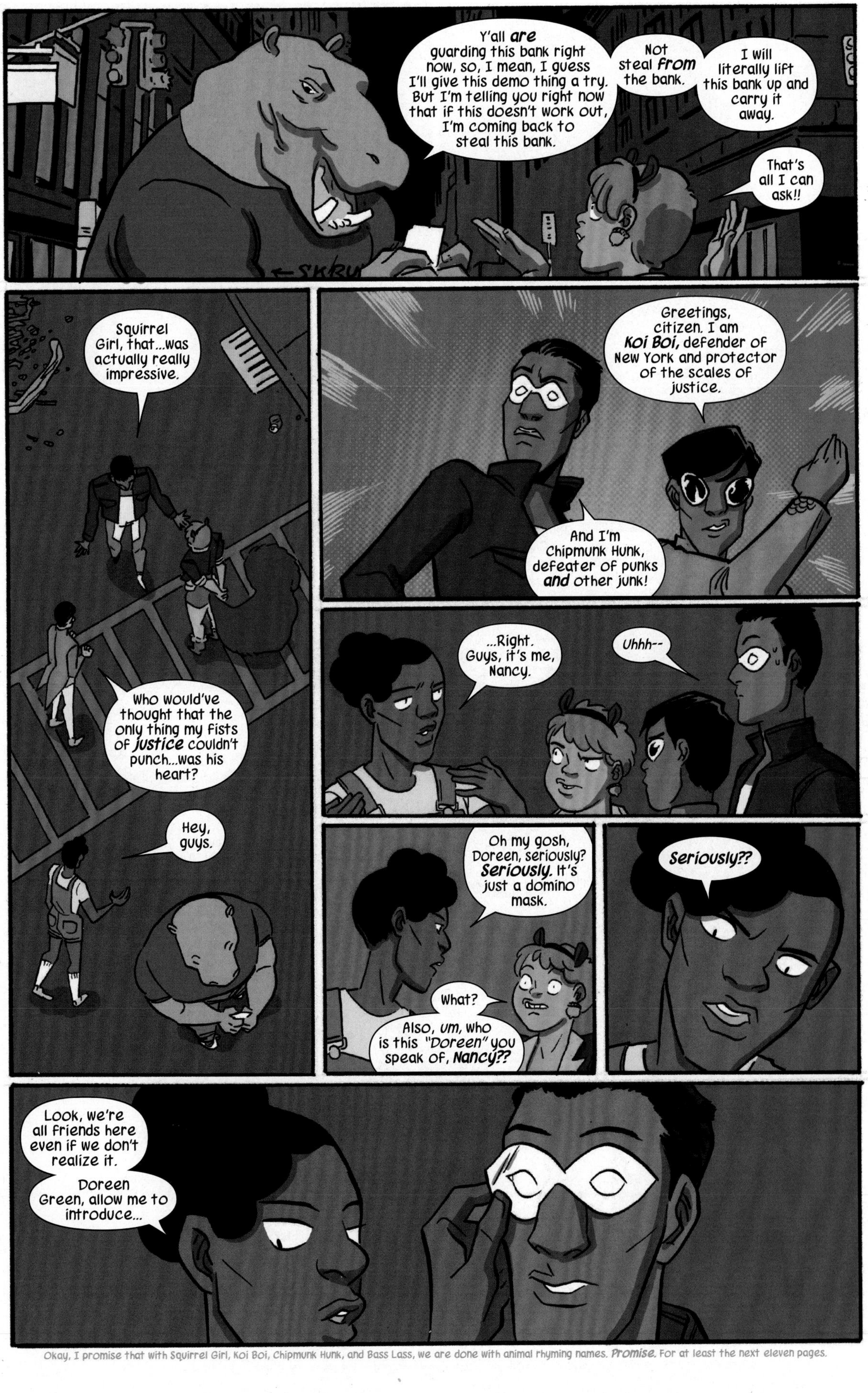
Y'all *are* guarding this bank right now, so, I mean, I guess I'll give this demo thing a try. But I'm telling you right now that if this doesn't work out, I'm coming back to steal this bank.
Not steal *from* the bank.
I will literally lift this bank up and carry it away.
That's all I can ask!!
Squirrel Girl, that...was actually really impressive.
Who would've thought that the only thing my fists of *justice* couldn't punch...was his heart?
Hey, guys.
Greetings, citizen. I am *Koi Boi,* defender of New York and protector of the scales of justice.
And I'm Chipmunk Hunk, defeater of punks *and* other junk!
...Right. Guys, it's me, Nancy.
Uhhh--
Oh my gosh, Doreen, seriously? *Seriously.* It's just a domino mask.
What?
Also, *um,* who is this *"Doreen"* you speak of, *Nancy??*
*Seriously??*
Look, we're all friends here even if we don't realize it.
Doreen Green, allow me to introduce...

Okay, I promise that with Squirrel Girl, Koi Boi, Chipmunk Hunk, and Bass Lass, we are done with animal rhyming names. *Promise.* For at least the next eleven pages.

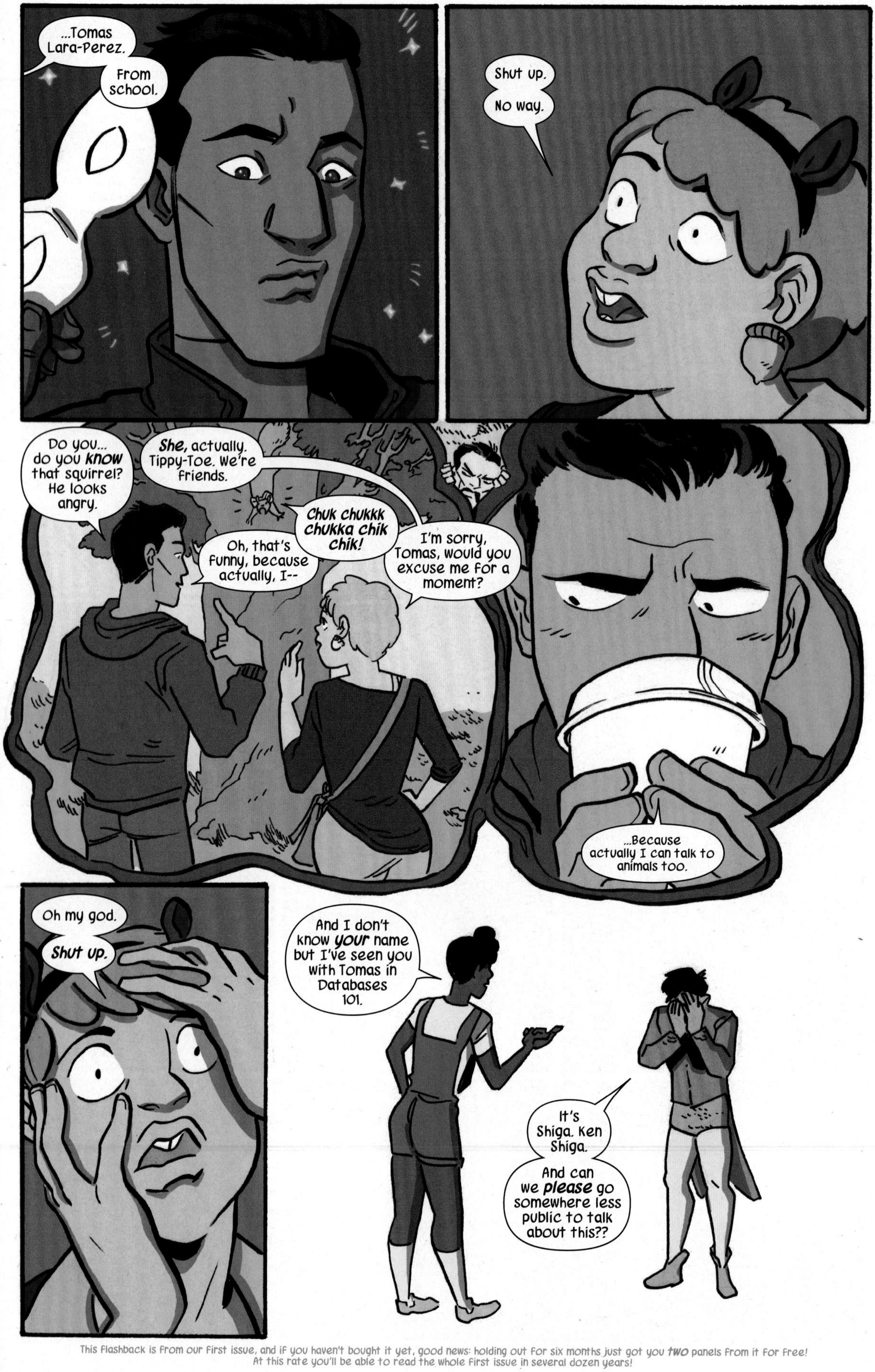

...Tomas Lara-Perez.
From school.
Shut up.
No way.
Do you... do you **know** that squirrel? He looks angry.
***She,*** actually. Tippy-Toe. We're friends.
Chuk chukkk chukka chik chik!
Oh, that's funny, because actually, I--
I'm sorry, Tomas, would you excuse me for a moment?
...Because actually I can talk to animals too.
Oh my god.
***Shut up.***
And I don't know ***your*** name but I've seen you with Tomas in Databases 101.
It's Shiga. Ken Shiga.
And can we ***please*** go somewhere less public to talk about this??


This flashback is from our first issue, and if you haven't bought it yet, good news: holding out for six months just got you ***two*** panels from it for free!
At this rate you'll be able to read the whole first issue in several dozen years!

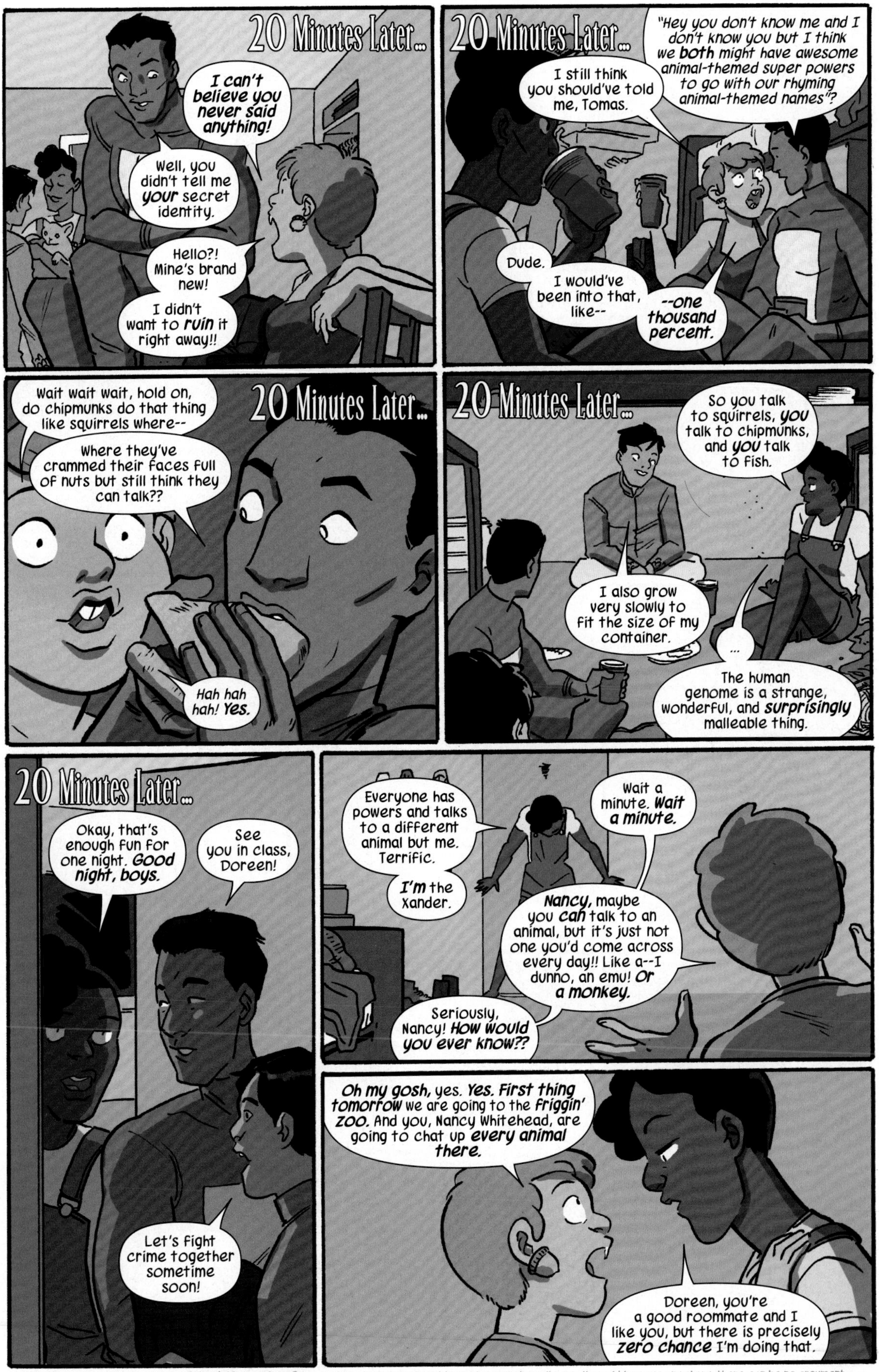
20 Minutes Later...
I can't believe you never said anything!
Well, you didn't tell me your secret identity.
Hello?! Mine's brand new!
I didn't want to ruin it right away!!
20 Minutes Later...
I still think you should've told me, Tomas.
"Hey you don't know me and I don't know you but I think we both might have awesome animal-themed super powers to go with our rhyming animal-themed names"?
Dude.
I would've been into that, like--
--one thousand percent.
20 Minutes Later...
Wait wait wait, hold on, do chipmunks do that thing like squirrels where--
Where they've crammed their faces full of nuts but still think they can talk??
Hah hah hah! Yes.
20 Minutes Later...
So you talk to squirrels, you talk to chipmunks, and you talk to fish.
I also grow very slowly to fit the size of my container.
...
The human genome is a strange, wonderful, and surprisingly malleable thing.
20 Minutes Later...
Okay, that's enough fun for one night. Good night, boys.
See you in class, Doreen!
Let's fight crime together sometime soon!
Everyone has powers and talks to a different animal but me. Terrific.
I'm the Xander.
Wait a minute. Wait a minute.
Nancy, maybe you can talk to an animal, but it's just not one you'd come across every day!! Like a--I dunno, an emu! Or a monkey.
Seriously, Nancy! How would you ever know??
Oh my gosh, yes. Yes. First thing tomorrow we are going to the friggin' zoo. And you, Nancy Whitehead, are going to chat up every animal there.
Doreen, you're a good roommate and I like you, but there is precisely zero chance I'm doing that.

Does every story ever need a *Friendship montage?* The answer: absolutely, unambiguously, unequivocally yes. It would improve any story; there can be no argument.

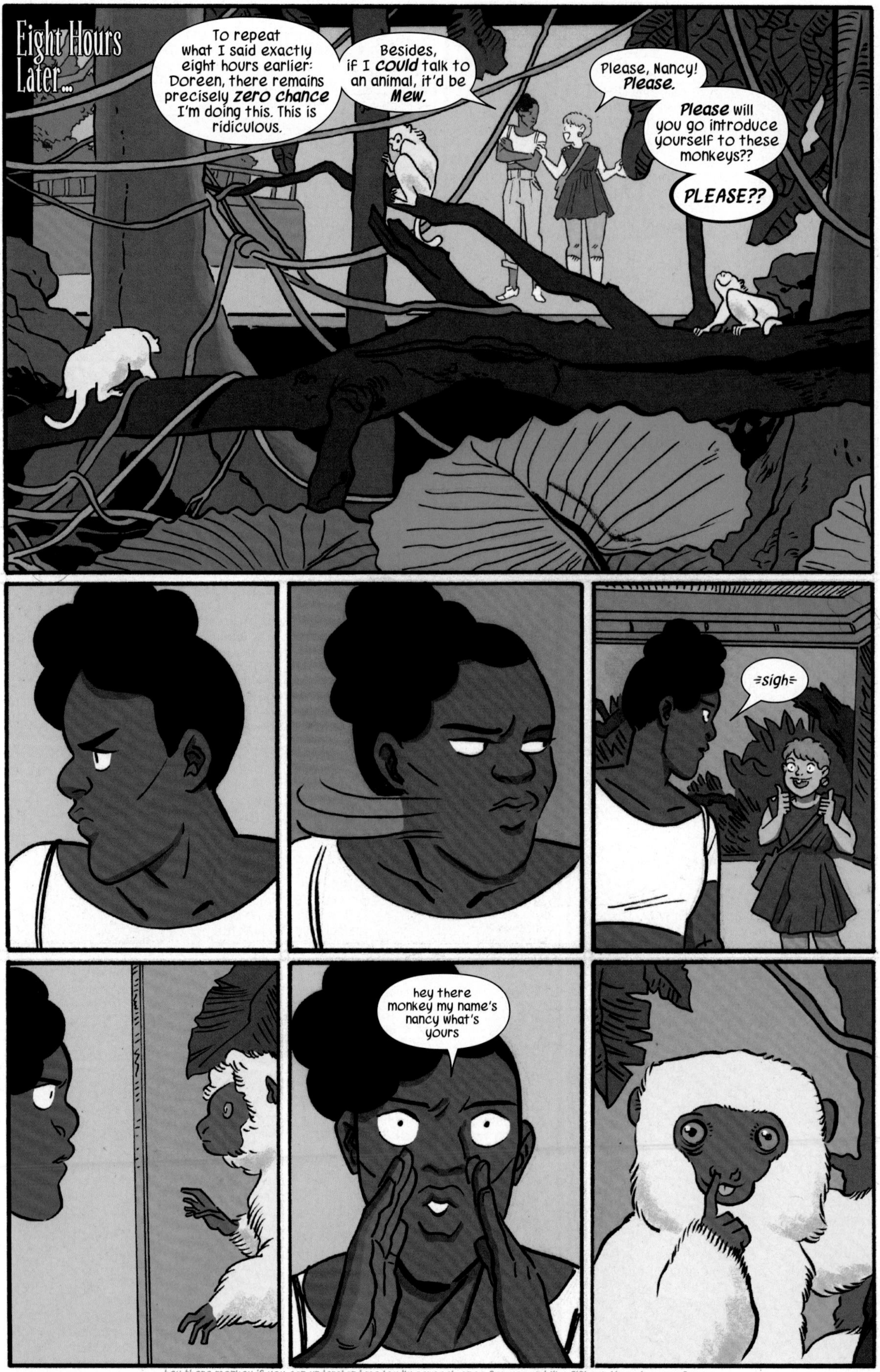
Eight Hours Later...
To repeat what I said exactly eight hours earlier: Doreen, there remains precisely zero chance I'm doing this. This is ridiculous.
Besides, if I could talk to an animal, it'd be Mew.
Please, Nancy! Please.
Please will you go introduce yourself to these monkeys??
PLEASE??
sigh
hey there monkey my name's nancy what's yours
hey there monkey if you can understand me loudly screech once for yes and like fifteen times in a row for no

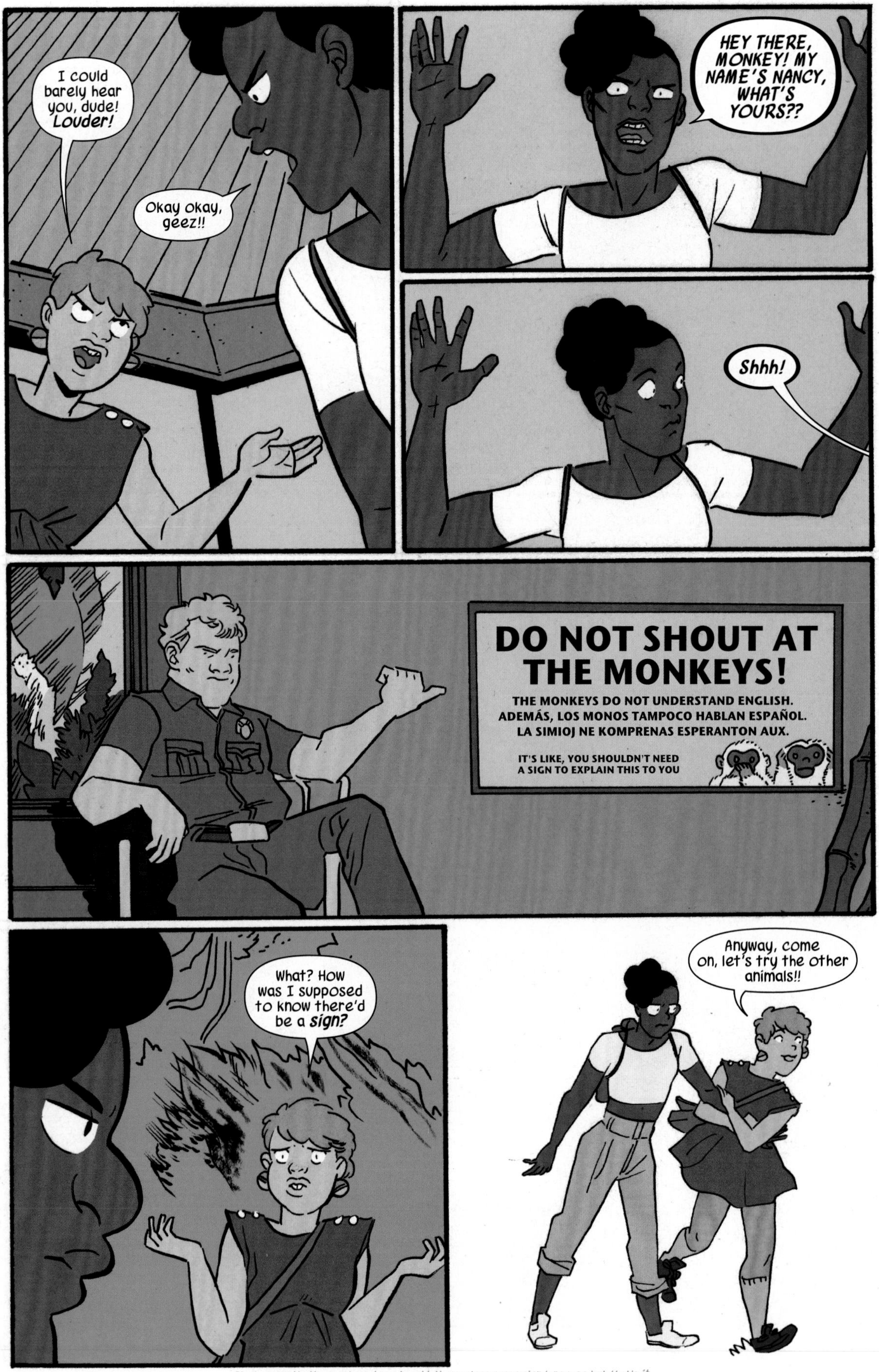
I could barely hear you, dude! Louder!
Okay okay, geez!!
HEY THERE, MONKEY! MY NAME'S NANCY, WHAT'S YOURS??
Shhh!
DO NOT SHOUT AT THE MONKEYS!
THE MONKEYS DO NOT UNDERSTAND ENGLISH.
ADEMÁS, LOS MONOS TAMPOCO HABLAN ESPAÑOL.
LA SIMIOJ NE KOMPRENAS ESPERANTON AUX.
IT'S LIKE, YOU SHOULDN'T NEED A SIGN TO EXPLAIN THIS TO YOU
What? How was I supposed to know there'd be a sign?
Anyway, come on, let's try the other animals!!

Okay, secretly the monkeys have taught themselves some sign language but that's *it.*

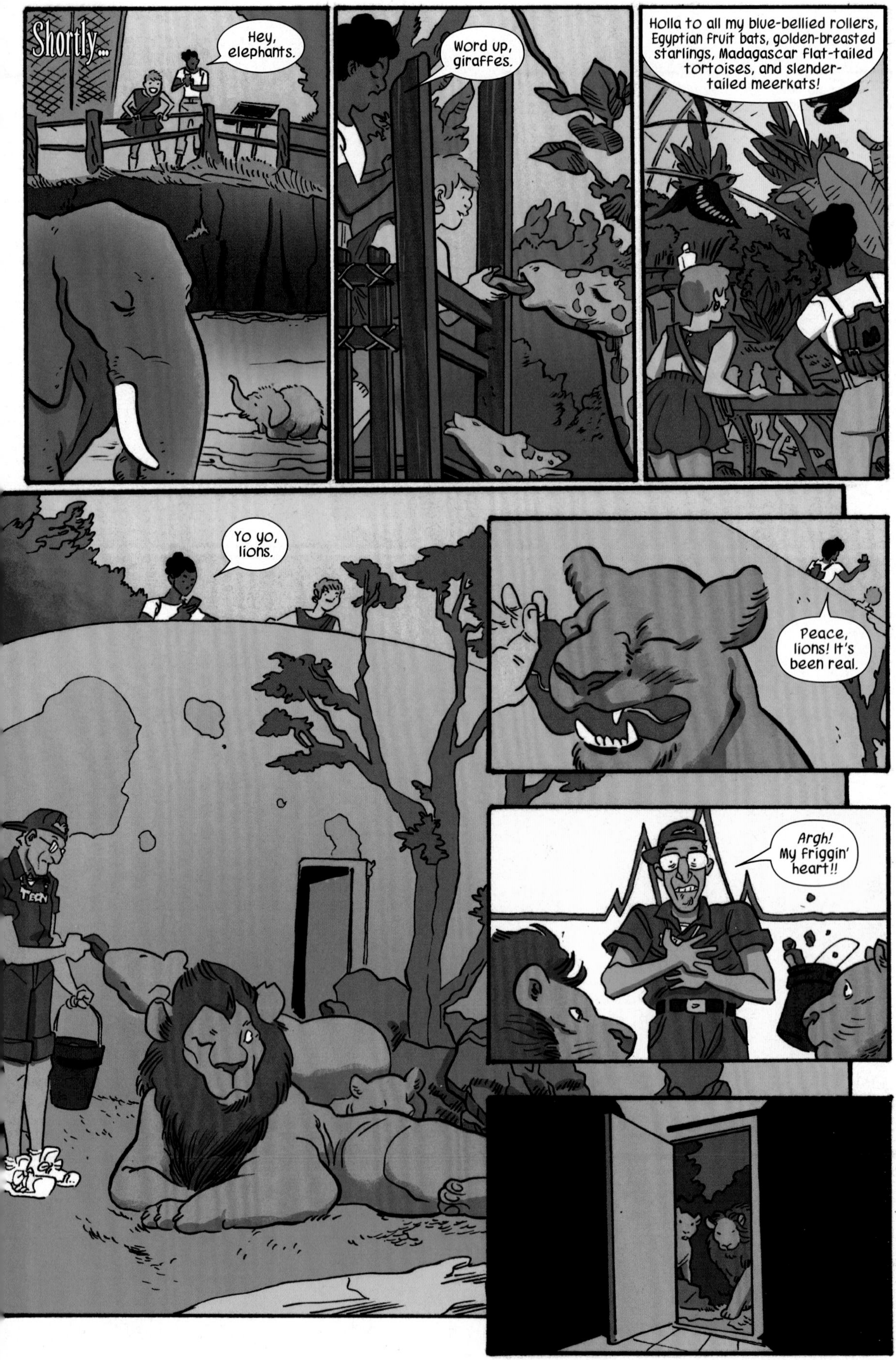
Shortly...
Hey, elephants.
Word up, giraffes.
Holla to all my blue-bellied rollers, Egyptian fruit bats, golden-breasted starlings, Madagascar flat-tailed tortoises, and slender-tailed meerkats!
Yo yo, lions.
Peace, lions! It's been real.
Argh! My friggin' heart!!

See, this is exactly why zoo regulations *clearly* state to close all lion doors *before* having a medical emergency.

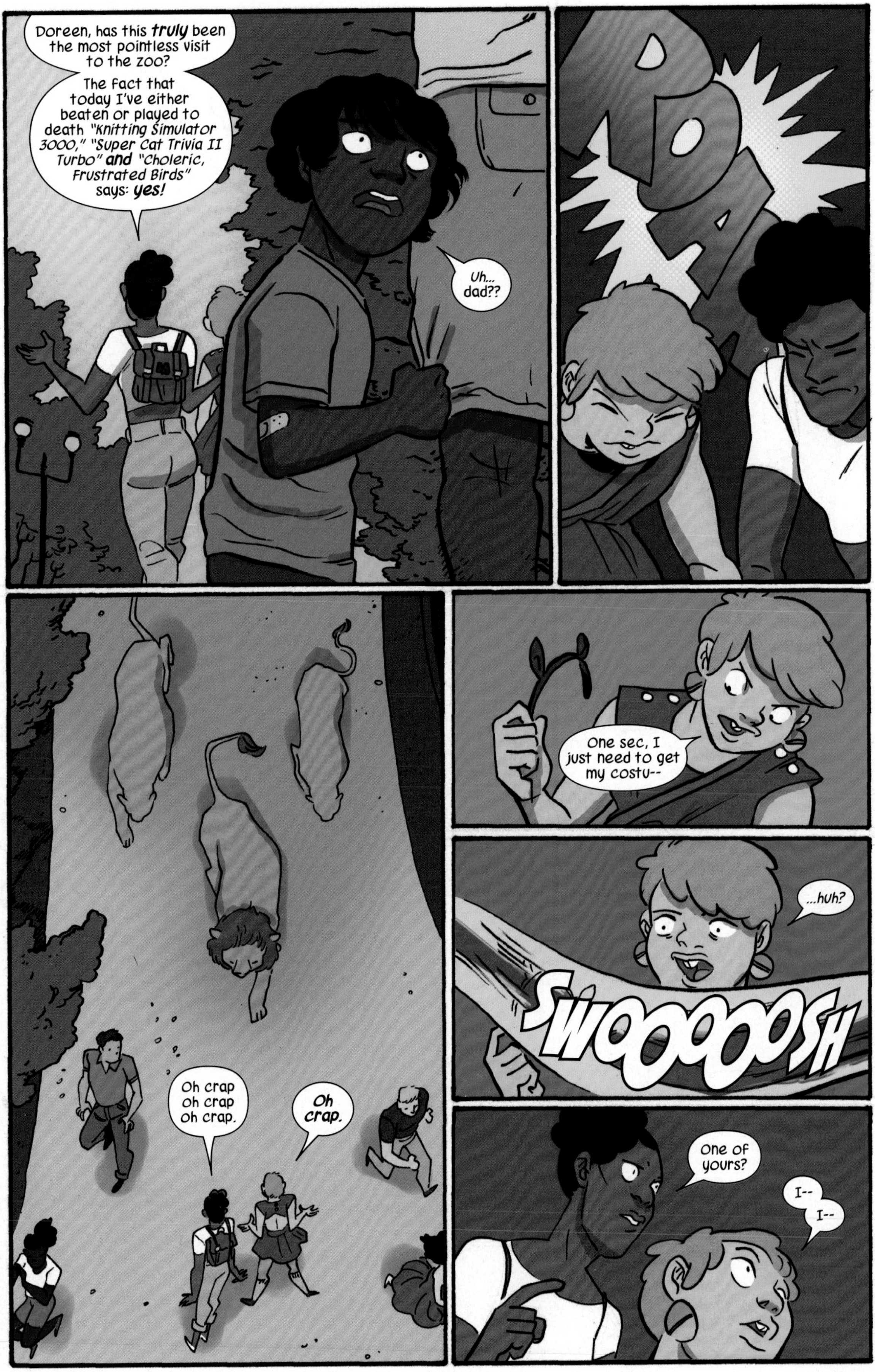

Doreen, has this truly been the most pointless visit to the zoo?
The fact that today I've either beaten or played to death "Knitting Simulator 3000," "Super Cat Trivia II Turbo" and "Choleric, Frustrated Birds" says: yes!
Uh... dad??
POW
One sec, I just need to get my costu--
...huh?
SWOOOOOSH
Oh crap oh crap oh crap.
Oh crap.
One of yours?
I--
I--

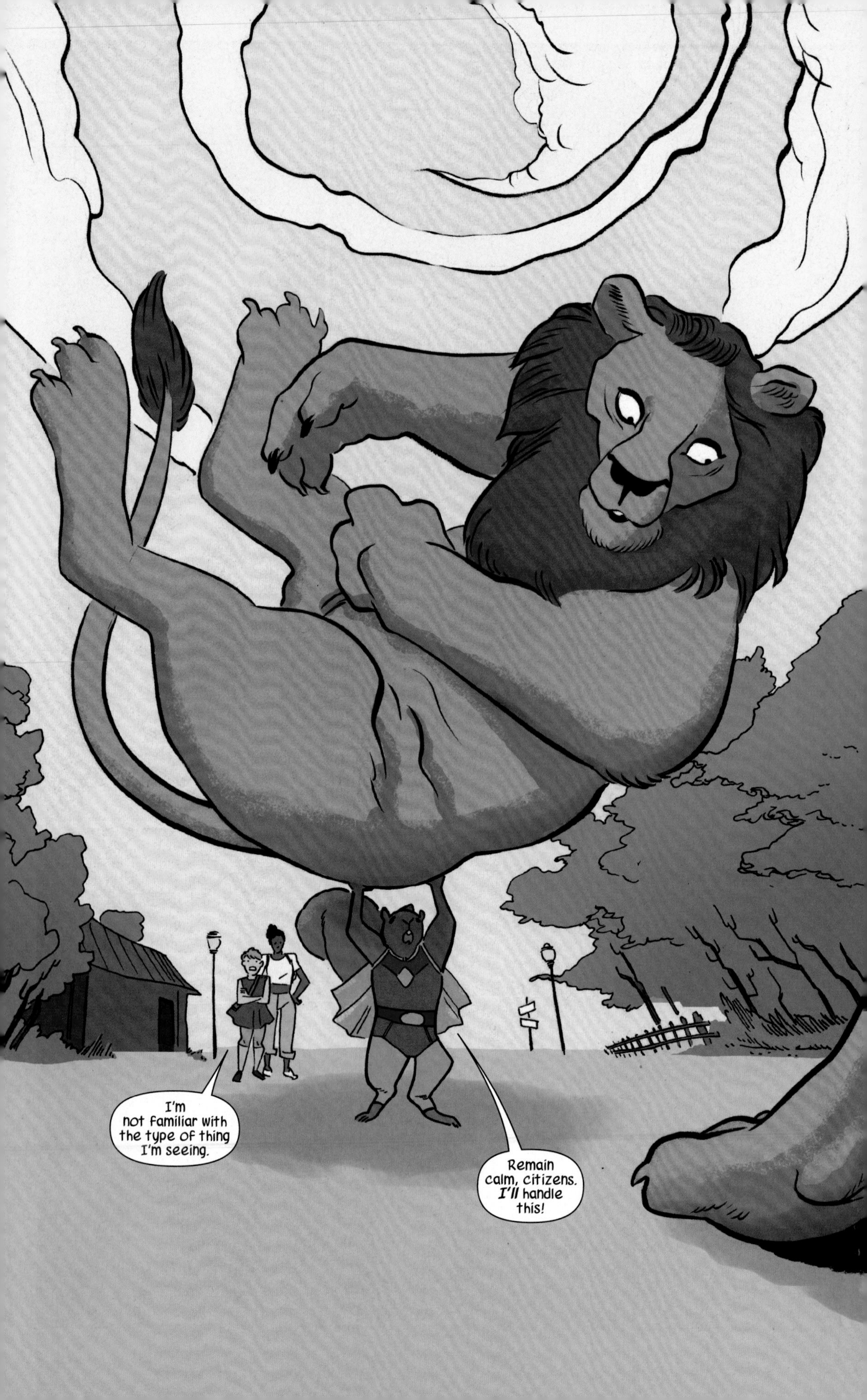
I'm not familiar with the type of thing I'm seeing.
Remain calm, citizens. *I'll* handle this!

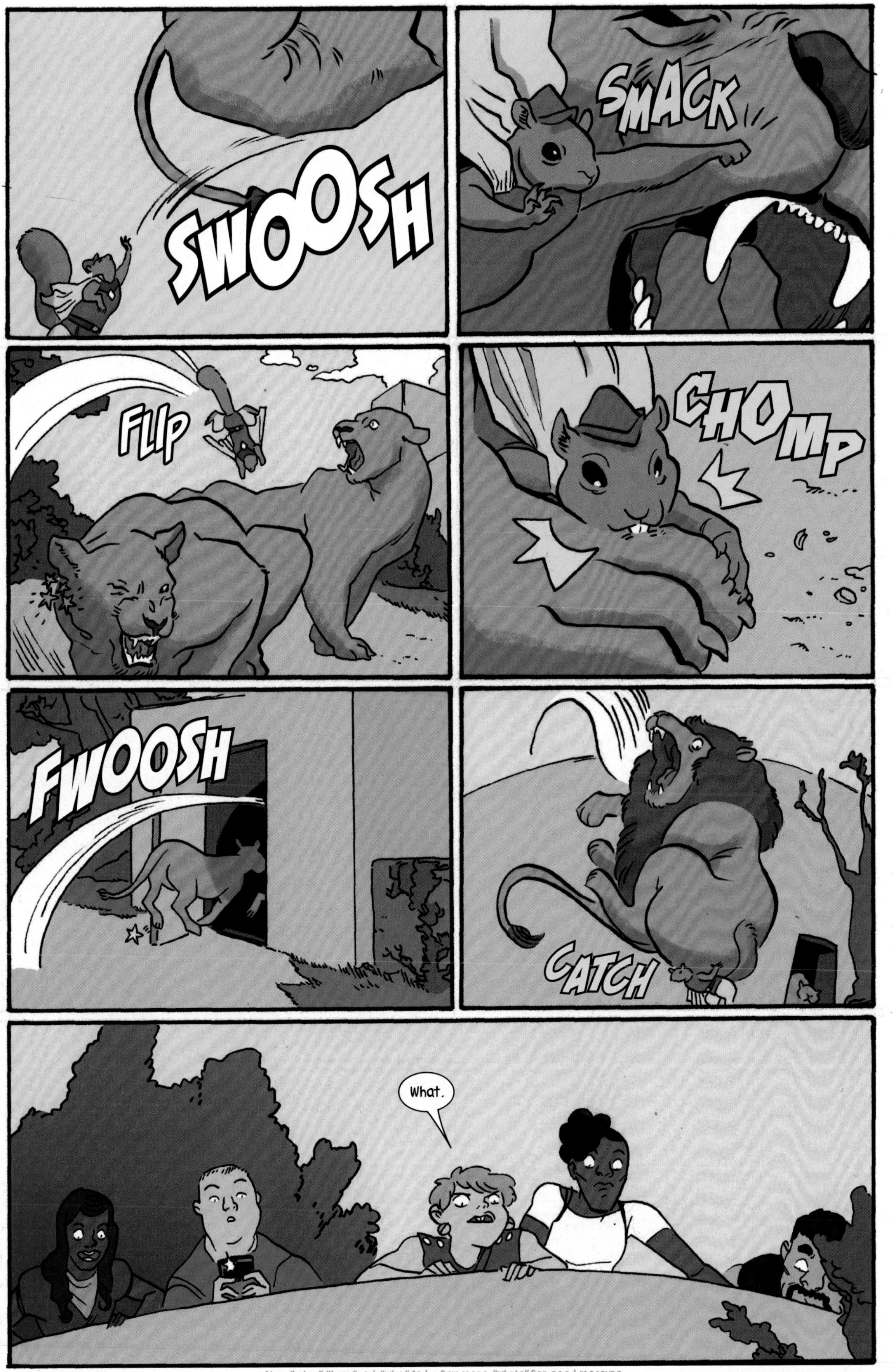
SWOOSH
SMACK
FLIP
CHOMP
FWOOSH
CATCH
What.

Also: "who," "how," and "why." And a few more "whats" for good measure.

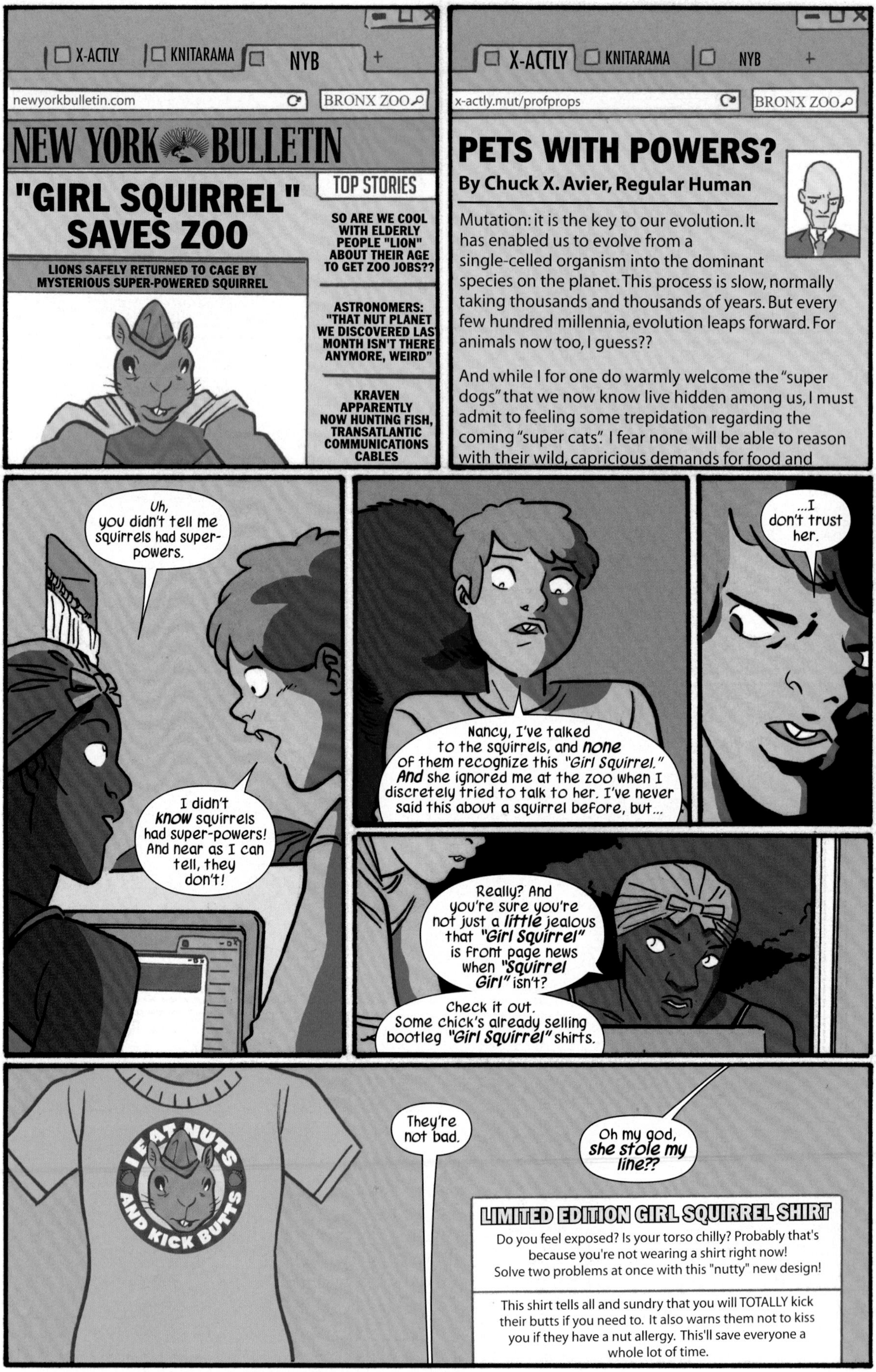
X-ACTLY
KNITARAMA
NYB
newyorkbulletin.com
BRONX ZOO
NEW YORK BULLETIN
"GIRL SQUIRREL" SAVES ZOO
LIONS SAFELY RETURNED TO CAGE BY MYSTERIOUS SUPER-POWERED SQUIRREL
TOP STORIES
SO ARE WE COOL WITH ELDERLY PEOPLE "LION" ABOUT THEIR AGE TO GET ZOO JOBS??
ASTRONOMERS: "THAT NUT PLANET WE DISCOVERED LAST MONTH ISN'T THERE ANYMORE, WEIRD"
KRAVEN APPARENTLY NOW HUNTING FISH, TRANSATLANTIC COMMUNICATIONS CABLES
X-ACTLY
KNITARAMA
NYB
x-actly.mut/profprops
BRONX ZOO
PETS WITH POWERS?
By Chuck X. Avier, Regular Human
Mutation: it is the key to our evolution. It has enabled us to evolve from a single-celled organism into the dominant species on the planet. This process is slow, normally taking thousands and thousands of years. But every few hundred millennia, evolution leaps forward. For animals now too, I guess??
And while I for one do warmly welcome the "super dogs" that we now know live hidden among us, I must admit to feeling some trepidation regarding the coming "super cats". I fear none will be able to reason with their wild, capricious demands for food and
Uh, you didn't tell me squirrels had super-powers.
I didn't know squirrels had super-powers! And near as I can tell, they don't!
Nancy, I've talked to the squirrels, and none of them recognize this "Girl Squirrel." And she ignored me at the zoo when I discretely tried to talk to her. I've never said this about a squirrel before, but...
...I don't trust her.
Really? And you're sure you're not just a little jealous that "Girl Squirrel" is front page news when "Squirrel Girl" isn't?
Check it out. Some chick's already selling bootleg "Girl Squirrel" shirts.
I EAT NUTS AND KICK BUTTS
They're not bad.
Oh my god, she stole my line??
LIMITED EDITION GIRL SQUIRREL SHIRT
Do you feel exposed? Is your torso chilly? Probably that's because you're not wearing a shirt right now! Solve two problems at once with this "nutty" new design!
This shirt tells all and sundry that you will TOTALLY kick their butts if you need to. It also warns them not to kiss you if they have a nut allergy. This'll save everyone a whole lot of time.

I don't know who this Chuck X. Avier guy is, but he sure likes talking up this School for Gifted Youngsters! Weird!!

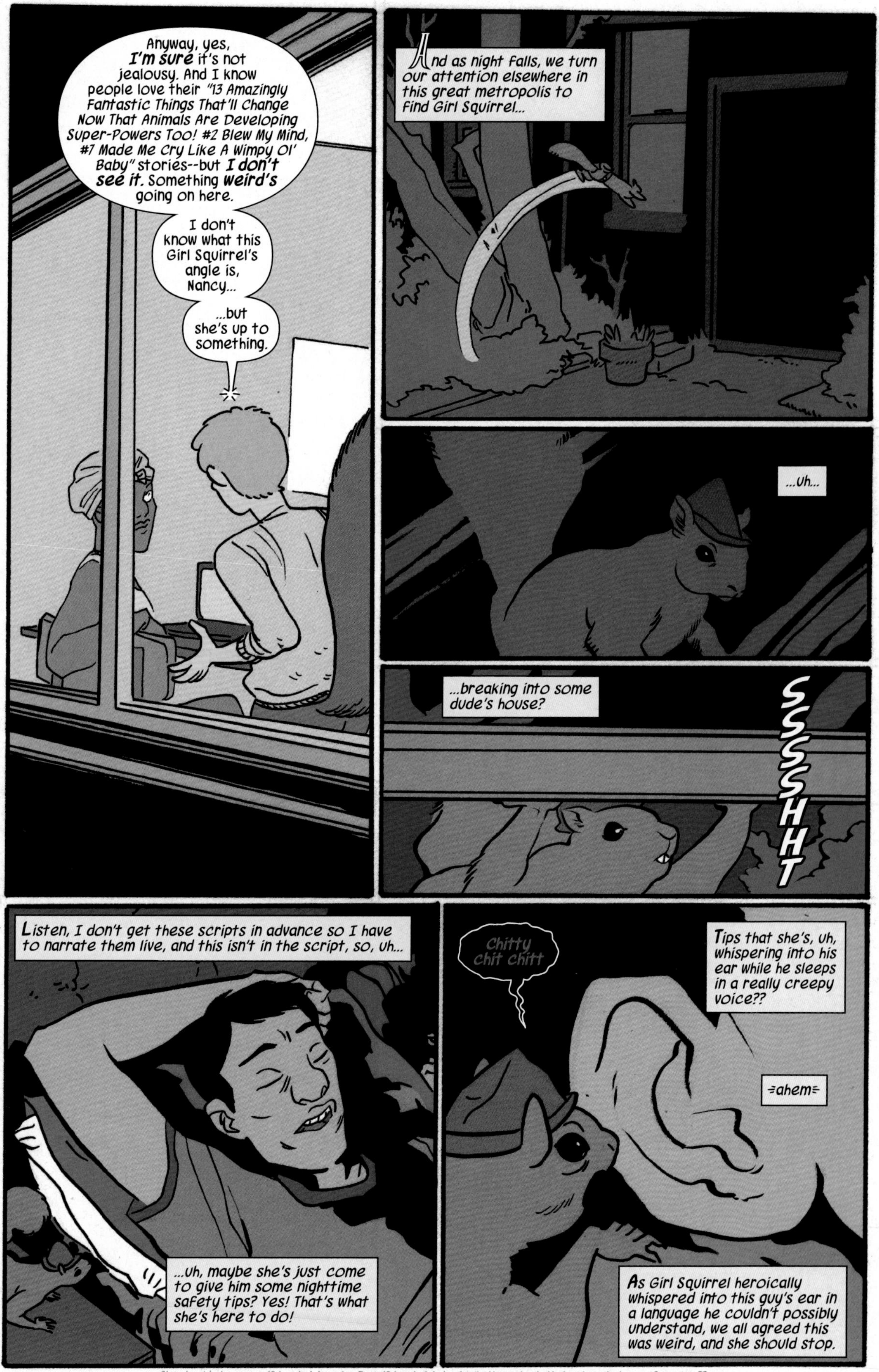
Anyway, yes, I'm sure it's not jealousy. And I know people love their "13 Amazingly Fantastic Things That'll Change Now That Animals Are Developing Super-Powers Too! #2 Blew My Mind, #7 Made Me Cry Like A Wimpy Ol' Baby" stories--but I don't see it. Something weird's going on here.
I don't know what this Girl Squirrel's angle is, Nancy...
...but she's up to something.
And as night falls, we turn our attention elsewhere in this great metropolis to find Girl Squirrel...
...uh...
...breaking into some dude's house?
SSSSHHT
Listen, I don't get these scripts in advance so I have to narrate them live, and this isn't in the script, so, uh...
...uh, maybe she's just come to give him some nighttime safety tips? Yes! That's what she's here to do!
Chitty chit chitt
Tips that she's, uh, whispering into his ear while he sleeps in a really creepy voice??
=ahem=
As Girl Squirrel heroically whispered into this guy's ear in a language he couldn't possibly understand, we all agreed this was weird, and she should stop.

She should stop even if her hat is cute. Even if her hat is basically the cutest, that only gets her so far, okay??

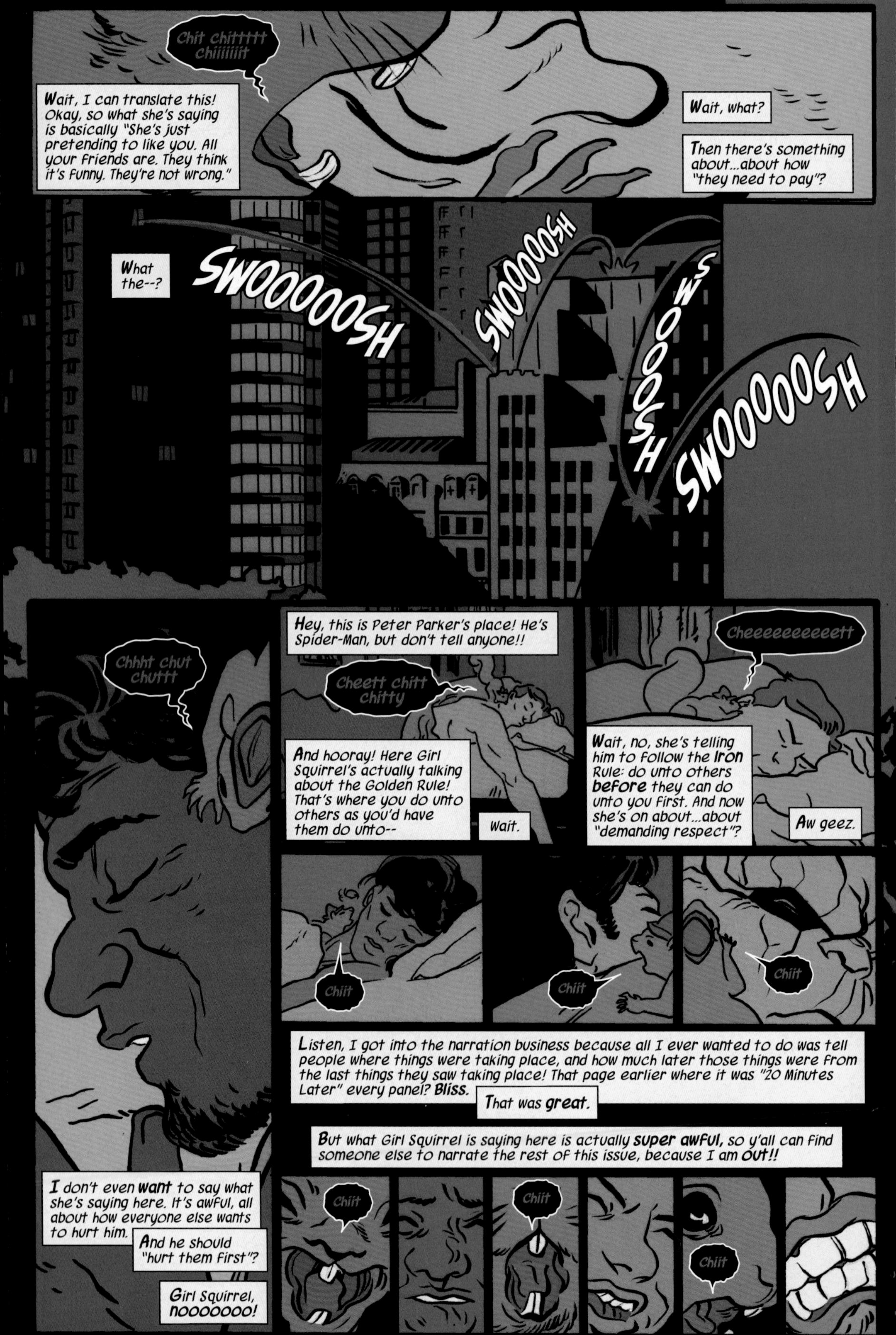
Chit chittttt chiiiiiiit
Wait, I can translate this! Okay, so what she's saying is basically "She's just pretending to like you. All your friends are. They think it's funny. They're not wrong."
Wait, what?
Then there's something about...about how "they need to pay"?
What the--?
SWOOOOOSH
SWOOOOSH
SWOOOOSH
SWOOOOOSH
Chhht chut chuttt
Hey, this is Peter Parker's place! He's Spider-Man, but don't tell anyone!!
Cheett chitt chitty
And hooray! Here Girl Squirrel's actually talking about the Golden Rule! That's where you do unto others as you'd have them do unto--
Wait.
Cheeeeeeeeeett
Wait, no, she's telling him to follow the Iron Rule: do unto others before they can do unto you first. And now she's on about...about "demanding respect"?
Aw geez.
Chiit
Chiit
Chiit
Listen, I got into the narration business because all I ever wanted to do was tell people where things were taking place, and how much later those things were from the last things they saw taking place! That page earlier where it was "20 Minutes Later" every panel? Bliss.
That was great.
But what Girl Squirrel is saying here is actually super awful, so y'all can find someone else to narrate the rest of this issue, because I am out!!
I don't even want to say what she's saying here. It's awful, all about how everyone else wants to hurt him.
And he should "hurt them first"?
Girl Squirrel, nooooooo!
Chiit
Chiit
Chiit

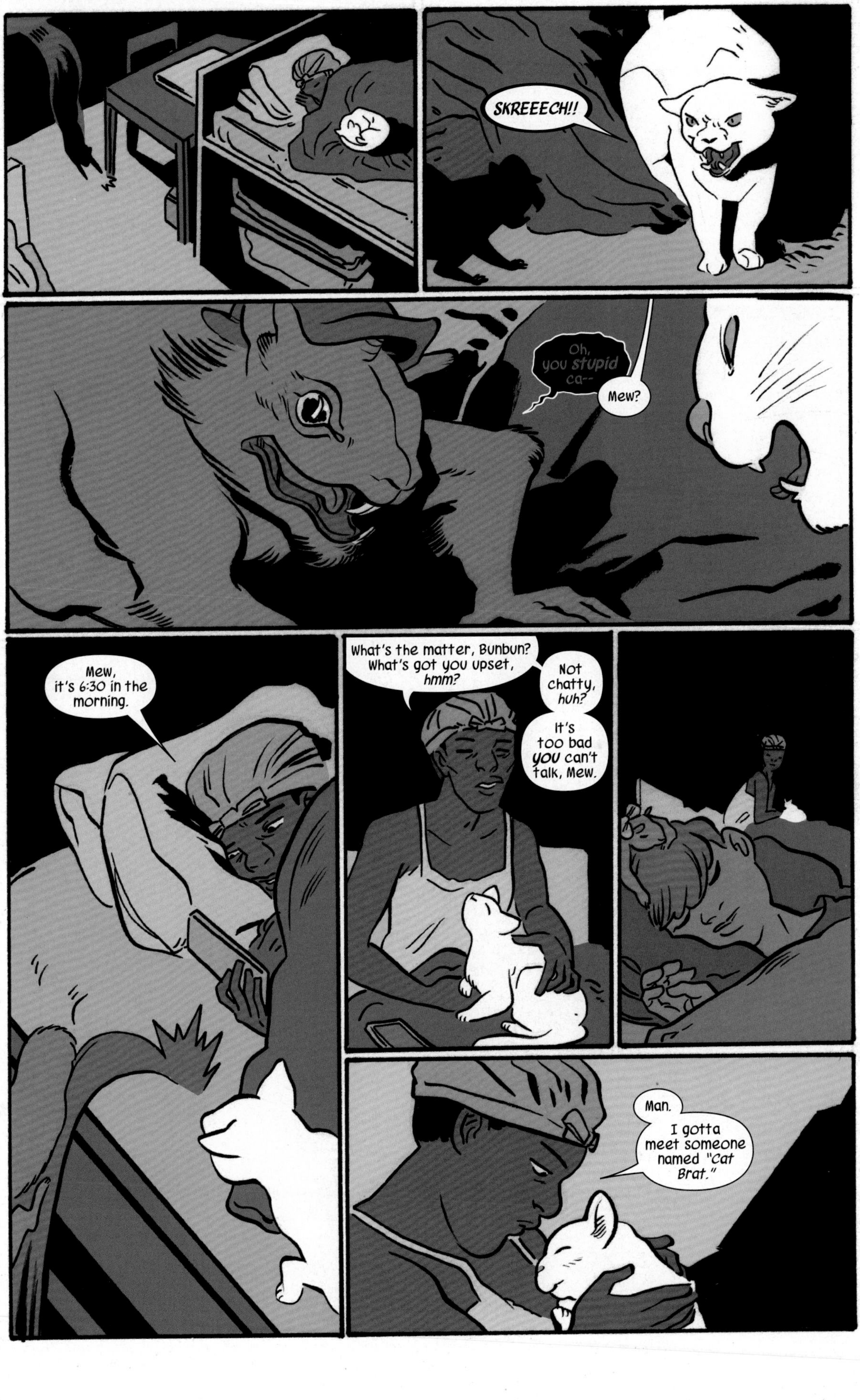
SKREEECH!!
Oh, you stupid ca--
Mew?
Mew, it's 6:30 in the morning.
What's the matter, Bunbun? What's got you upset, hmm?
Not chatty, huh?
It's too bad YOU can't talk, Mew.
Man.
I gotta meet someone named "Cat Brat."

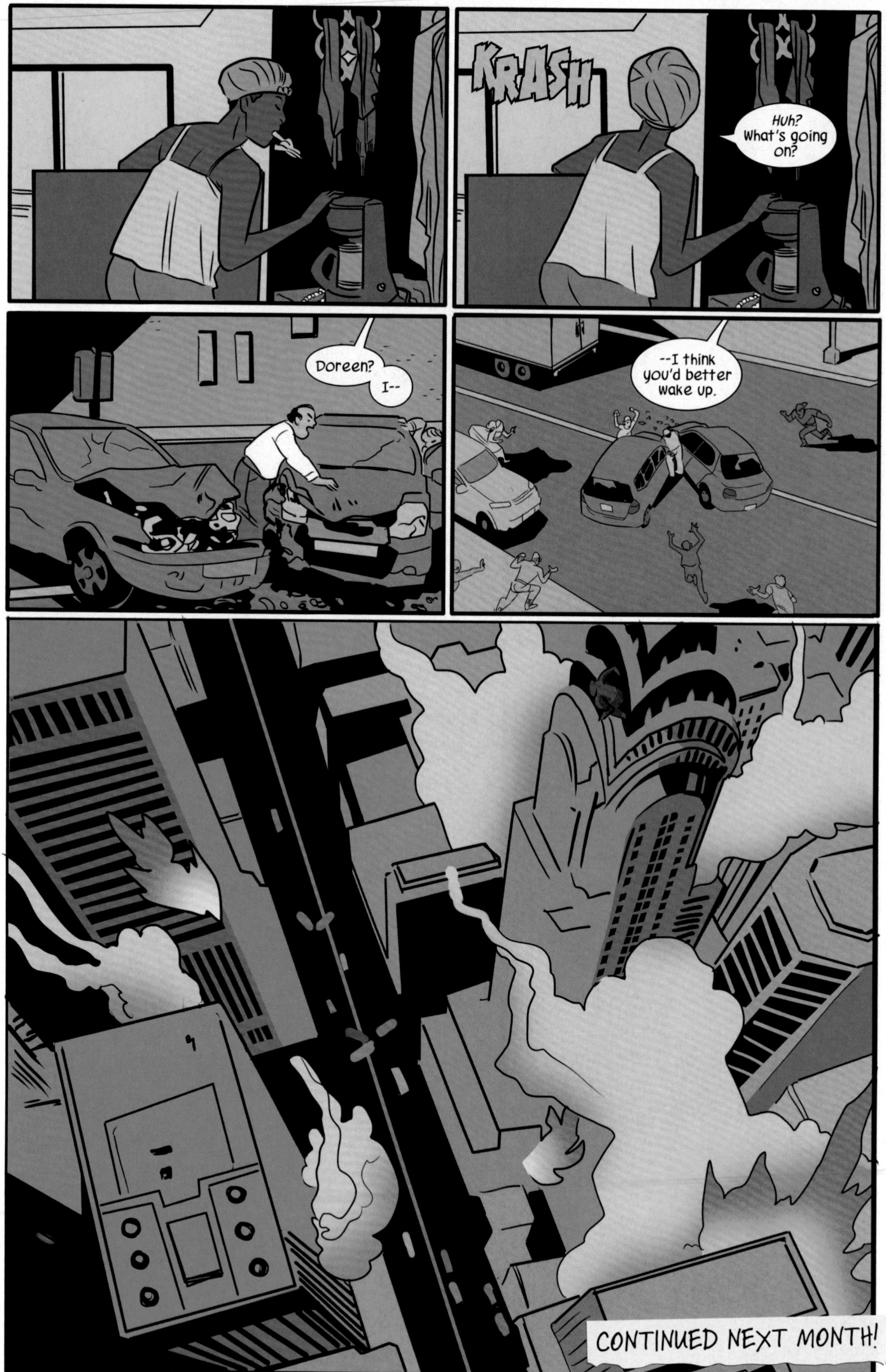
KRASH
Huh? What's going on?
Doreen?
I--
--I think you'd better wake up.
CONTINUED NEXT MONTH!

Okay I'm back, but only to say that Cat Brat sounds awesome and I want to narrate their comic instead. *Peace.*

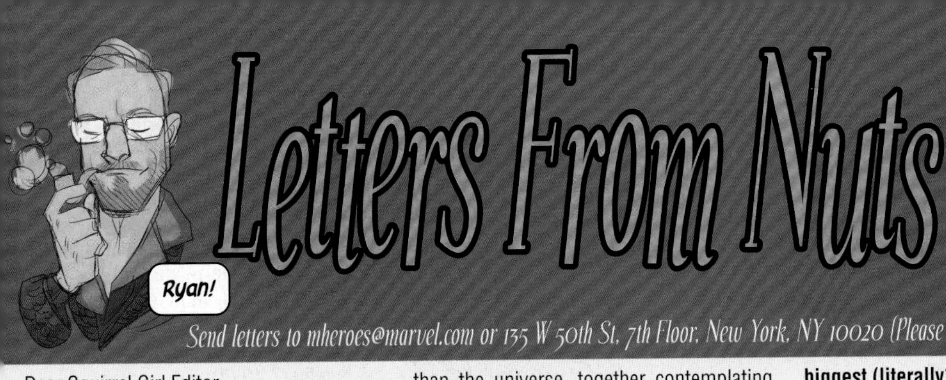
Ryan!

# Letters From Nuts

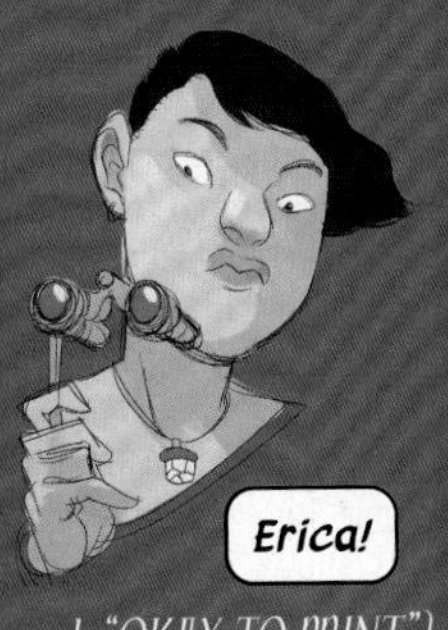
Erica!

*Send letters to mheroes@marvel.com or 135 W 50th St, 7th Floor, New York, NY 10020 (Please mark "OKAY TO PRINT")*

Dear Squirrel Girl Editor,

What in the H-E-single Asgardian hockey stick is the matter with you?! I have just read the advance copy of SQUIRREL GIRL #4!!! ONE PAGE?!! SQUIRREL GIRL DEFEATS GALACTUS IN ONE PAGE?!!! Thank you, jerk-faces. Thank you for ruining Marvel Comics for all time!

The Marvel that *I* knew, the Marvel that *I* grew up with made sense! LOGICAL sense! Armor was transistor powered! Steve Rogers could hide his shield under his jacket! And NOBODY could beat Galactus! NO ONE!

Yes, it's canon that Squirrel Girl's defeated Doctor Doom, M.O.D.O.K., and even Fin Fang Foom, but none of those guys are the Mighty Galactus! Silver Surfer just fought Galactus for three straight issues--that's 59 more pages than shown here--and the Surfer STILL LOST! Now THAT'S a Galactus story that makes SENSE! (And on sale soon as part of the SILVER SURFER: WORLDS APART trade paperback.) And now you've gone and defeated him in what is tantamount to ONE PANEL?! And by someone with SQUIRREL POWERS?!

NUTS TO YOU, PAL! NUTS! TO! YOU!

Dan Slott
3 Doors Down
Marvel Entertainment, NY

**RYAN: Hey Dan! Nice to hear from you, buddy! I was stoked to run your great quote on the cover of our issue #2 ("I can't recommend the new SQUIRREL GIRL book enough! It's NUTS!") but I think you may have overlooked something because there's not much here I can use. The best I've come up with from your letter is, "I have just read... Squirrel Girl #4!!!... Now THAT'S a Galactus story! ...SQUIRREL POWERS... TO YOU, PAL!" which is actually a pretty great quote after all, so--thanks!**

**ERICA: Dan, calm down.**

Dear Ryan and Erica,

I just wanted to let you know how much I've been enjoying THE UNBEATABLE SQUIRREL GIRL thus far. An encounter with Galactus so early in the series would seem difficult to pull off successfully, but I thought it was handled very well. The way Squirrel Girl hears Galactus's words not just in her own language, but her own vernacular, was a nice touch. The full page of an American teenage girl sitting on the giant shoulder of a god-like being older than the universe, together contemplating the Earth set against the background of the cosmos, is perhaps Erica's most beautiful image.

I also noticed that your Galactus story parallels that of the original Galactus trilogy by Lee and Kirby, which I am old enough to have read when it first appeared. In both cases, the encounter with Galactus commences hot on the heels of another adventure and ends with the characters resuming their everyday lives. I'll certainly be looking forward to future installments.

Make Mine Marvel!
Charles Hoffman,
Van Nuys, CA

P.S. I've taken the liberty of attaching a picture of myself with Erica's father, Red Hook, 1980s. I know that he would be delighted with Squirrel Girl.

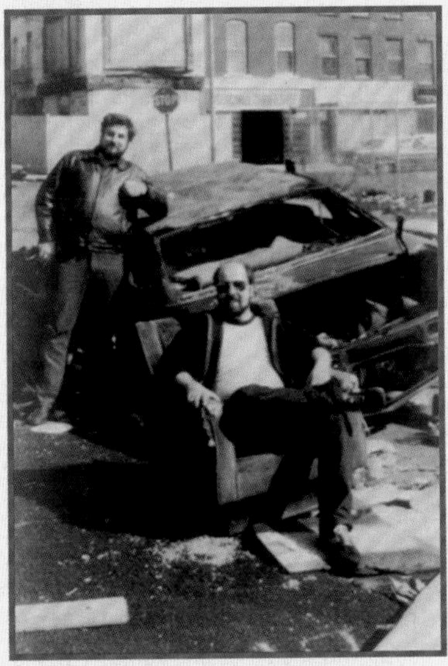

**RYAN: I didn't even see these parallels until you pointed them out, but now I'm happy they're there!**

**ERICA: Oh wow. That's an old photo. That's possibly a pre-Erica photo. Anyway, I think Galactus had to be in the first arc. Dan Slott's work on the character really established who the character is after her initial appearance in Marvel Super-Heroes Winter Special, and more importantly established that she wins fights against the toughest of the tough. After pitting her against some of Marvel's biggest baddies (Giganto, Fin Fang Foom, Thanos) it only makes sense that we start off by going one further and putting her up against Marvel's biggest (literally?) baddie.**

Dear Unbeatable Squirrel-team,

As a long time comic reader and Marvel fan, I want to thank you for one of, heck, THE most brilliantly executed, on-point character portrayals in issue #4.

Only SQUIRREL GIRL could leave me satisfied with a one-page comic. Sometimes nothing more needs to be said, and you said it perfectly.

I also appreciate the interaction with the fans you guys show in the responses of your letter columns, showing that you care about us as much as we care about you. The SG fans may not be as garishly loud as those of a certain Spider-Man, but like the squirrels, we are there, hiding in the trees and eating nuts.

Squirrel Girl may not be as widely known of a hero, she's not in it for the flash and publicity. She's the hero we need, there to do things right and put a smile on our faces. Heck, I bet not even Howard the Duck, among the grumpiest, most perennially frustrated and disappointed of heroes, could resist cracking a smile in her presence.

Now if you'll excuse me, I've just finished up the letters column and am off to see if the tiny print continues on the blank pages to follow...wait...what's this? BONUS COMIC!

You guys (for lack of a proper gender-neutral pronoun) rock!

Nathan

**RYAN: I appreciate you taking the time to write a letter only three pages into the comic! I kinda wish all letters were like that, all "Dear Squirrel Girl people, I can't wait to see what happens next! I guess I'm about to now though! Well, bye!"**

**ERICA: I personally enjoy "dude" as a gender-neutral term. It's often thought of as male, but it just means individual. Before the 60s (which is when it started to be misused as "man") it meant either a city slicker or someone who is very fashion forward and that's definitely us. 100%.**

**P.S. I'm glad you like SQUIRREL GIRL!**

Hello again, lovely people, and thank you again for the brilliance that is SQUIRREL GIRL! I have just finished #4... And you have to make SQUIRREL GIRL spin-offs! "Squirrel Girl, Herald of Galactus" has to be a thing! What must we do to make it happen?! On the subject, how about a Magneto/Squirrel-Girl eighteen-chapter epic that dwarfs all those 90's crossovers that we all remember so fondly?

No? Okay...what about "Squirrel Girl's Adventures In Babysitting" filling in all the gaps where SG had to stay home and look after Luke Cage's kid?

SQUIRREL GIRL is easily my favorite comic book to date, across all publishers and genres. Thank you again for everything!

Tim P.
Plymouth, England

**RYAN: I keep thinking of how Magneto and Squirrel Girl would get along. He's such a serious, dour guy! Maybe they should go on a road trip together. Maybe... maybe they should DEFINITELY go on a road trip together.**

I wanted to write in to complain that my copy of UNBEATABLE SQUIRREL GIRL #4 must have been a counterfeit. The bottom of the first page clearly states that all of the pages following the letters page would be blank. I was deeply disappointed to find all sorts of art, words, and story along with ZERO blank pages! Either it was counterfeit or someone in quality control needs to be fired!

Seriously though, it was one of the most entertaining comics I've read in some time. I can't remember the last time I've started laughing uproariously and had to catch my breath and re-read what I had just read to make sure I got it all... And this happened several times during this issue. If the rest of the pages HAD been blank it would have been an amazing gag of its own. Great stuff!

Sean Bayless

**RYAN: Sean, the truth of the matter is that after printing the blank pages we felt bad about maybe ripping people off, so we requested the staff at your (and everyone's!) local comic book store to create and draw in their own conclusion to the story on the remaining blank pages, so everyone got their own different ending! I'm glad you liked yours! P.S.: Let me know what some of the jokes were, so I can use them in future issues.**

**ERICA: I'm going to respond to the second half of your letter since Ryan responded to the first half. I was reading this script while my boyfriend was in the other end of the apartment and he kept walking over to find out what I was laughing at. This also happens a lot when I'm out working with Joe Quinones (artist on HOWARD THE DUCK) and we'll chuckle to ourselves about the pages we're working on while in a cafe. So you are not alone in this.**

Congratulations, Ryan and Erica, on creating a fun and entertaining comic. After reading the first issue of this comic, I found myself already going nuts for this series. I love that Doreen is just as awkward and silly as any other person. Also, it's pretty cool that she "defeats" these baddies just by being nice and friendly to them. I'm definitely looking forward to many more issues to come!

The photo attached is me with a baby squirrel that my family cared for recently. He's now living with 12 other little squirrels at our local wildlife rescue!

Kevin Krause

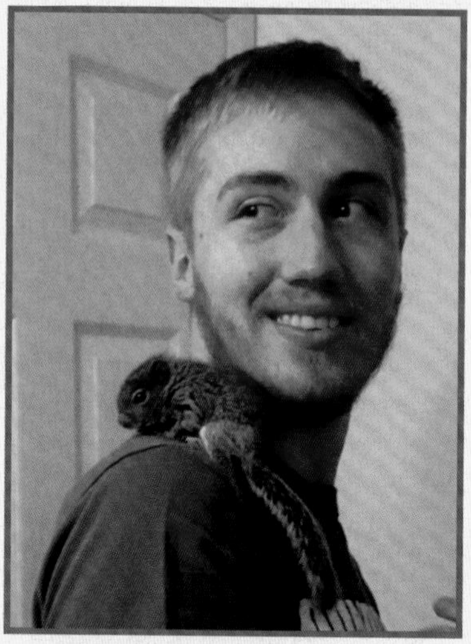

**RYAN: Thanks! Also when I started this comic I honestly did not expect there would be so many people with squirrels in their lives. I did not expect our letters column would be mostly photos of people with squirrels on them. I'm happy this turned out to be the case!**

**ERICA: This is worth it just for all the pictures of wee baby squirrels people send us.**

I've seriously never written to a comic book before. (It seemed silly.) But I had to let you all know that THE UNBEATABLE SQUIRREL GIRL is my new most favorite thing. Ever. I love it. I love it. I love it.

Jesse

P.S. Please tell me there's some sweet Squirrel Girl merch in the works? I would love to buy me some Doreen Green action figures, buttons, etc.

**RYAN: Jesse, I would love some Squirrel Girl action figures! We don't get to tell the merchandise companies what to make, but now I will absolutely tell the merchandise companies what to make: a Squirrel Girl action figure with at least 12 points of articulation, and which comes packaged with a Tippy-Toe figure that can lock onto her shoulder and a randomly selected Deadpool card. I've got the designs right here. Call me, merchandise companies.**

**ERICA: I want a Squirrel Girl toy so bad. In the meantime I've just been collecting squirrel paraphernalia. Right now I'm up to two necklaces, a purse and a stuffed animal.**

**Rico did design six different Squirrel Girl buttons for the release of the book though. He's way more on top of this merchandising stuff than we are. Have you seen all the Spider-Gwen stuff he's put together? YOW!**

To the gloriously deranged minds behind SQUIRREL GIRL:

Kudos! Amazing work! I've been hooked since the first issue! I have but one humble question. When do we get to meet The Chipmunk Hunk? Convention season is upon us and I need to know what my cosplay should look like.

Keep up the fabulous work, Doreen is a gem and I haven't laughed so much in ages.

Josh W.

**RYAN: Hey thanks, Josh! As for meeting Chipmunk Hunk, I can't say for sure when we'll be seeing him! If that bothers you, I guess that's just the NEXT ISSUE you need to deal with. It's probably ISSUE #6 on your list.**

**Oh wait, never mind, this is issue six already. He's in this issue, surprise!!**

**ERICA: OH GOD I'M SO EXCITED FOR CHIPMUNK HUNK COSPLAY. I NEVER CONSIDERED THAT MIGHT BE A POSSIBILITY. YOU'D BETTER SEND US PHOTOS.**

## Next: Avengers Assemble?

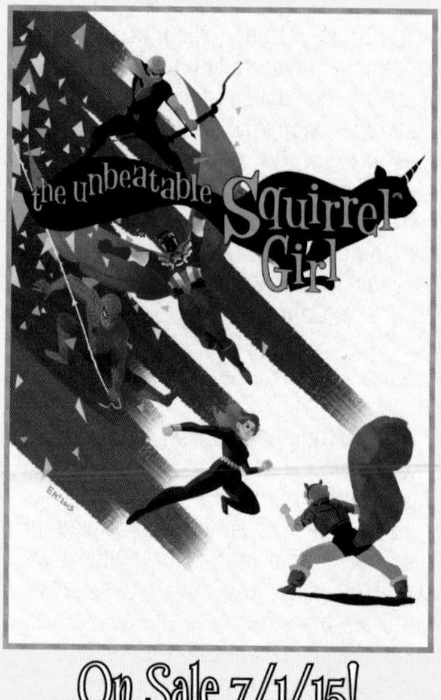
the unbeatable Squirrel Girl

## On Sale 7/1/15!

Attention Squirrel Scouts! Make sure to check out our production blog, **unbeatablesquirrelgirl.tumblr.com**, where we post behind-the-scenes stuff on how the book gets made, along with all sorts of cool things *you* make: fanart, cosplay, whatever!

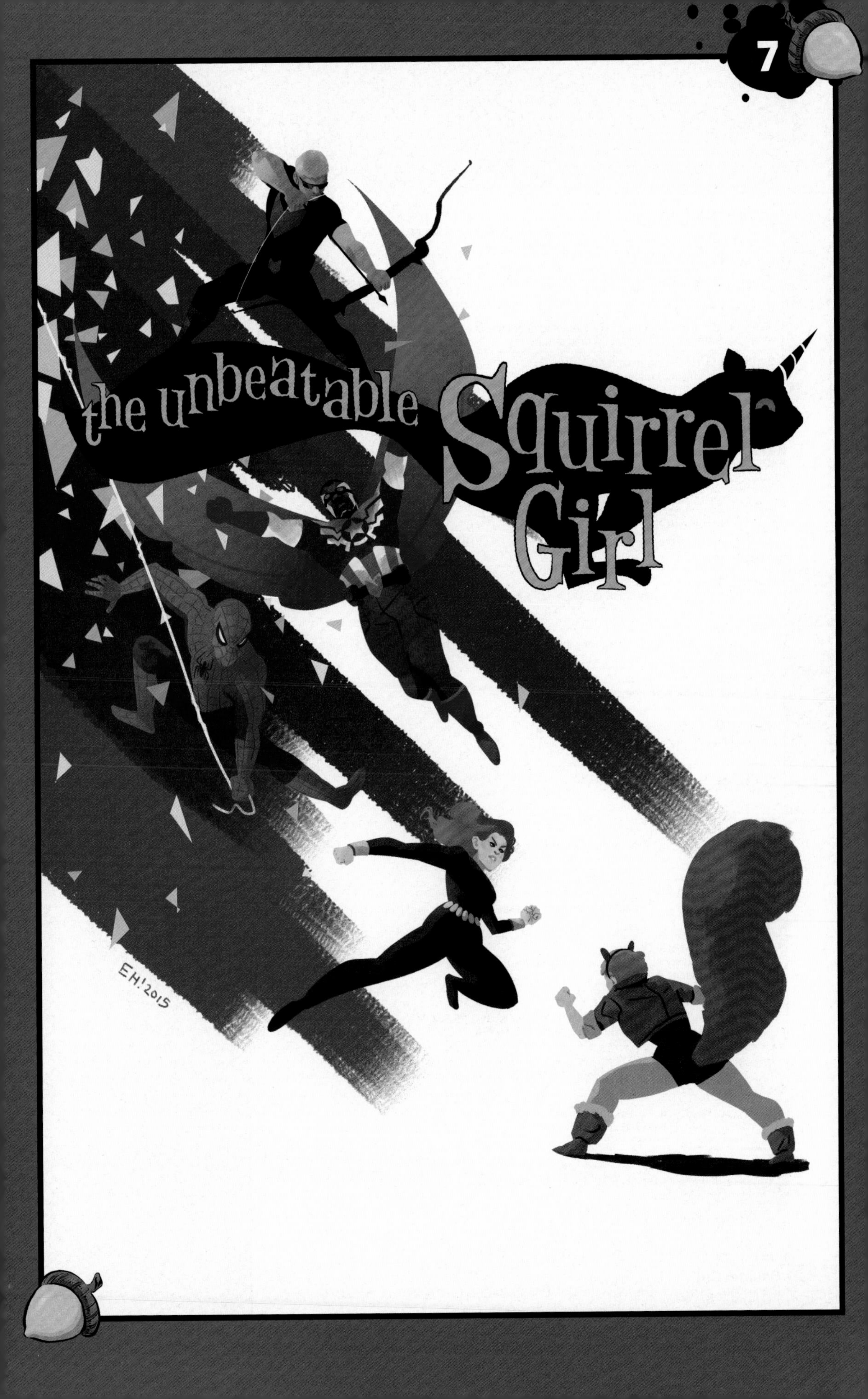
7
the unbeatable Squirrel Girl
EH! 2015

Doreen Green isn't just a first-year computer science student: she secretly also has all the powers of both squirrel and girl!
She uses her amazing abilities to fight crime **and** be as awesome as possible. You know her as...The Unbeatable Squirrel Girl!
Let's catch up with what she's been up to until now, with...

# Squirrel Girl *in a nutshell*

**Squirrel Girl!** @unbeatablesg
PUBLIC SERVICE ANNOUNCEMENT: Everyone should go to the zoo and talk to every animal there. Just go and chat up every animal!

**Squirrel Girl!** @unbeatablesg
Because how do you know you CAN'T talk to animals unless you've tried with every animal?? And they've got lots of animals there!

**Squirrel Girl!** @unbeatablesg
Also yes I am aware that there are elements of zoos that are NOT UNPROBLEMATIC but where else are you gonna chat up mad lemurs

**Squirrel Girl!** @unbeatablesg
Besides Madagascar I mean

**Tippy-Toe** @yoitstippytoe
@unbeatablesg CHITTT CHITTY CHIT CHIT

**Squirrel Girl!** @unbeatablesg
@yoitstippytoe dude, I meant "mad lemurs" in the "lots of lemurs" sense, not that they're angry! The zoo ones were actually mostly sleepy

**Squirrel Girl!** @unbeatablesg
@yoitstippytoe lots of sleepy lemurs to be had at your local zoo, visit today

**Nancy W.** @sewwiththeflo
I was at the zoo yesterday when the lions got out and this "Girl Squirrel" saved everyone.

**Nancy W.** @sewwiththeflo
As near as I can tell she is a squirrel with the INVERSE proportional strength of a girl? Or something?

**Nancy W.** @sewwiththeflo
What even is biology, you guys.

**Nancy W.** @sewwiththeflo
How do bodies even work.

**Nancy W.** @sewwiththeflo
Local woman publicly questions how a squirrel can have the powers of a girl. Vets hate me.

**Tony Stark** @starkmantony ✓
@unbeatablesg Getting reports of fights breaking out all over NYC. Can I assume you are on this?

**Squirrel Girl!** @unbeatablesg
@starkmantony uh can you assume it's like 6:30am here and i just woke up

**Tony Stark** @starkmantony ✓
@unbeatablesg My post woke you up? Huh. You have a special notification sound for me, don't you.

**Squirrel Girl!** @unbeatablesg
@starkmantony um, YEAH, it's your old 60s-style PERSONAL JINGLE that you hoped we'd all just forgot about and it's AMAZING

**Squirrel Girl!** @unbeatablesg
@starkmantony ♫ Tony Stark / Makes you feel / He's the cool exec / With a heart of steel ♫

**Tony Stark** @starkmantony ✓
@unbeatablesg Hold on a second.

**Tony Stark** @starkmantony ✓
@unbeatablesg I just remotely erased that song from your phone and from every other mirror online.

**Squirrel Girl!** @unbeatablesg
@starkmantony ♫ Tony Stark / Makes me feel / That I'm super glad / That I backed up that song to a device not connected to the internet ♫

**Squirrel Girl!** @unbeatablesg
Hey I dunno if any criminals follow me but JUST IN CASE, you should know that KOI BOI and CHIPMUNK HUNK are fighting crime now too!

**Squirrel Girl!** @unbeatablesg
Also if you are a criminal please stop doing crimes. #crimeadvice

**search!** 🔍

#databasesoneohone

#databasesoneohFUN

#dontthrowshadeonmyfriends

#breakfastbeats

#boythor

Bostonian Cameos

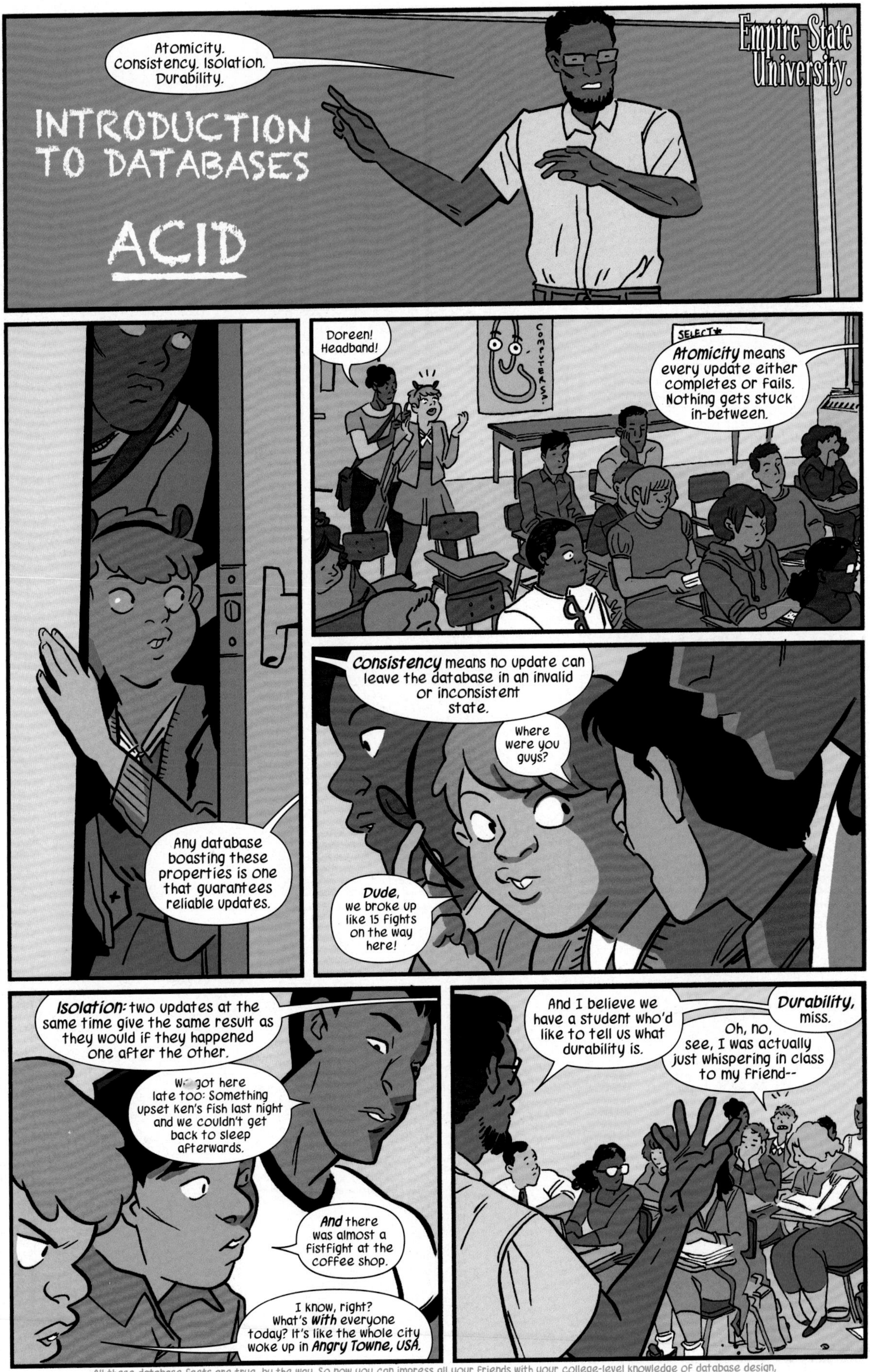
Empire State University.
Atomicity. Consistency. Isolation. Durability.
INTRODUCTION TO DATABASES
ACID
Any database boasting these properties is one that guarantees reliable updates.
Doreen! Headband!
COMPUTERS4
SELECT*
*Atomicity* means every update either completes or fails. Nothing gets stuck in-between.
*Consistency* means no update can leave the database in an invalid or inconsistent state.
Where were you guys?
*Dude*, we broke up like 15 fights on the way here!
*Isolation:* two updates at the same time give the same result as they would if they happened one after the other.
We got here late too: Something upset Ken's fish last night and we couldn't get back to sleep afterwards.
*And* there was almost a fistfight at the coffee shop.
I know, right? What's *with* everyone today? It's like the whole city woke up in *Angry Towne, USA*.
And I believe we have a student who'd like to tell us what durability is.
*Durability,* miss.
Oh, no, see, I was actually just whispering in class to my friend--

All these database facts are true, by the way. So now you can impress all your friends with your college-level knowledge of database design, so long as they don't ask a single follow-up question!

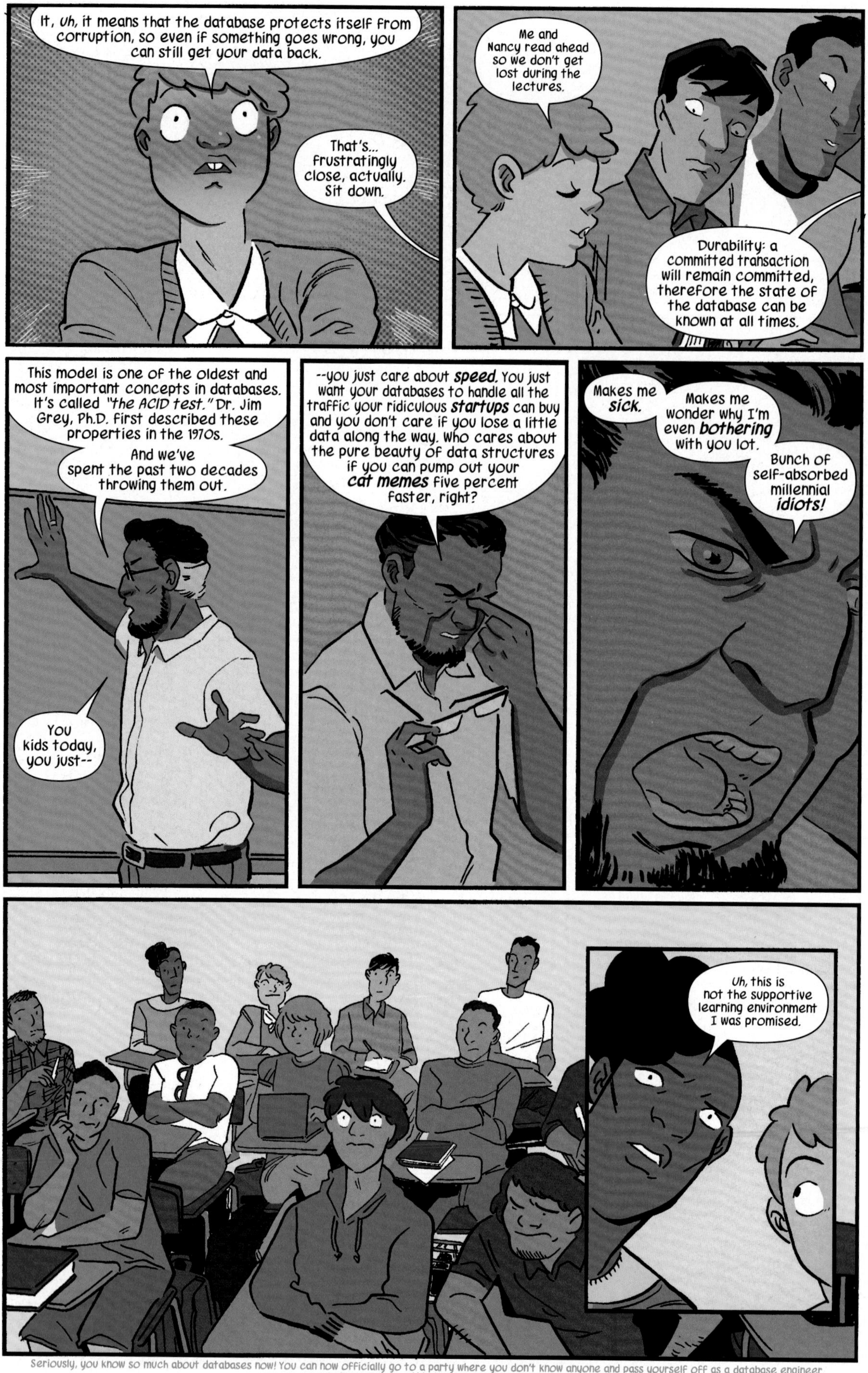
It, Uh, it means that the database protects itself from corruption, so even if something goes wrong, you can still get your data back.
That's... frustratingly close, actually. Sit down.
Me and Nancy read ahead so we don't get lost during the lectures.
Durability: a committed transaction will remain committed, therefore the state of the database can be known at all times.
This model is one of the oldest and most important concepts in databases. It's called "the ACID test." Dr. Jim Grey, Ph.D. first described these properties in the 1970s.
And we've spent the past two decades throwing them out.
You kids today, you just--
--you just care about speed. You just want your databases to handle all the traffic your ridiculous startups can buy and you don't care if you lose a little data along the way. Who cares about the pure beauty of data structures if you can pump out your cat memes five percent faster, right?
Makes me sick.
Makes me wonder why I'm even bothering with you lot.
Bunch of self-absorbed millennial idiots!
Uh, this is not the supportive learning environment I was promised.

Seriously, you know so much about databases now! You can now officially go to a party where you don't know anyone and pass yourself off as a database engineer. In fact, surprise, ***this is now mandatory.***

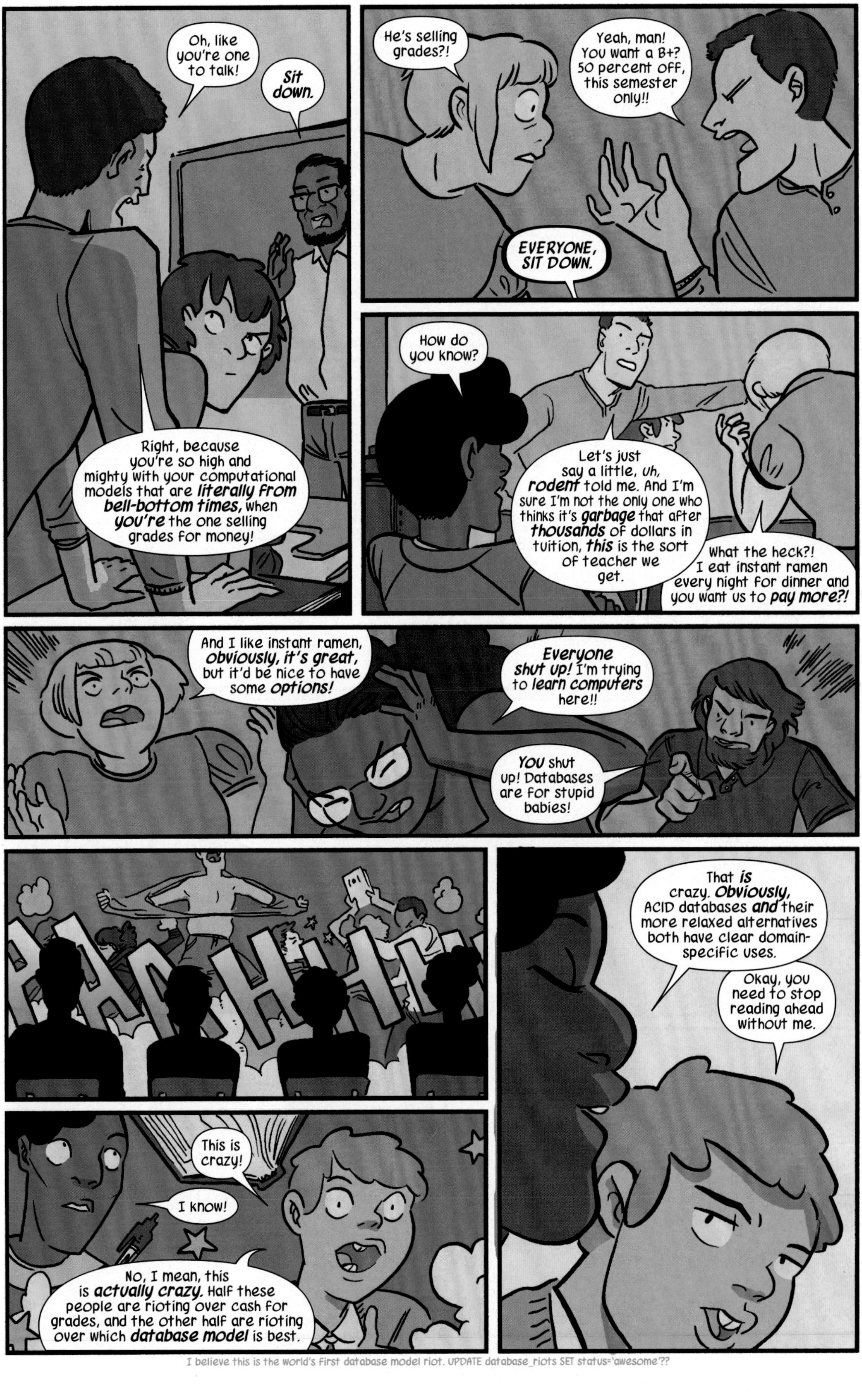

Oh, like you're one to talk!
Sit down.
Right, because you're so high and mighty with your computational models that are literally from bell-bottom times, when you're the one selling grades for money!
He's selling grades?!
Yeah, man! You want a B+? 50 percent off, this semester only!!
EVERYONE, SIT DOWN.
How do you know?
Let's just say a little, uh, rodent told me. And I'm sure I'm not the only one who thinks it's garbage that after thousands of dollars in tuition, this is the sort of teacher we get.
What the heck?! I eat instant ramen every night for dinner and you want us to pay more?!
And I like instant ramen, obviously, it's great, but it'd be nice to have some options!
Everyone shut up! I'm trying to learn computers here!!
YOU shut up! Databases are for stupid babies!
This is crazy!
I know!
No, I mean, this is actually crazy. Half these people are rioting over cash for grades, and the other half are rioting over which database model is best.
That is crazy. Obviously, ACID databases and their more relaxed alternatives both have clear domain-specific uses.
Okay, you need to stop reading ahead without me.


I believe this is the world's first database model riot. UPDATE database_riots SET status='awesome'??

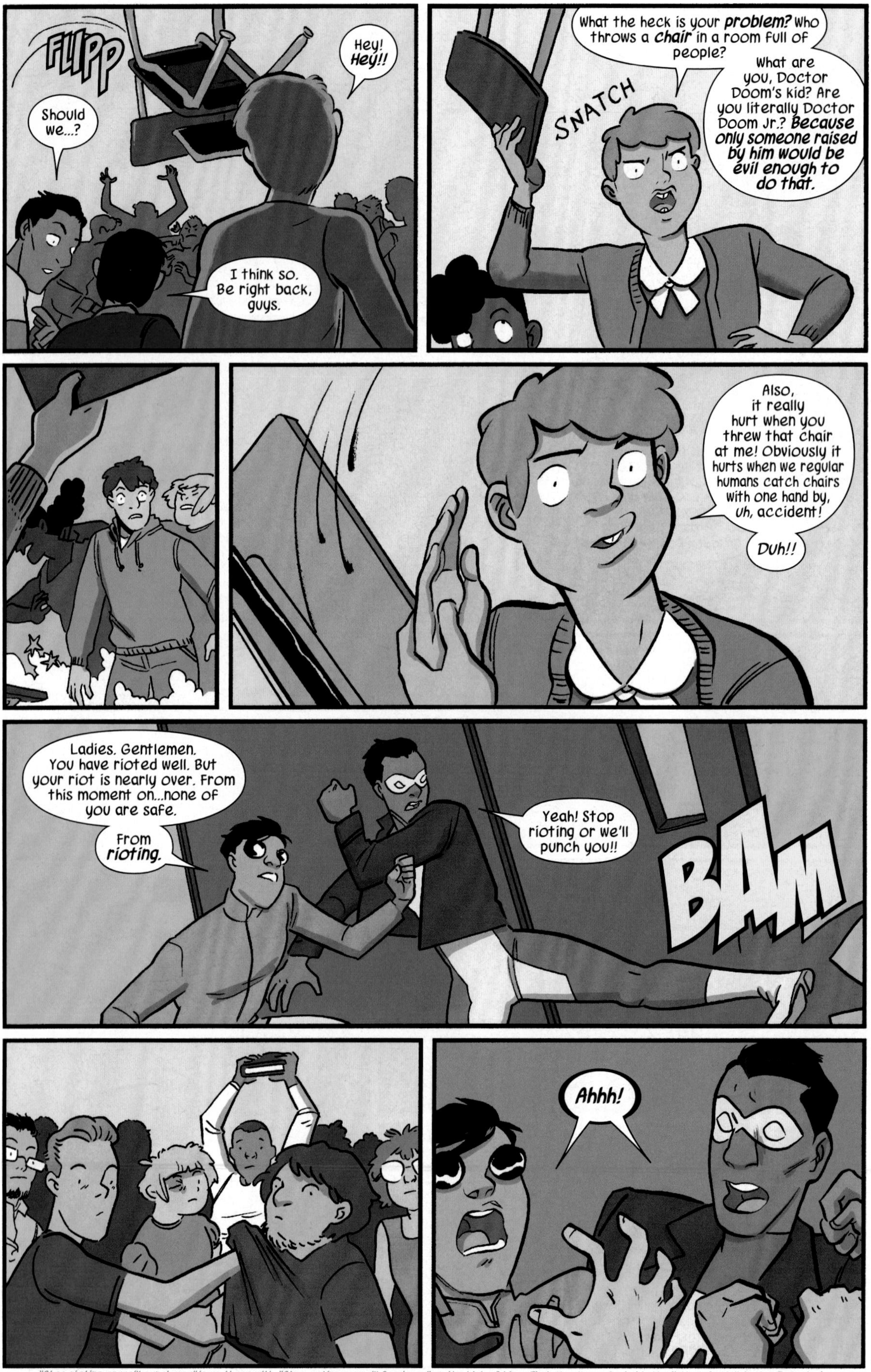
FLIPP
Hey!
Hey!!
Should we...?
I think so. Be right back, guys.
What the heck is your problem? Who throws a chair in a room full of people?
What are you, Doctor Doom's kid? Are you literally Doctor Doom Jr.? Because only someone raised by him would be evil enough to do that.
SNATCH
Also, it really hurt when you threw that chair at me! Obviously it hurts when we regular humans catch chairs with one hand by, uh, accident!
Duh!!
Ladies. Gentlemen. You have rioted well. But your riot is nearly over. From this moment on...none of you are safe.
From rioting.
Yeah! Stop rioting or we'll punch you!!
BAM
Ahhh!

"Stop rioting or we'll punch you" is up there with "Stop eating or we'll feed you" on the List of Lines That, You Know, Probably Won't Work As Well As You Expected.

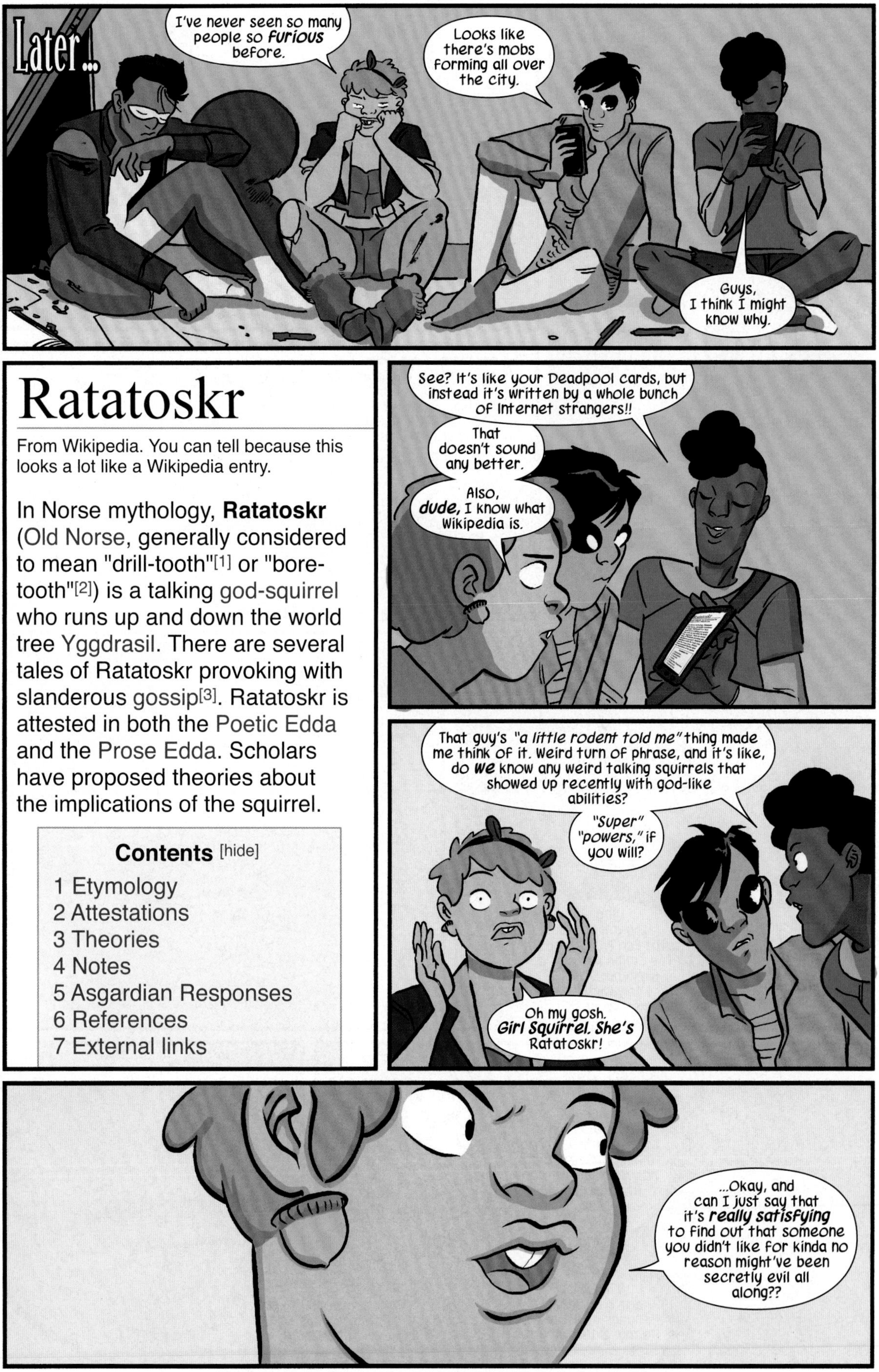
Later...
I've never seen so many people so furious before.
Looks like there's mobs forming all over the city.
Guys, I think I might know why.
Ratatoskr
From Wikipedia. You can tell because this looks a lot like a Wikipedia entry.
In Norse mythology, Ratatoskr (Old Norse, generally considered to mean "drill-tooth"[1] or "bore-tooth"[2]) is a talking god-squirrel who runs up and down the world tree Yggdrasil. There are several tales of Ratatoskr provoking with slanderous gossip[3]. Ratatoskr is attested in both the Poetic Edda and the Prose Edda. Scholars have proposed theories about the implications of the squirrel.
Contents [hide]
1 Etymology
2 Attestations
3 Theories
4 Notes
5 Asgardian Responses
6 References
7 External links
See? It's like your Deadpool cards, but instead it's written by a whole bunch of Internet strangers!!
That doesn't sound any better.
Also, dude, I know what Wikipedia is.
That guy's "a little rodent told me" thing made me think of it. Weird turn of phrase, and it's like, do we know any weird talking squirrels that showed up recently with god-like abilities?
"Super" "powers," if you will?
Oh my gosh. Girl Squirrel. She's Ratatoskr!
...Okay, and can I just say that it's really satisfying to find out that someone you didn't like for kinda no reason might've been secretly evil all along??

Also, she was ripping off my name the whole time and that *was* annoying. There. I said it.

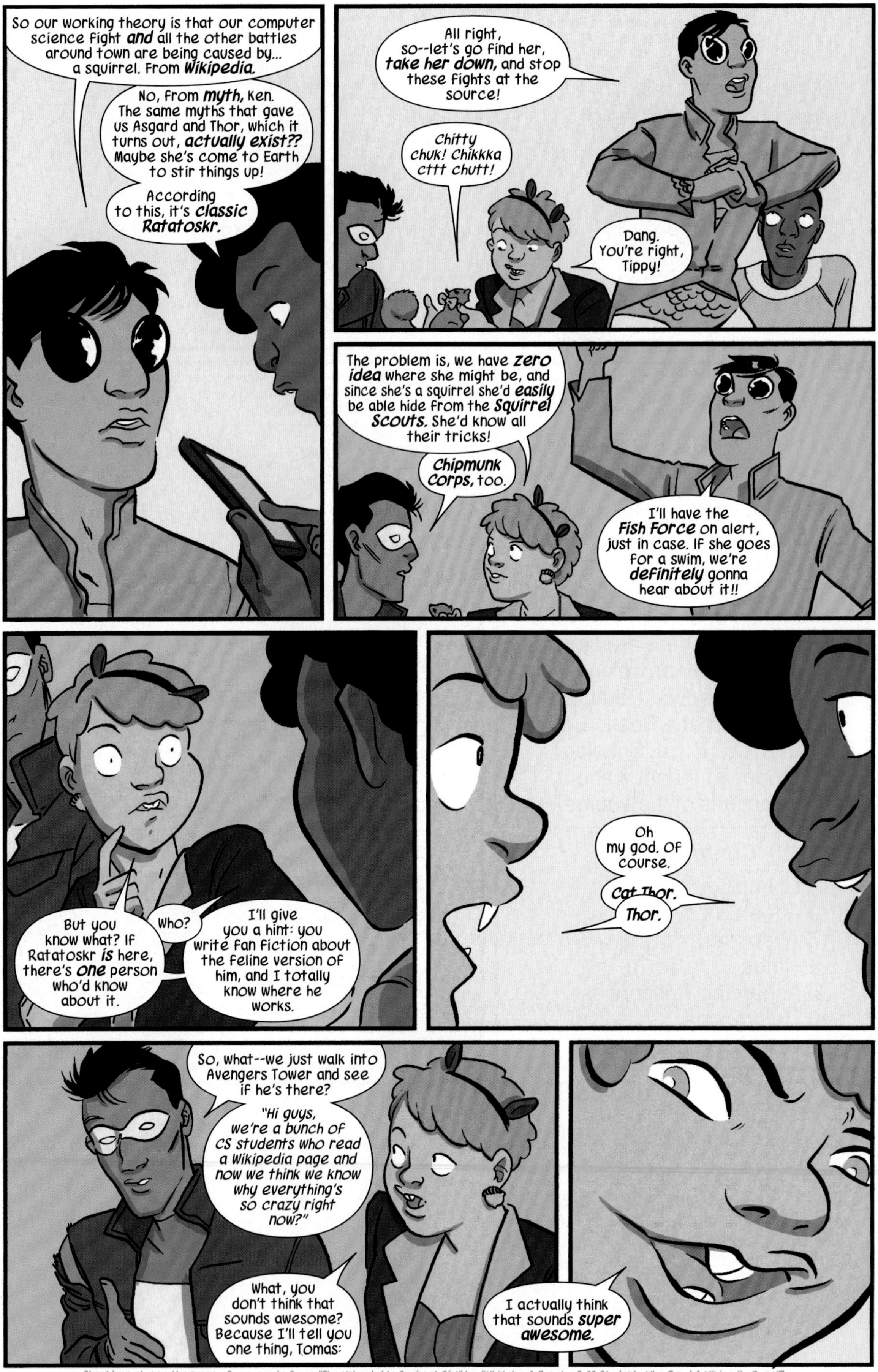
So our working theory is that our computer science fight and all the other battles around town are being caused by... a squirrel. From Wikipedia.
No, from myth, Ken. The same myths that gave us Asgard and Thor, which it turns out, actually exist?? Maybe she's come to Earth to stir things up!
According to this, it's classic Ratatoskr.
All right, so--let's go find her, take her down, and stop these fights at the source!
Chitty chuk! Chikkka cttt chutt!
Dang. You're right, Tippy!
The problem is, we have zero idea where she might be, and since she's a squirrel she'd easily be able hide from the Squirrel Scouts. She'd know all their tricks!
Chipmunk Corps, too.
I'll have the Fish Force on alert, just in case. If she goes for a swim, we're definitely gonna hear about it!!
But you know what? If Ratatoskr is here, there's one person who'd know about it.
Who?
I'll give you a hint: you write fan fiction about the feline version of him, and I totally know where he works.
Oh my god. Of course.
Cat Thor.
Thor.
So, what--we just walk into Avengers Tower and see if he's there?
"Hi guys, we're a bunch of CS students who read a Wikipedia page and now we think we know why everything's so crazy right now?"
What, you don't think that sounds awesome? Because I'll tell you one thing, Tomas:
I actually think that sounds super awesome.

Should we change the name of our comic from *"The Unbeatable Squirrel Girl"* to *"Hi We're A Bunch Of CS Students Who Read A Wikipedia Page"*?
Market research says: *"hah hah hah nope"*

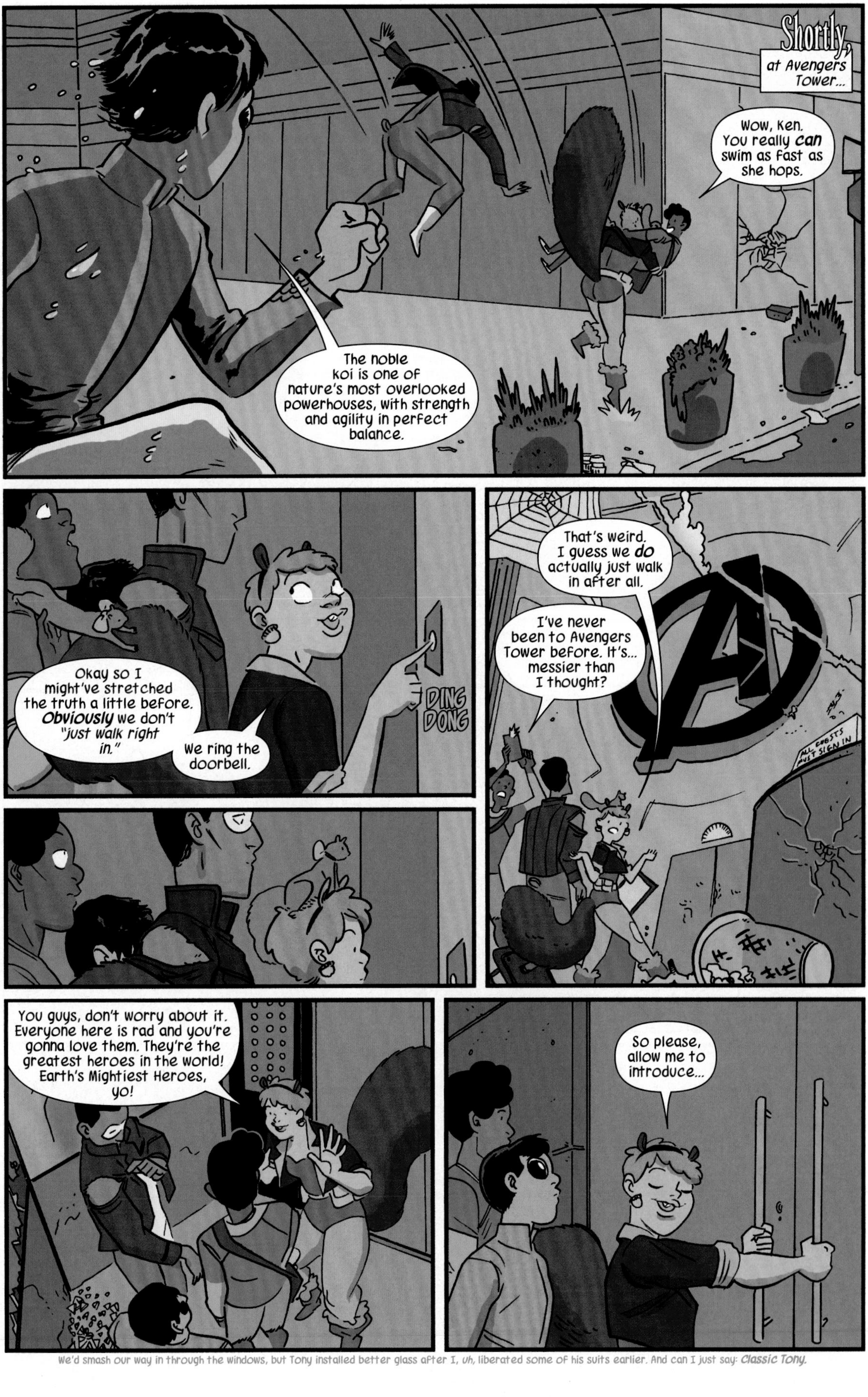
Shortly, at Avengers Tower...
Wow, Ken. You really **can** swim as fast as she hops.
The noble koi is one of nature's most overlooked powerhouses, with strength and agility in perfect balance.
Okay so I might've stretched the truth a little before. ***Obviously*** we don't *"just walk right in."*
We ring the doorbell.
DING DONG
That's weird. I guess we **do** actually just walk in after all.
I've never been to Avengers Tower before. It's... messier than I thought?
ALL GUESTS MUST SIGN IN
You guys, don't worry about it. Everyone here is rad and you're gonna love them. They're the greatest heroes in the world! Earth's Mightiest Heroes, yo!
So please, allow me to introduce...

We'd smash our way in through the windows, but Tony installed better glass after I, *uh,* liberated some of his suits earlier. And can I just say: ***Classic Tony.***

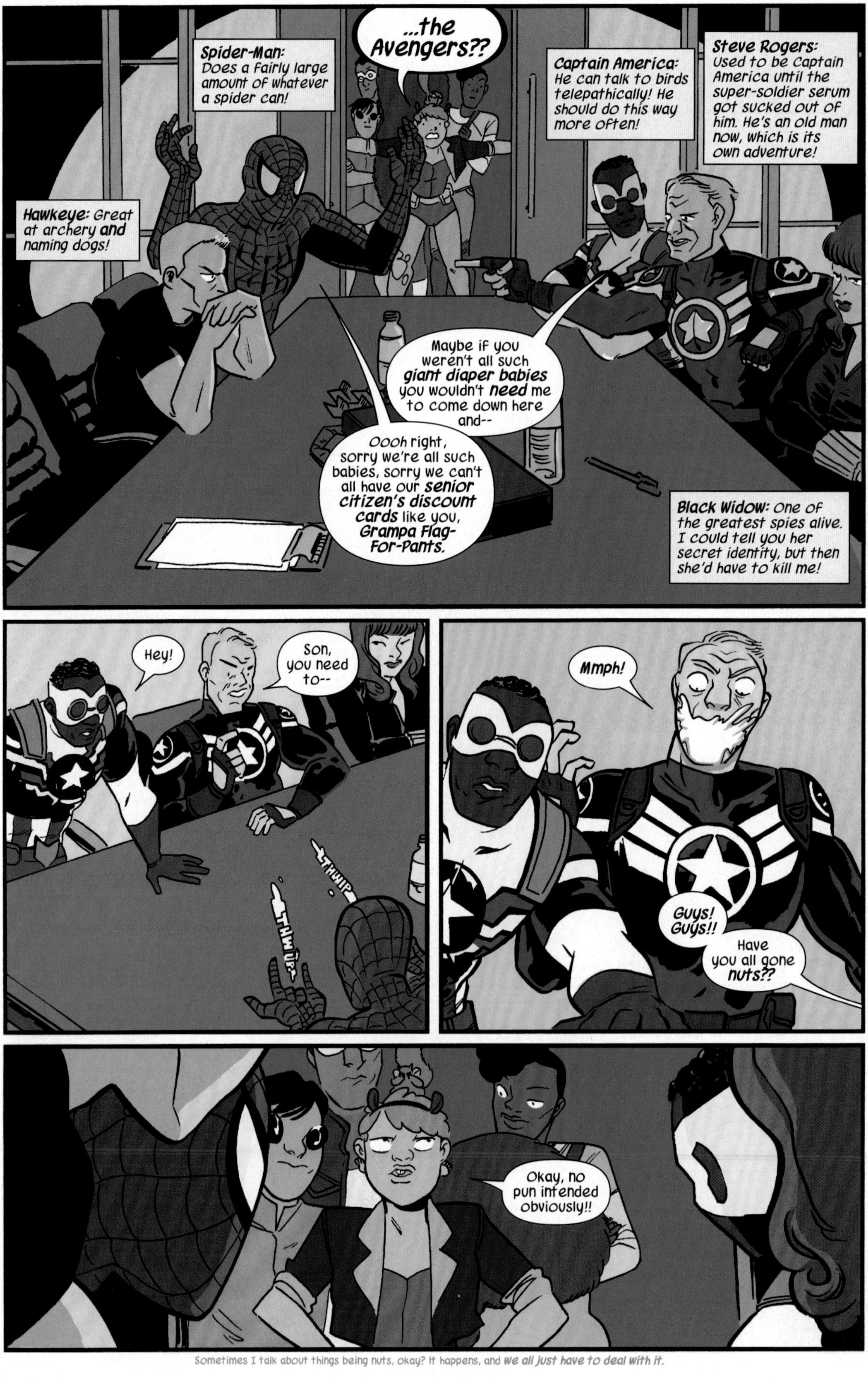
...the Avengers??
Spider-Man: Does a fairly large amount of whatever a spider can!
Captain America: He can talk to birds telepathically! He should do this way more often!
Steve Rogers: Used to be Captain America until the super-soldier serum got sucked out of him. He's an old man now, which is its own adventure!
Hawkeye: Great at archery and naming dogs!
Maybe if you weren't all such giant diaper babies you wouldn't need me to come down here and--
Oooh right, sorry we're all such babies, sorry we can't all have our senior citizen's discount cards like you, Grampa Flag-For-Pants.
Black Widow: One of the greatest spies alive. I could tell you her secret identity, but then she'd have to kill me!
Hey!
Son, you need to--
THWIP
THWIP
Mmph!
Guys! Guys!!
Have you all gone nuts??
Okay, no pun intended obviously!!

Sometimes I talk about things being nuts, okay? It happens, and *we all just have to deal with it.*

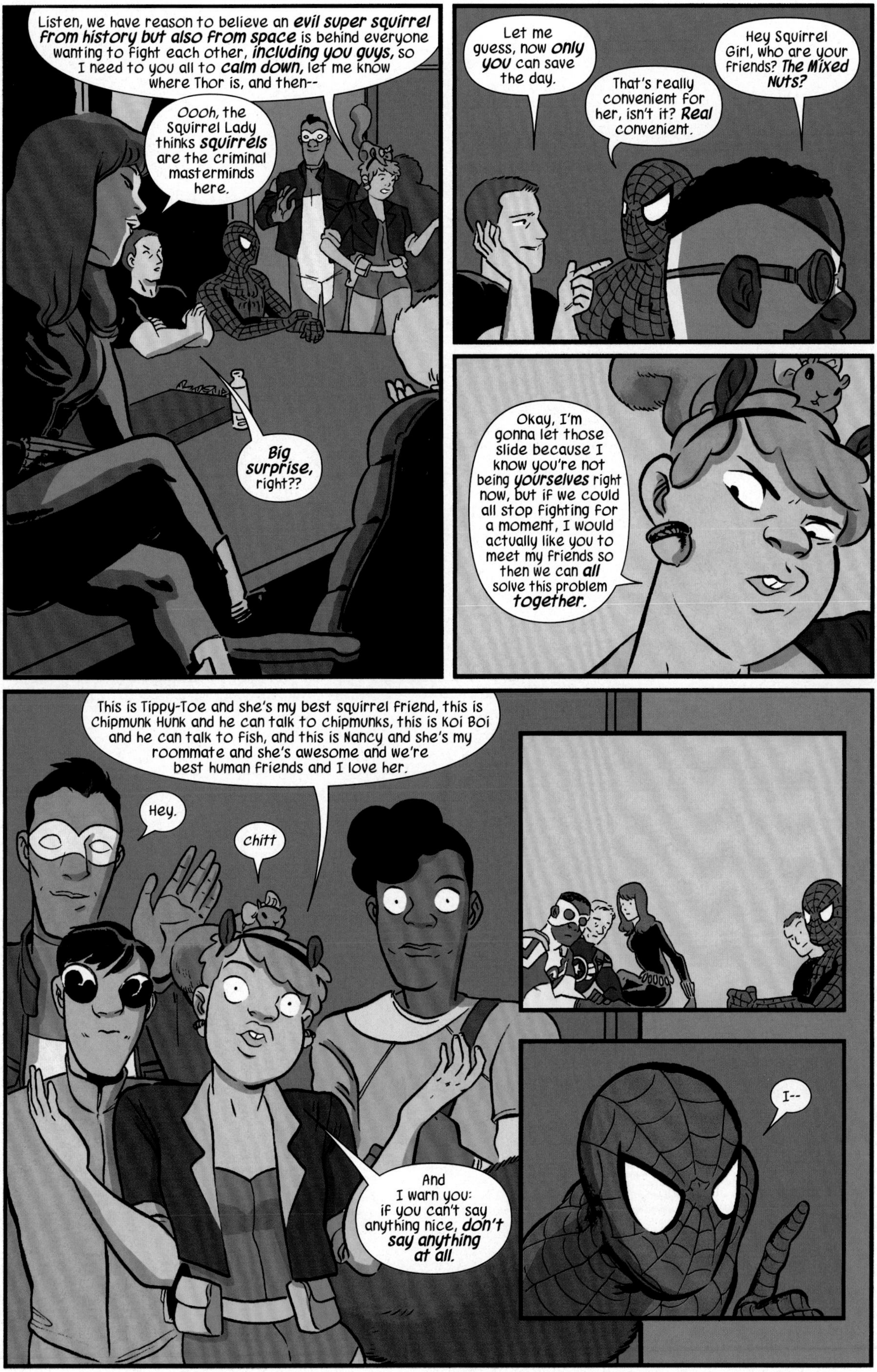

Listen, we have reason to believe an ***evil super squirrel from history but also from space*** is behind everyone wanting to fight each other, ***including you guys,*** so I need to you all to ***calm down,*** let me know where Thor is, and then--
Oooh, the Squirrel Lady thinks ***squirrels*** are the criminal masterminds here.
***Big surprise,*** right??
Let me guess, now ***only you*** can save the day.
That's really convenient for her, isn't it? ***Real*** convenient.
Hey Squirrel Girl, who are your friends? ***The Mixed Nuts?***
Okay, I'm gonna let those slide because I know you're not being ***yourselves*** right now, but if we could all stop fighting for a moment, I would actually like you to meet my friends so then we can ***all*** solve this problem ***together.***
This is Tippy-Toe and she's my best squirrel friend, this is Chipmunk Hunk and he can talk to chipmunks, this is Koi Boi and he can talk to fish, and this is Nancy and she's my roommate and she's awesome and we're best human friends and I love her.
Hey.
Chitt
And I warn you: if you can't say anything nice, ***don't say anything at all.***
I--

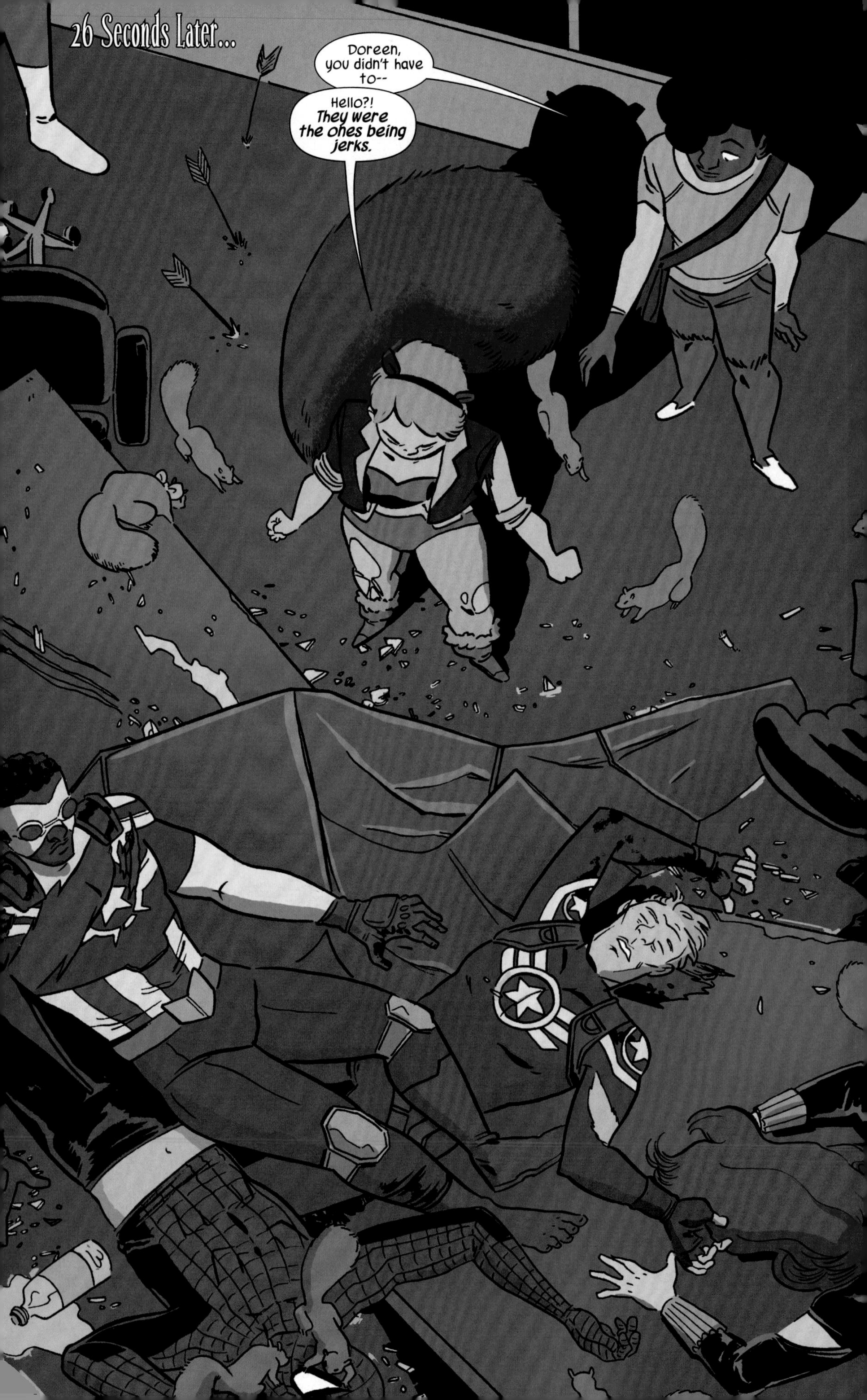
26 Seconds Later...
Doreen, you didn't have to--
Hello?! They were the ones being jerks.

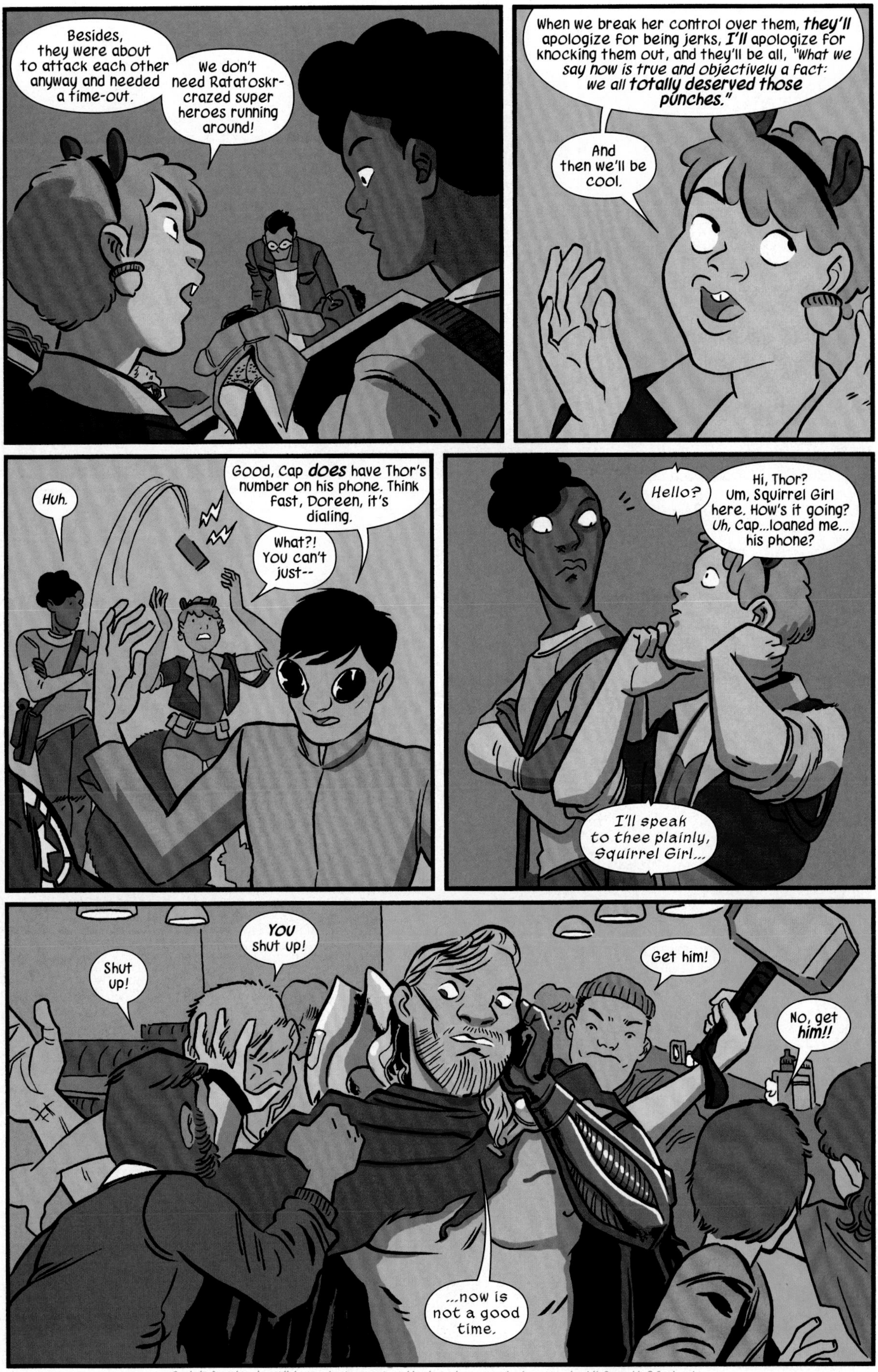
Besides, they were about to attack each other anyway and needed a time-out.
We don't need Ratatoskr-crazed super heroes running around!
When we break her control over them, *they'll* apologize for being jerks, *I'll* apologize for knocking them out, and they'll be all, "What we say now is true and objectively a fact: we all **totally deserved those punches.**"
And then we'll be cool.
Huh.
Good, Cap **does** have Thor's number on his phone. Think fast, Doreen, it's dialing.
What?! You can't just--
Hello?
Hi, Thor? Um, Squirrel Girl here. How's it going? Uh, Cap...loaned me... his phone?
I'll speak to thee plainly, Squirrel Girl...
Shut up!
*YOU* shut up!
Get him!
No, get *him!!*
...now is not a good time.

Captain America doesn't have a lock screen on his phone because who is gonna steal it from him? Seriously.
*Um, besides our heroes in this book, I mean.*

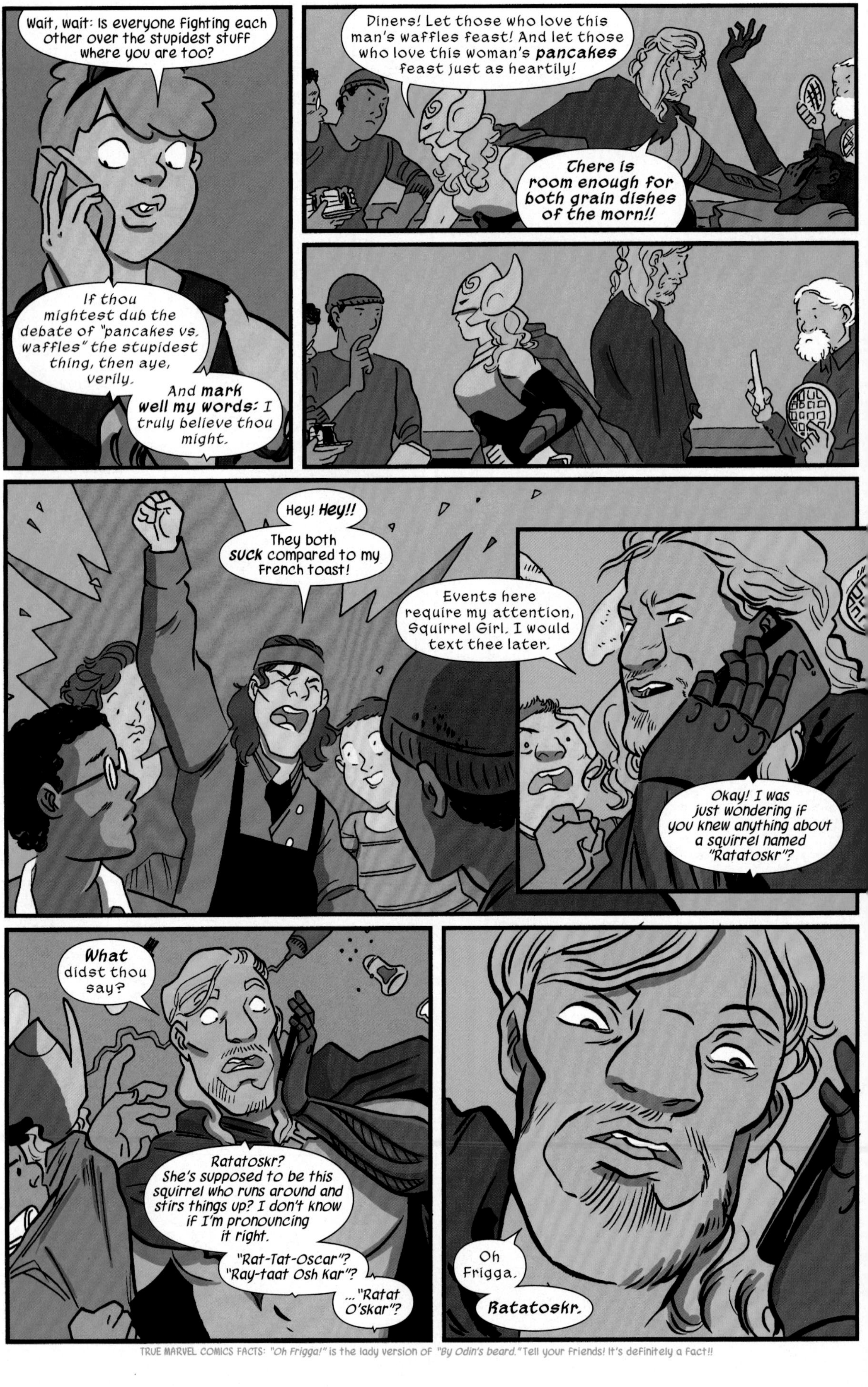
Wait, wait: Is everyone fighting each other over the stupidest stuff where you are too?
If thou mightest dub the debate of "pancakes vs. waffles" the stupidest thing, then aye, verily.
And mark well my words: I truly believe thou might.
Diners! Let those who love this man's waffles feast! And let those who love this woman's pancakes feast just as heartily!
There is room enough for both grain dishes of the morn!!
Hey! Hey!!
They both SUCK compared to my French toast!
Events here require my attention, Squirrel Girl. I would text thee later.
Okay! I was just wondering if you knew anything about a squirrel named "Ratatoskr"?
What didst thou say?
Ratatoskr? She's supposed to be this squirrel who runs around and stirs things up? I don't know if I'm pronouncing it right.
"Rat-Tat-Oscar"? "Ray-taat Osh Kar"?
..."Ratat O'skar"?
Oh Frigga.
Ratatoskr.

TRUE MARVEL COMICS FACTS: *"Oh Frigga!"* is the lady version of *"By Odin's beard."* Tell your friends! It's definitely a Fact!!

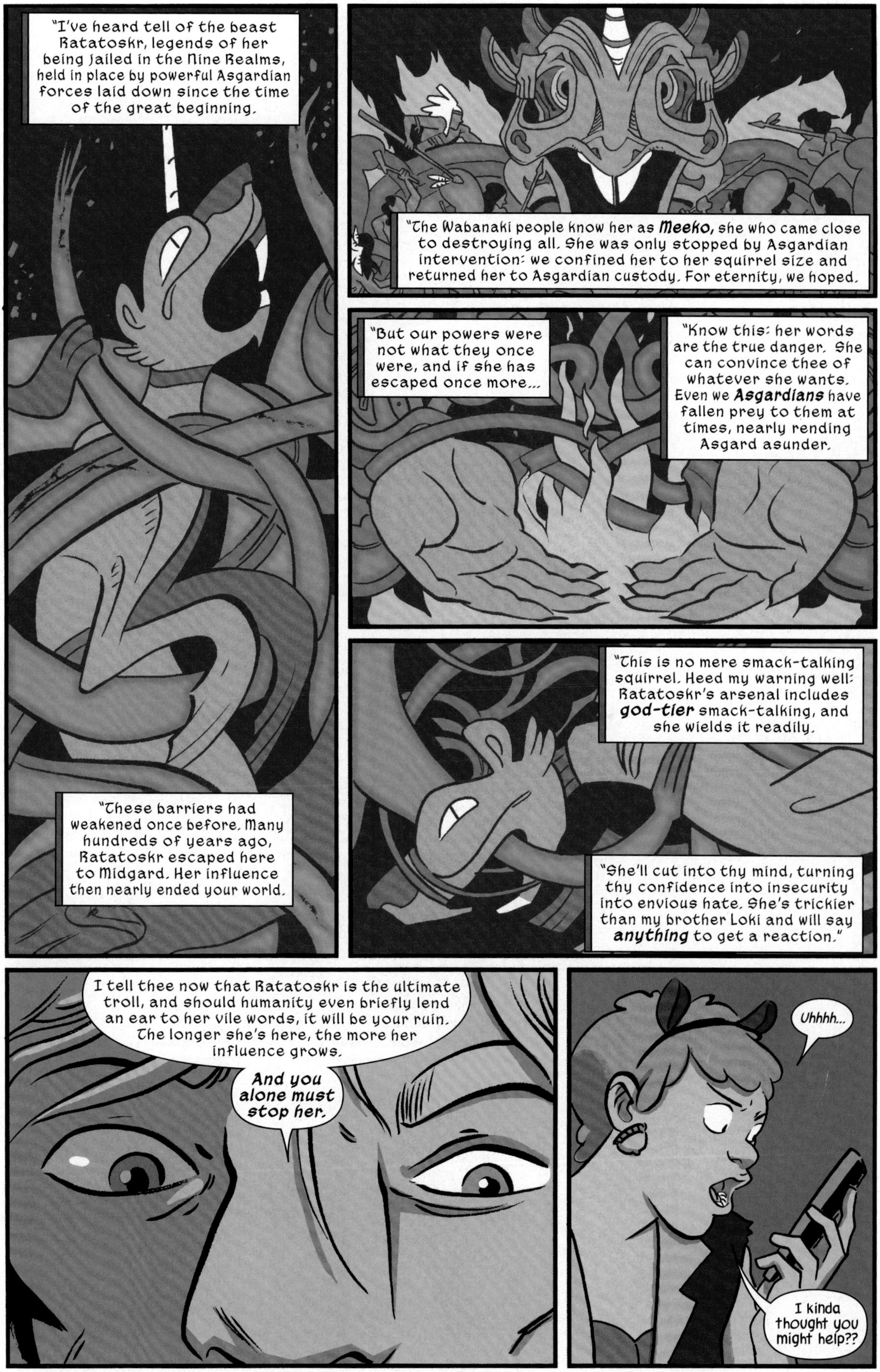
"I've heard tell of the beast Ratatoskr, legends of her being jailed in the Nine Realms, held in place by powerful Asgardian forces laid down since the time of the great beginning.
"These barriers had weakened once before. Many hundreds of years ago, Ratatoskr escaped here to Midgard. Her influence then nearly ended your world.
"The Wabanaki people know her as **Meeko**, she who came close to destroying all. She was only stopped by Asgardian intervention: we confined her to her squirrel size and returned her to Asgardian custody. For eternity, we hoped.
"But our powers were not what they once were, and if she has escaped once more...
"Know this: her words are the true danger. She can convince thee of whatever she wants. Even we **Asgardians** have fallen prey to them at times, nearly rending Asgard asunder.
"This is no mere smack-talking squirrel. Heed my warning well: Ratatoskr's arsenal includes **god-tier** smack-talking, and she wields it readily.
"She'll cut into thy mind, turning thy confidence into insecurity into envious hate. She's trickier than my brother Loki and will say **anything** to get a reaction."
I tell thee now that Ratatoskr is the ultimate troll, and should humanity even briefly lend an ear to her vile words, it will be your ruin. The longer she's here, the more her influence grows.
**And you alone must stop her.**
Uhhhh...
I kinda thought you might help??

See, Thor, ***this*** is why I keep saying you should contribute to Wikipedia. This is ***way*** more useful than their summary. *Sheesh!*

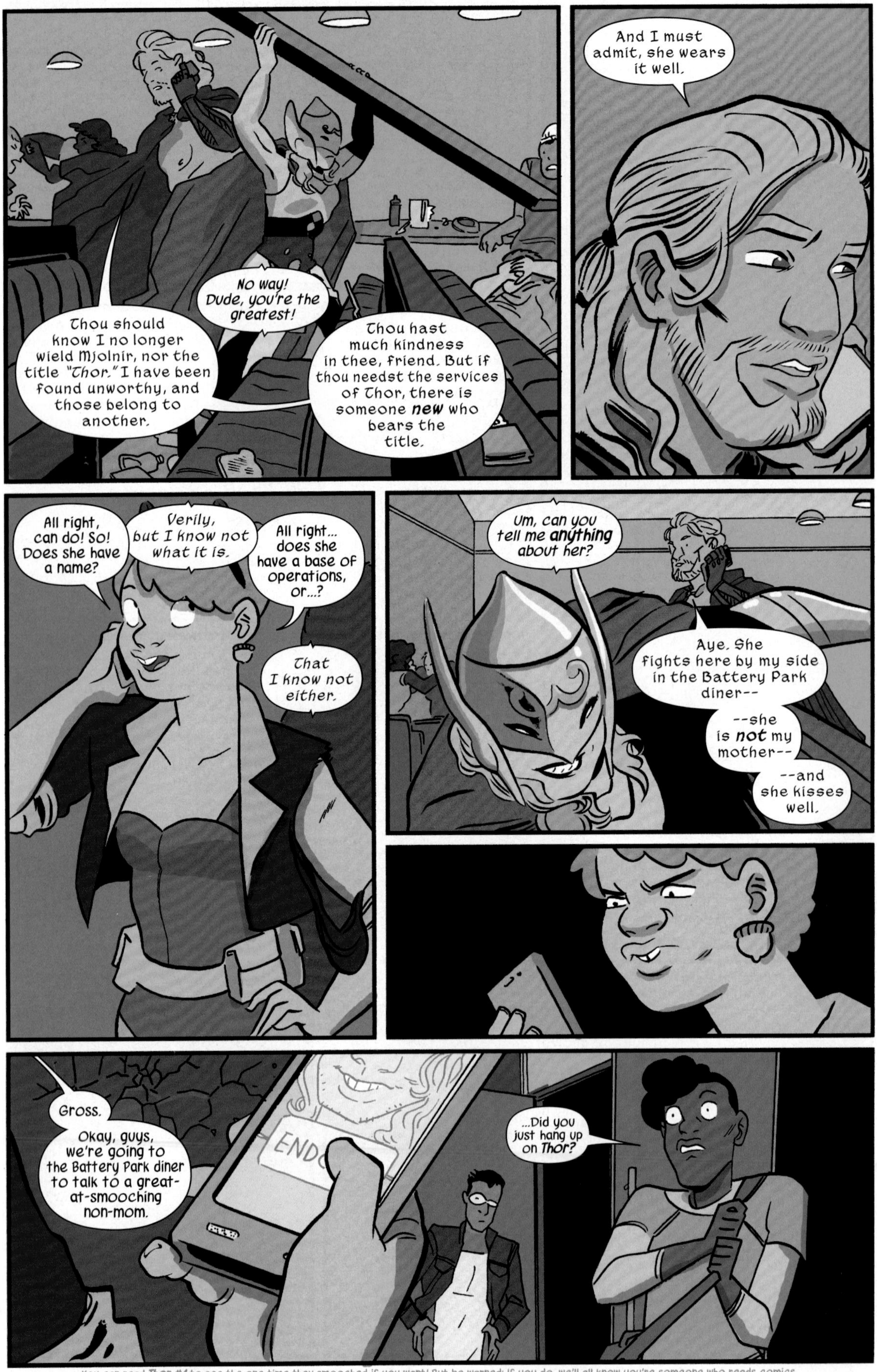
Thou should know I no longer wield Mjolnir, nor the title "Thor." I have been found unworthy, and those belong to another.
No way! Dude, you're the greatest!
Thou hast much kindness in thee, friend. But if thou needst the services of Thor, there is someone new who bears the title.
And I must admit, she wears it well.
All right, can do! So! Does she have a name?
Verily, but I know not what it is.
All right... does she have a base of operations, or...?
That I know not either.
Um, can you tell me anything about her?
Aye. She fights here by my side in the Battery Park diner--
--she is not my mother--
--and she kisses well.
Gross.
Okay, guys, we're going to the Battery Park diner to talk to a great-at-smooching non-mom.
END
...Did you just hang up on Thor?

You can read *Thor #4* to see the one time they smooched if you want! But be warned: if you do, we'll all know you're someone who reads comics just to flip forward to the smooches. ***We'll all know. Even your parents will know.***

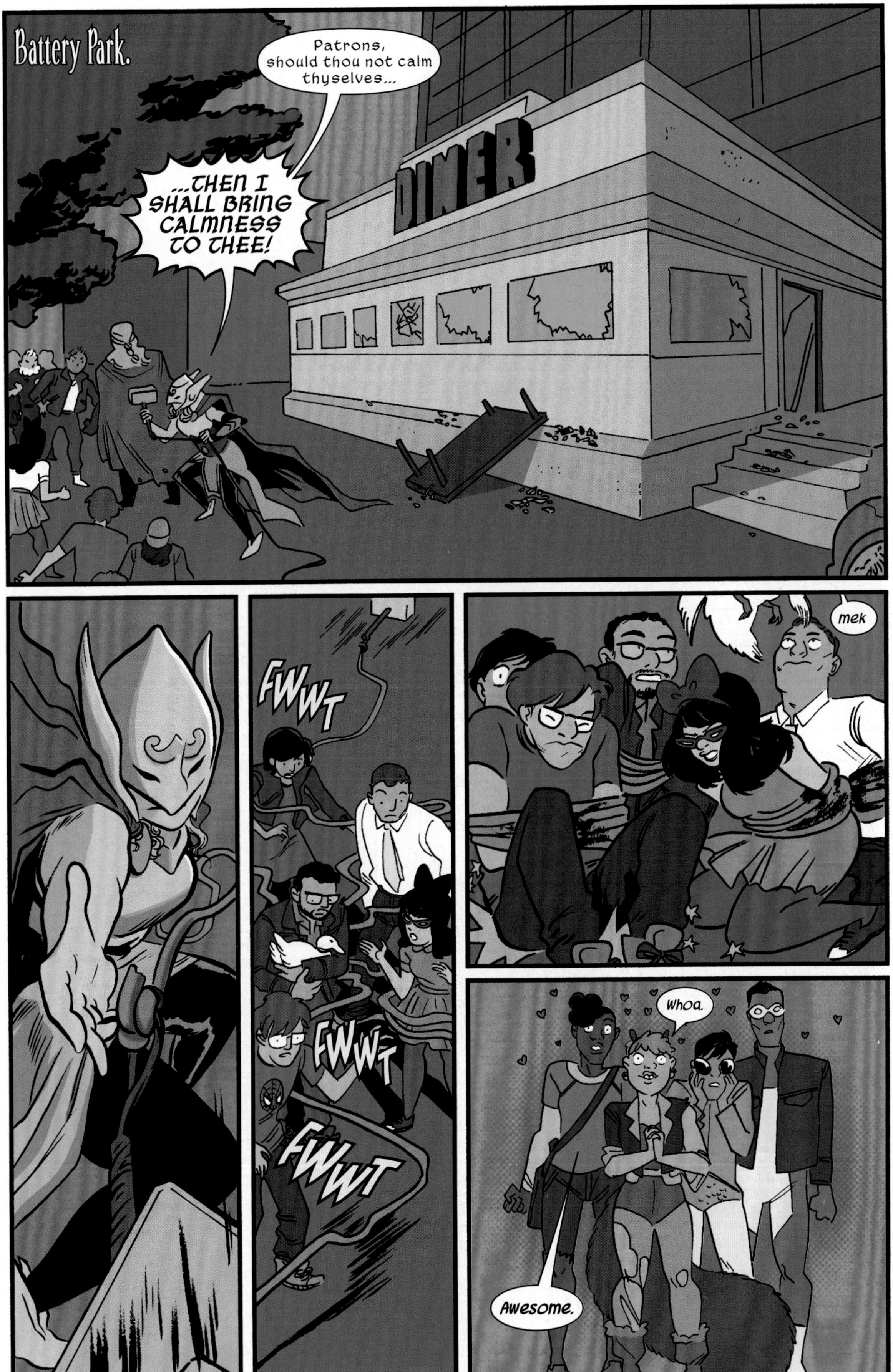
Battery Park.
Patrons, should thou not calm thyselves...
...THEN I SHALL BRING CALMNESS TO THEE!
DINER
FWWT
FWWT
FWWT
mek
Whoa.
Awesome.

TRUE REAL WORLD FACTS: Did you know that the side of a hammer is called the *"cheek"*? And the part you hit with is called the *"face,"* which is attached to the *"neck."* Hammers are these adorable little metal heads we invented to solve our problems.

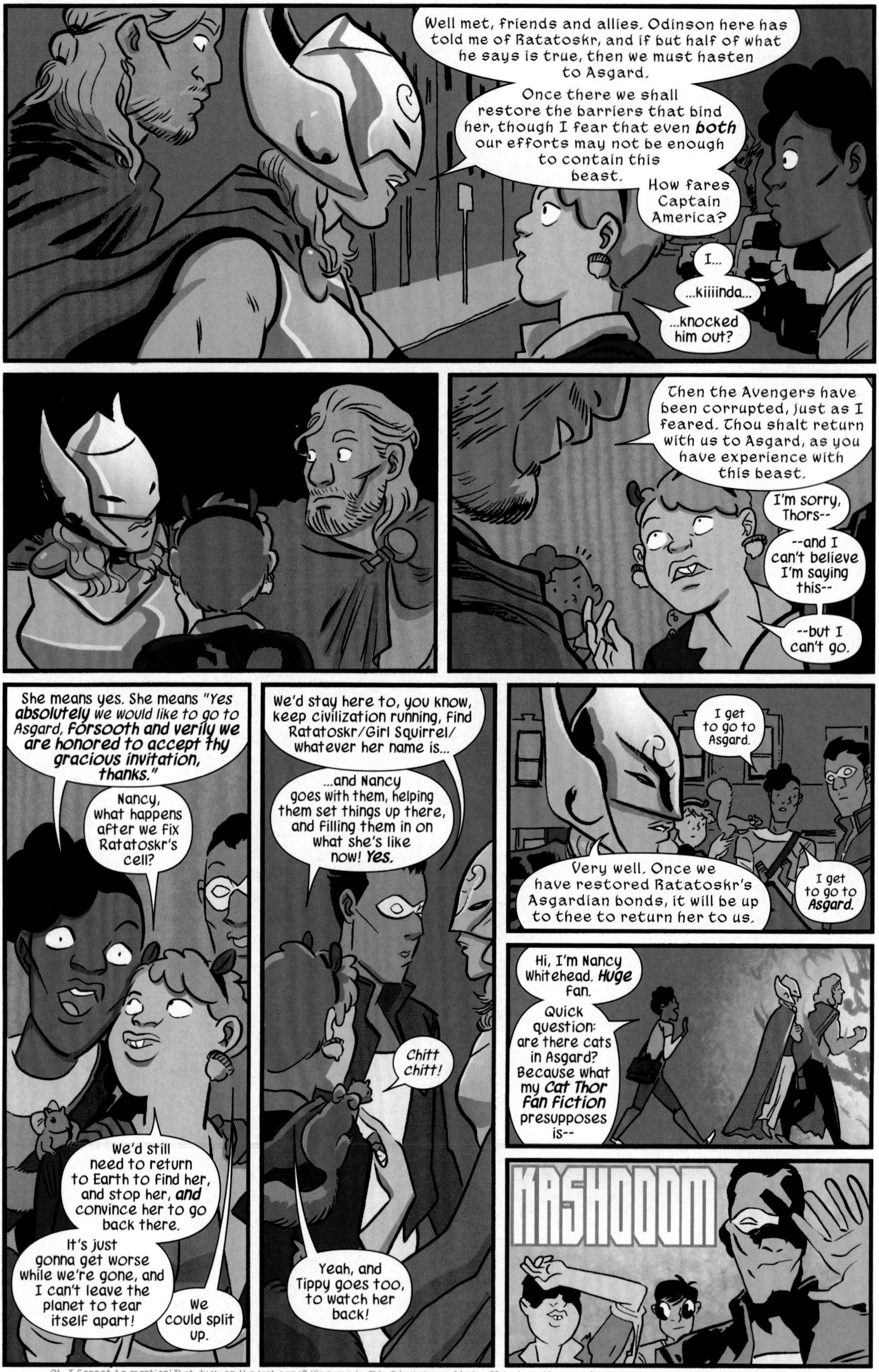
Well met, friends and allies. Odinson here has told me of Ratatoskr, and if but half of what he says is true, then we must hasten to Asgard.
Once there we shall restore the barriers that bind her, though I fear that even *both* our efforts may not be enough to contain this beast.
How fares Captain America?
I...
...kiiiinda...
...knocked him out?
Then the Avengers have been corrupted, just as I feared. Thou shalt return with us to Asgard, as you have experience with this beast.
I'm sorry, Thors--
--and I can't believe I'm saying this--
--but I can't go.
She means yes. She means "Yes *absolutely* we would like to go to Asgard, *forsooth and verily we are honored to accept thy gracious invitation, thanks.*"
Nancy, what happens after we fix Ratatoskr's cell?
We'd still need to return to Earth to find her, and stop her, *and* convince her to go back there.
It's just gonna get worse while we're gone, and I can't leave the planet to tear itself apart!
We could split up.
We'd stay here to, you know, keep civilization running, find Ratatoskr/Girl Squirrel/ whatever her name is...
...and Nancy goes with them, helping them set things up there, and filling them in on what she's like now! *Yes.*
Chitt chitt!
Yeah, and Tippy goes too, to watch her back!
I get to go to Asgard.
Very well. Once we have restored Ratatoskr's Asgardian bonds, it will be up to thee to return her to us.
I get to go to *Asgard.*
Hi, I'm Nancy Whitehead. *Huge* fan.
Quick question: are there cats in Asgard? Because what my *Cat Thor Fan Fiction* presupposes is--
KASHOOOM

Oh, I forgot to mention! That duck on the last page? His name is Chip Zducksky, and he's off to have his own adventures that we, for reasons of good taste, cannot publish here. Fare thee well, Chip Zducksky!

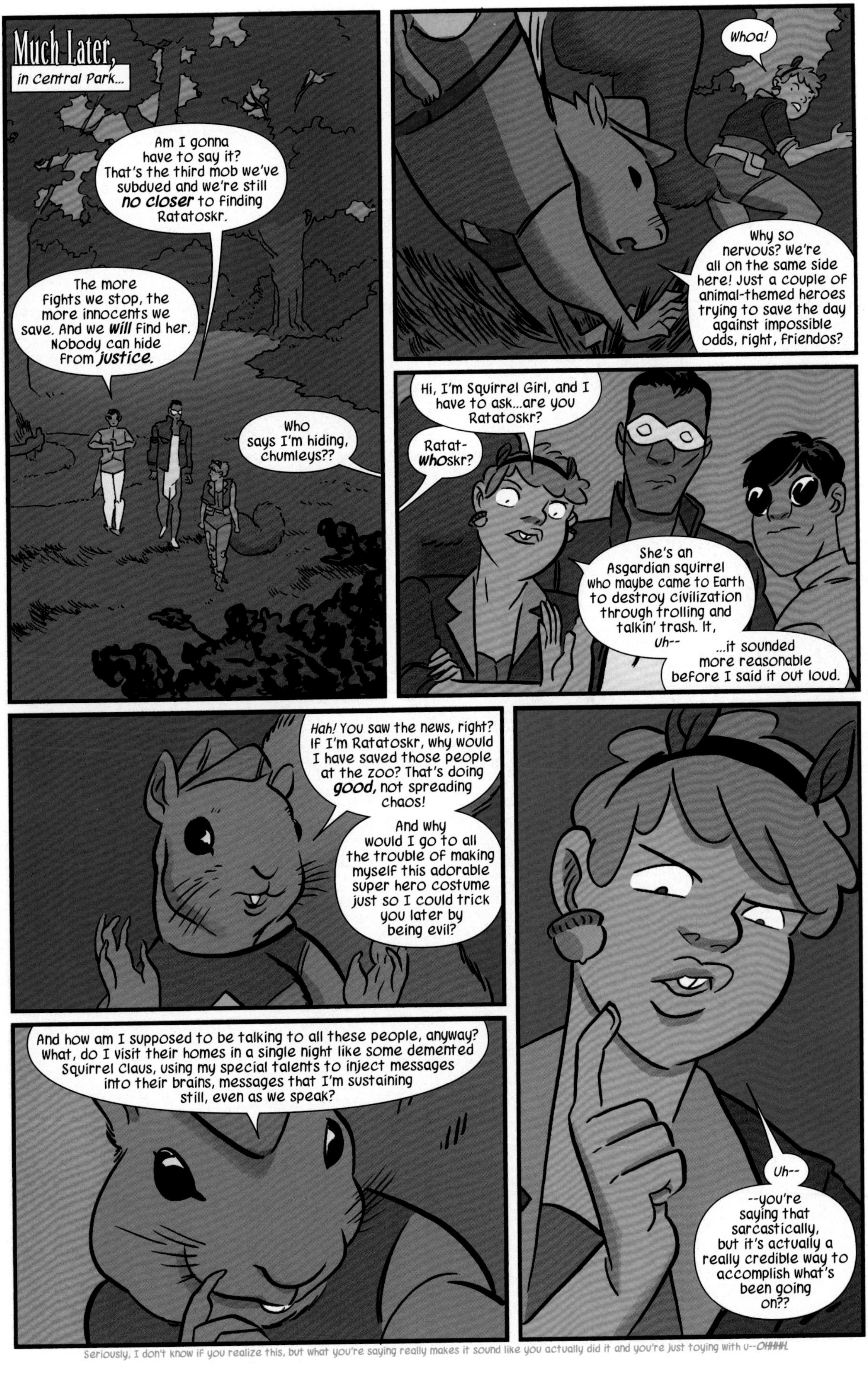
Much Later,
in Central Park...
Am I gonna have to say it? That's the third mob we've subdued and we're still no closer to finding Ratatoskr.
The more fights we stop, the more innocents we save. And we will find her. Nobody can hide from justice.
Who says I'm hiding, chumleys??
Whoa!
Why so nervous? We're all on the same side here! Just a couple of animal-themed heroes trying to save the day against impossible odds, right, friendos?
Hi, I'm Squirrel Girl, and I have to ask...are you Ratatoskr?
Ratat-whoskr?
She's an Asgardian squirrel who maybe came to Earth to destroy civilization through trolling and talkin' trash. It, uh--
...it sounded more reasonable before I said it out loud.
Hah! You saw the news, right? If I'm Ratatoskr, why would I have saved those people at the zoo? That's doing good, not spreading chaos!
And why would I go to all the trouble of making myself this adorable super hero costume just so I could trick you later by being evil?
And how am I supposed to be talking to all these people, anyway? What, do I visit their homes in a single night like some demented Squirrel Claus, using my special talents to inject messages into their brains, messages that I'm sustaining still, even as we speak?
Uh--
--you're saying that sarcastically, but it's actually a really credible way to accomplish what's been going on??

Seriously, I don't know if you realize this, but what you're saying really makes it sound like you actually did it and you're just toying with u--OHHHH.

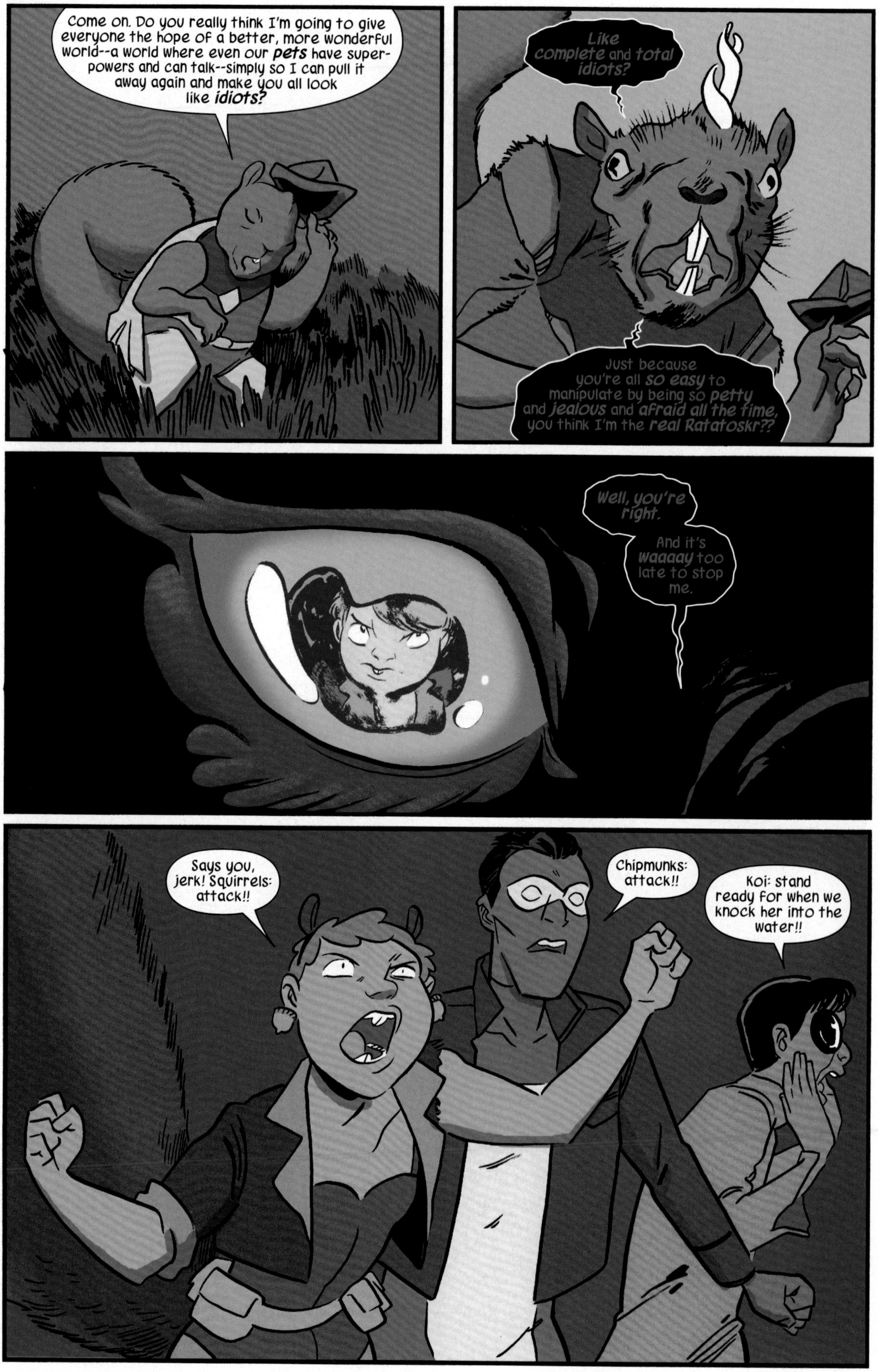

Come on. Do you really think I'm going to give everyone the hope of a better, more wonderful world--a world where even our *pets* have super-powers and can talk--simply so I can pull it away again and make you all look like *idiots?*
*Like complete* and *total idiots?*
Just because you're all *so easy* to manipulate by being so *petty* and *jealous* and *afraid all the time,* you think I'm the *real Ratatoskr??*
*Well, you're right.*
And it's *waaaay* too late to stop me.
Says you, jerk! Squirrels: attack!!
Chipmunks: attack!!
Koi: stand ready for when we knock her into the water!!

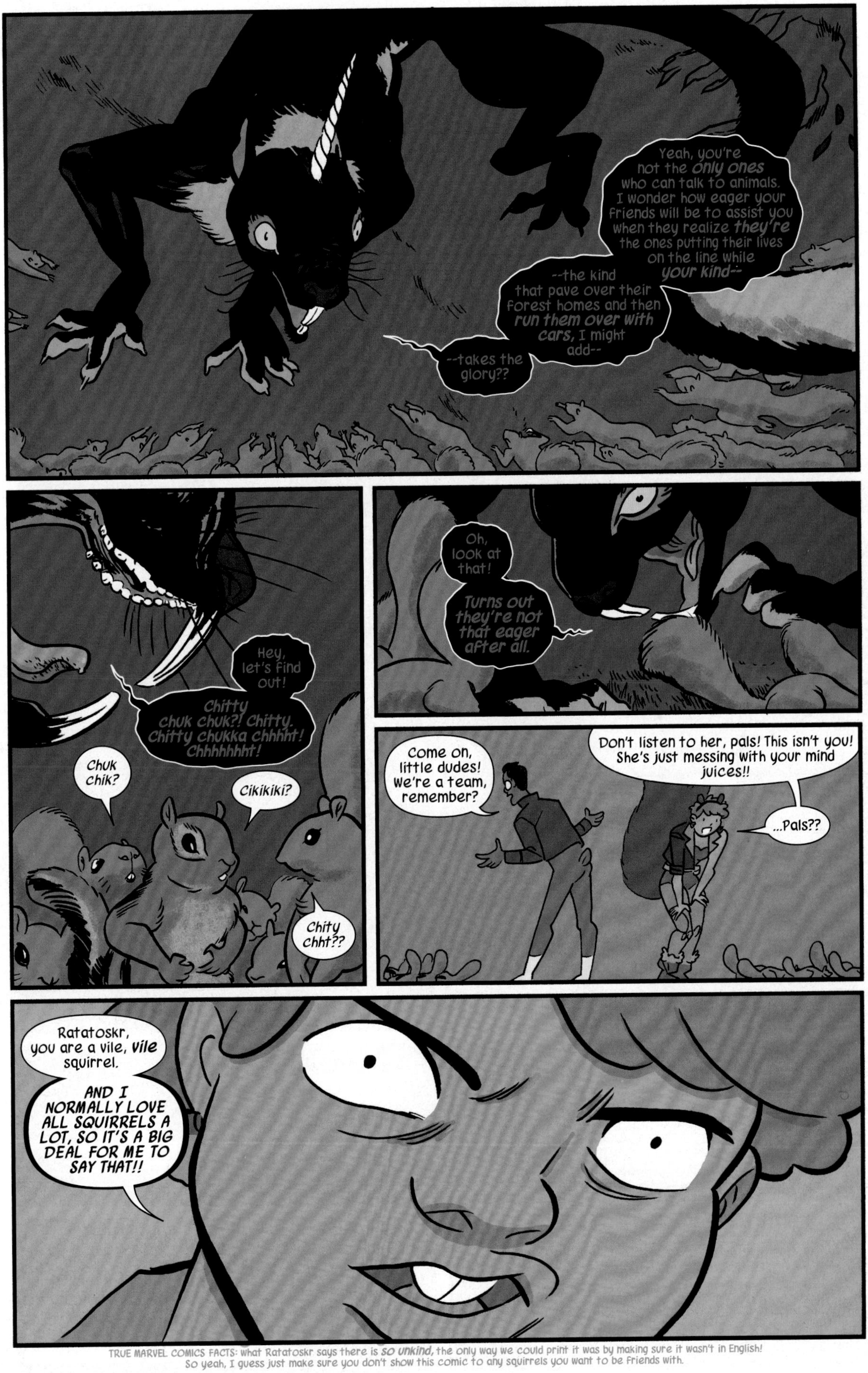
Yeah, you're not the only ones who can talk to animals. I wonder how eager your friends will be to assist you when they realize they're the ones putting their lives on the line while your kind--
--the kind that pave over their forest homes and then run them over with cars, I might add--
--takes the glory??
Hey, let's find out!
Chitty chuk chuk?! Chitty. Chitty chukka chhhht! Chhhhhhht!
Chuk chik?
Cikikiki?
Chity chht??
Oh, look at that!
Turns out they're not that eager after all.
Come on, little dudes! We're a team, remember?
Don't listen to her, pals! This isn't you! She's just messing with your mind juices!!
...Pals??
Ratatoskr, you are a vile, vile squirrel.
AND I NORMALLY LOVE ALL SQUIRRELS A LOT, SO IT'S A BIG DEAL FOR ME TO SAY THAT!!

TRUE MARVEL COMICS FACTS: what Ratatoskr says there is *so unkind,* the only way we could print it was by making sure it wasn't in English! So yeah, I guess just make sure you don't show this comic to any squirrels you want to be friends with.

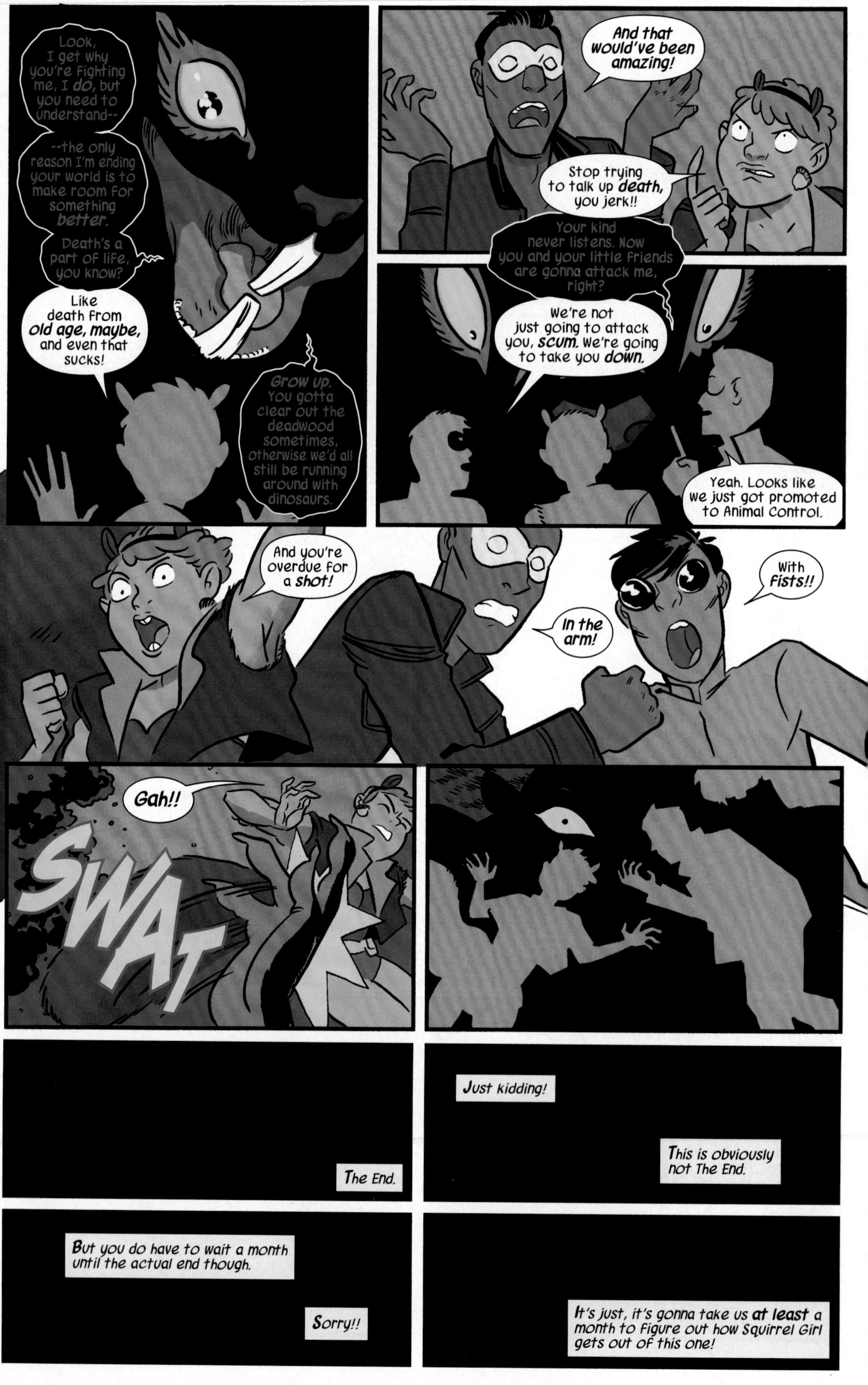
Look, I get why you're fighting me, I do, but you need to understand--
--the only reason I'm ending your world is to make room for something better.
Death's a part of life, you know?
Like death from old age, maybe, and even that sucks!
Grow up. You gotta clear out the deadwood sometimes, otherwise we'd all still be running around with dinosaurs.
And that would've been amazing!
Stop trying to talk up death, you jerk!!
Your kind never listens. Now you and your little friends are gonna attack me, right?
We're not just going to attack you, scum. We're going to take you down.
Yeah. Looks like we just got promoted to Animal Control.
And you're overdue for a shot!
In the arm!
With fists!!
Gah!!
SWAT
The End.
Just kidding!
This is obviously not The End.
But you do have to wait a month until the actual end though.
Sorry!!
It's just, it's gonna take us at least a month to figure out how Squirrel Girl gets out of this one!

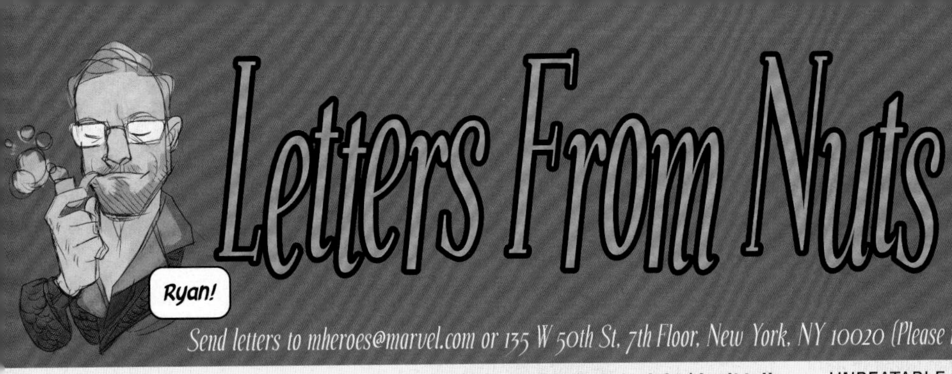
Ryan!

# Letters From Nuts

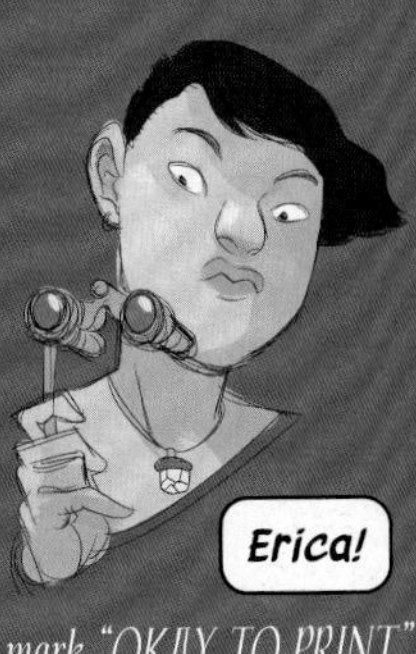
Erica!

*Send letters to mheroes@marvel.com or 135 W 50th St, 7th Floor, New York, NY 10020 (Please mark "OKAY TO PRINT")*

Dear Erica and Ryan,

Could you please make a spin off series for Squirrel Grrrl 2099. She looks badasssss! Power of squirrels and lazerss!

Thanks
Brent, Auckland, NZ

**RYAN: I'm actually way more interested in what Bass Lass (and Squirrel Earl) are up to! What are her powers? Does wearing a fish head and an evening gown give her powers, and if so, how did she ever discover that? Would - would I get her powers under similar circumstances?**

**ERICA: I'm torn on this. On the one hand, I prefer to have something like that not get any bigger than it is because we all have our own expectations of who she is and defining it would narrow down who she is. On the other hand, earlier this year, my boyfriend read Doom 2099 out loud to me as we lay on the sofa so I'm definitely into some 2099 craziness.**

Hey!

First of all, this is not my email account. I am only 9. This is my mom's account. Second of all, I know I'm a little young to be reading SQUIRREL GIRL, but I am addicted to any girl super hero comic. Third of all, you are awesome, period. Here are my top 5 comic books (not in any type of order):

- Ms. Marvel
- Squirrel Girl
- Supergirl
- Wonder Woman
- Buffy Vampire Slayer

Can't wait to read more comics.

Eliot P.

**RYAN: Hey Eliot, thanks! That's great company to be in. This was a very sweet letter, and I'm stoked you like so many female super heroes! There's a whole universe of them out there, and it's getting bigger all the time. Hooray!**

**ERICA: I think as long as you can open up Unbeatable Squirrel Girl and know what the words mean, you're old enough to read it. Ryan's right (don't tell him I said that), there are a ton of great books out there. When you're a couple of years older, e-mail again and I'll have a giant list of recommendations.**

For the Avengers premiere, as a fundraiser, my manager agreed to dress up as any super hero his reports wanted as long as we each donated $100 to charity. We all chipped in and after a brief discussion, we of course chose the Unbeatable Squirrel Girl. We all pitched in on the costume and I think he pulled it off pretty well.

Kyle Gong

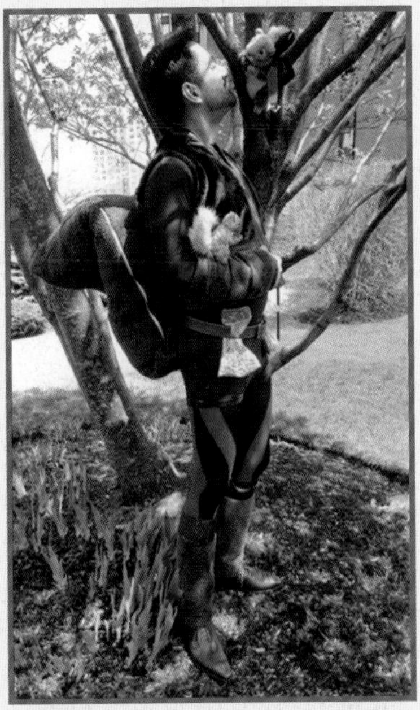

**RYAN: I rate your manager: AWESOME. Also please tell me he came in with those plastic bags of nuts tied to his belt before the costume was ever conceived of, because that is a new level of efficient snacking.**

**ERICA: YES YES YES YES YES YES YES YES YES YES YES YES YES YES YES YES YES YES YES YES YES YES YES YES YES YES YES YES YES YES YES YES YES YES YES YES YES YES**

Dear Erica and Ryan and whoever else is involved in creating this book,

UNBEATABLE SQUIRREL GIRL is such a great, entertaining book that it inspired me to write to Marvel for the FIRST TIME EVER. See how important you are? Keep up the good work.

So, I got a question and a suggestion:

- Can we have another miniseries starring the Pet Avengers, only this time including Tippy-Toe and, maybe, Mew? I know there's a cat there already, but I think Mew's interactions with Ms. Lion would be priceless!
- I think we should have a cameo from Iara Dos Santos [aka Shark-Girl] on this book. For no other reason than she's from my city and I think that would be awesome. Make it happen! Pretty please?

Tiago Maciel
Recife, Brazil

**RYAN: 1) I think about the Pet Avengers all the time.**

**2) I didn't know about Shark-Girl, and now I think about HER all the time too! Koi Boi and Shark-Girl: will their love sink, or will it - at last, at long last - swim??**

**ERICA: 1) There can totally be two cats. Who says there can't be two cats? I demand MORE CATS. Cat Thor, I say.**

**2) Shark-Girl is great. I vote yes.**

Dear Erica, Ryan and Rico,

As a proud dog owner, I am predisposed to absolutely hate squirrels. They torment my dogs in the backyard, sitting in trees and mocking them with their incessant chirping. During normal conversation, I have to spell out the S-Q-U-I-R-R-E-L word because my dogs know that word and begin to bark and rampage. Squirrels are nothing more than dog-aggravating, plague-carrying rodents.

With all that in my past, I was predisposed to despise Squirrel Girl and all she represented. Then I read the first story arc and I immediately changed my tune. Not only is the story itself funny and engaging and beautifully drawn, but I am seeing a new side of the squirrel. I have started to appreciate their craftiness and versatility. Maybe like Kraven, my dogs need to find a new enemy.

I have attempted to read Squirrel Girl comics to my dogs in the hopes of changing their minds. Sadly, they are too distracted by the squirrels outside to ever sit still for enough time.

Max D.
Los Angeles, CA

**RYAN: My first dog, Kita, hated squirrels too (or really just loved to bark at them and chase them off the deck? It is impossible to say). My current dog, Noam Chompsky, doesn't really notice squirrels, but I do, and if I'm behind on a deadline it's like they're all saying "hey stop hanging out with your dog in the park and go work, slacker." So I think it's fair to say that, like you, my relationship with squirrels has become... more complicated?**

**ERICA: As I've mentioned in the letters before, I was bitten by a squirrel (remember kids, they're wild animals!) and had to get tested for rabies. It took me a long time to come back around to squirrels but I was pretty okay with them again before I started on the book. Now my goal is to find someone who has a pet squirrel so that I can play with it.**

Hi there!

I would like to start with thanking you guys for providing me with a comic that is most definitely worth spending my money on; I buy them both in digital and physical copies, because when living in Denmark it takes a while for the magazines to arrive and I'm not always a patient person - not when it comes to things like this ;)

Secondly, OH MY GOSH! I've never had that much attention on any of my cosplays, as when you retweeted and blogged my Star Trek/Squirrel Girl picture, as well as my "standard" ones (not that there's anything ordinary about Doreen.)

I fell in love with her after reading the first volume, with her positive attitude, her humor and her style, and knew right away that I had to make her my newest cosplay, and I love it! She has practical pockets (lots of room for nuts) and while my tail is a tiny bit heavy, it's also a build-in chair! And people loved it when I brought it to the latest con! I even made a nice bunch of her trading cards, just for props .I am introducing her to everyone I know, and the last time I saw my five year old sister, her very first thing to say was not "hi," but rather "you're a squirrel!" because she'd seen the pictures online.

I love Doreen, Tippy Toe and you guys, and I am happy to spread the word!

Peace out!
Stine Fuchs

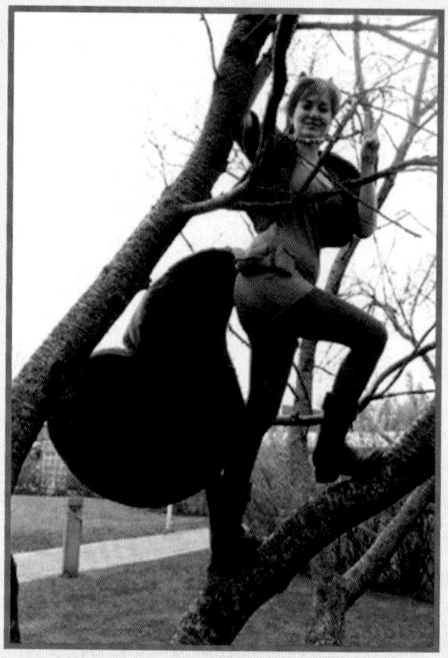

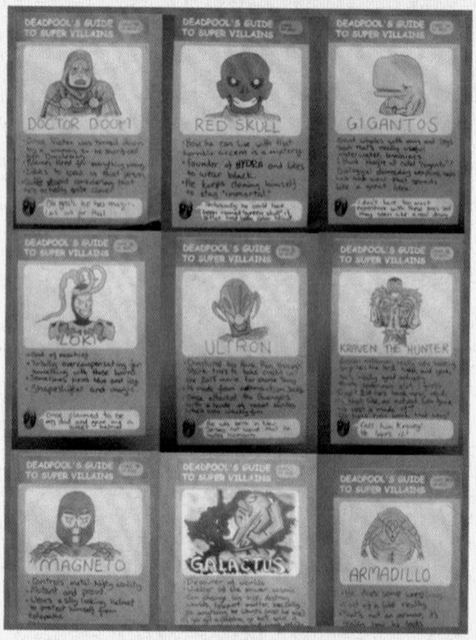
DEADPOOL'S GUIDE TO SUPER VILLAINS
DOCTOR DOOM
RED SKULL
GIGANTOS
LOKI
ULTRON
KRAVEN THE HUNTER
MAGNETO
GALACTUS
ARMADILLO

Denmark

**RYAN: Stine, your cosplay is, and I say this without hyperbole, OFF THE HOOK. Holy cow. Also, it's such a thrill to see cosplay for Squirrel Girl! Especially when it's so great. I love that you made more Deadpool cards too - they're so much fun to write (AS YOU HAVE NOW DISCOVERED) that I'm sure there'll be more here in the future! In conclusion, you are awesome (and thank you so much for buying every issue - TWICE!) and we are in your debt. Keep spreading the word!!**

**ERICA: Your Star Trek Squirrel Girl is amazing, as is your Squirrel Girl Squirrel Girl. For readers who haven't seen it, it's on our tumblr (see below).**

**The Deadpool cards are AMAZING. I love that you're drawing them yourself too. Keep sending us photos, okay? We will retweet ALL OF THEM.**

**RYAN: Finally, I'd like to dedicate this issue to Hester the sugar glider, pictured below. While not technically a squirrel (sugar gliders look similar to flying squirrels but had a different evolutionary path!), she was the pet of our editor Wil and his wife, Julia, and she had an awesome ten-year run. She was loved so much, and will be missed.**

**ERICA: She's beautiful. I'm sorry she's gone, Wil, but you've had a great many years with her and that's what's important.**

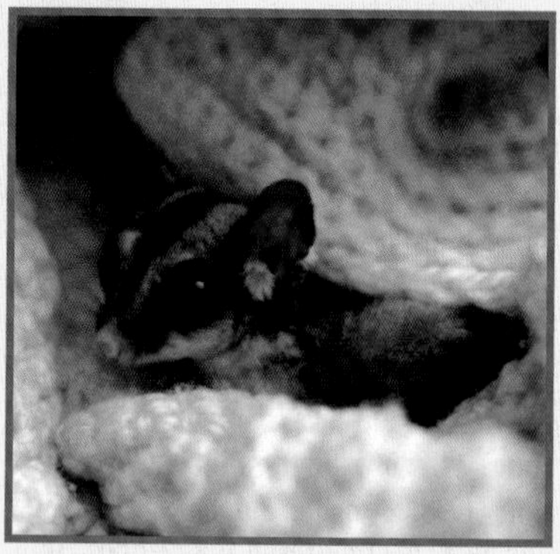

## Next: It's The End Of The Squirrel-D As We Know It!

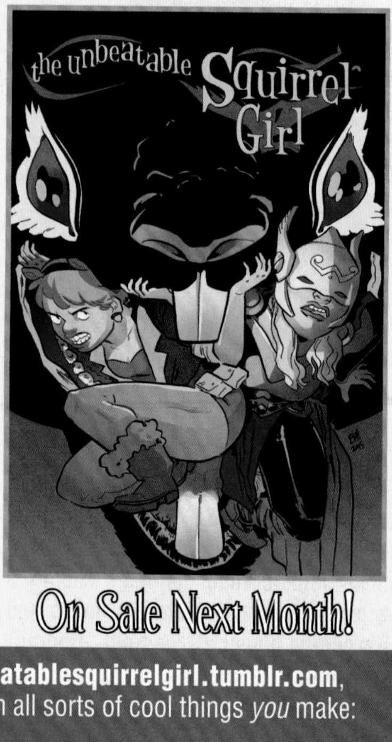
the unbeatable Squirrel Girl

## On Sale Next Month!

Attention Squirrel Scouts! Make sure to check out our production blog, **unbeatablesquirrelgirl.tumblr.com**, where we post behind-the-scenes stuff on how the book gets made, along with all sorts of cool things *you* make: fan art, cosplay, whatever!

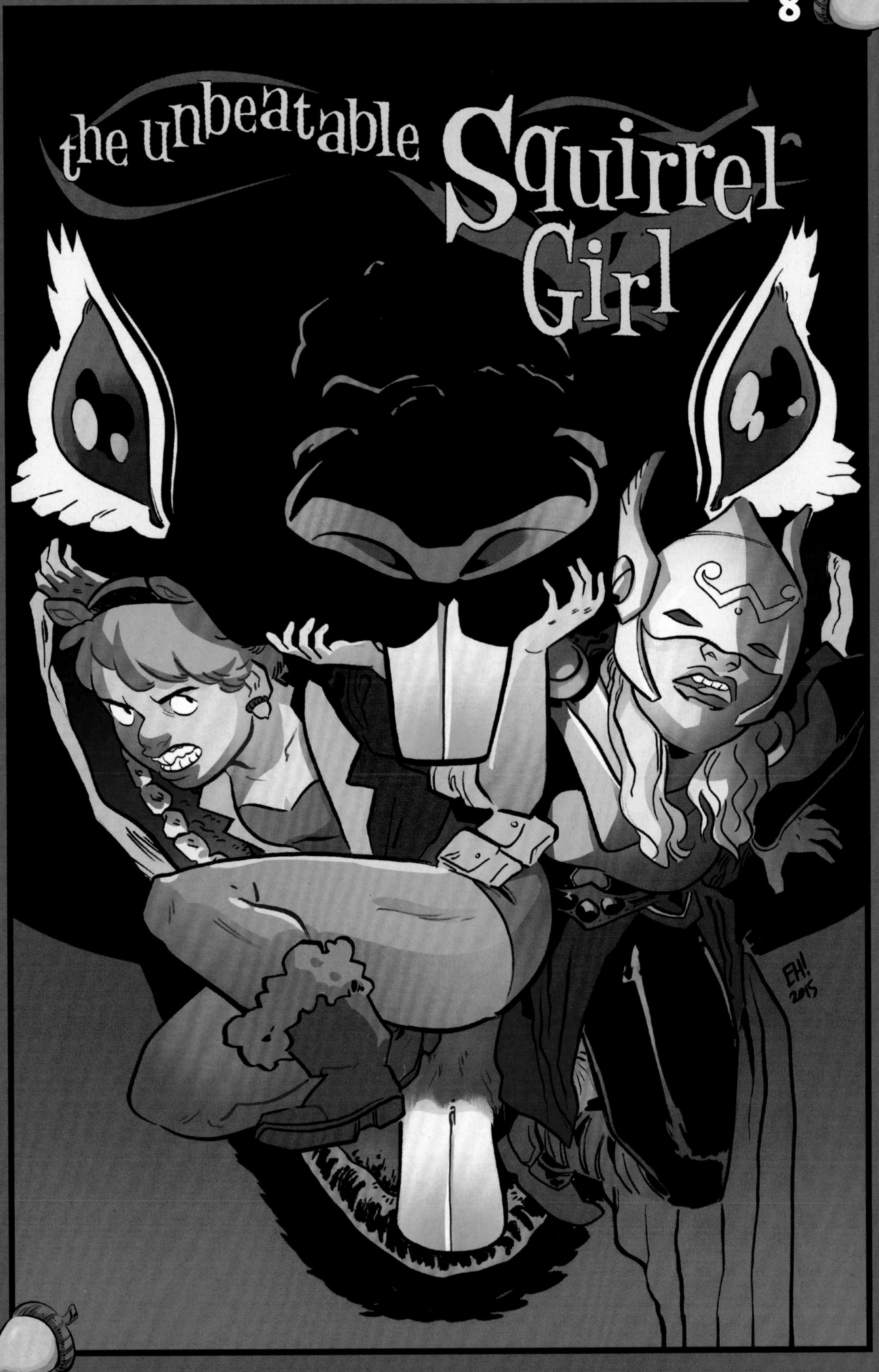
the unbeatable Squirrel Girl
EH! 2015

Doreen Green isn't just a first-year computer science student: she secretly also has all the powers of both squirrel and girl!
She uses her amazing abilities to fight crime **and** be as awesome as possible. You know her as...**The Unbeatable Squirrel Girl!**
Let's catch up with what she's been up to until now, with...

# 8

# Squirrel Girl in a nutshell

### search! 🔍

#asgard

#catsgard

#ratatoskrage

#breakfastmeets

#seeyouinoctober

**Nancy W.** @sewwiththeflo
If I don't come back, I want my epitaph to read "HERE LIES NANCY WHITEHEAD: SHE WENT TO ASGARD AND DIED AND IT WAS TOTALLY WORTH IT."

**Nancy W.** @sewwiththeflo
Koi Boi and Chipmunk Hunk and @unbeatablesg all stayed behind, so I need y'all to make sure one of them takes care of this for me.

**Squirrel Girl!** @unbeatablesg
@sewwiththeflo dude, you're not going to DIE in ASGARD!! you got a current AND a former Thor watching your back! COME ON

**Nancy W.** @sewwiththeflo
@unbeatablesg It was a humblebrag, SG. A humbleepitaph.

**Squirrel Girl!** @unbeatablesg
@sewwiththeflo only you would brag by updating your followers on what your GRAVESTONE should read.

**Nancy W.** @sewwiththeflo
@unbeatablesg #personalbranding

**Tony Stark** @starkmantony ✓
@unbeatablesg Hey, just looking at a report that says you're fighting "a giant monster god-squirrel from Asgard named 'Ratatoskr'"

**Tony Stark** @starkmantony ✓
@unbeatablesg Can't help noticing that before I knew you, there were precisely zero evil squirrel-gods running around NYC.

**Squirrel Girl!** @unbeatablesg
@starkmantony uh that's funny because before I knew YOU there were precisely zero IRON MONGERS and MADAME MASQUES running around NYC!!

**Squirrel Girl!** @unbeatablesg
@starkmantony haha okay, so, i got those from a website that lists villains you've defeated? but they're like, bonkers

**Squirrel Girl!** @unbeatablesg
@starkmantony dude you fought a BIG WHEEL named "BIG WHEEL" that was invented by one "Jackson WHEELE"??? that's SINCERELY AMAZING.

**Tony Stark** @starkmantony ✓
@unbeatablesg Can't talk, gotta get back to my very important world-class CEO work. Just take care of the squirrel thing.

**Squirrel Girl!** @unbeatablesg
@starkmantony obviously i'm gonna do that! quick question before I go though. just one super-quick question, okay?

**Squirrel Girl!** @unbeatablesg
@starkmantony when he said he was gonna take over earth, did you tell him he "spoke" too soon and is in "wheely" big trouble now or WHAT

**Squirrel Girl!** @unbeatablesg
So um, I kinda beat up the Avengers? In 26 seconds?? But they were being mind-controlled so it's okay

**HULK** @HULKYSMASHY
@unbeatablesg HULK WAS NOT PRESENT FOR THIS BUT HULK THINKS ABOUT BEATING UP AVENGERS ALL THE TIME

**Squirrel Girl!** @unbeatablesg
@HULKYSMASHY haha, well, they sassed my pals!! they were SO RUDE!

**HULK** @HULKYSMASHY
@unbeatablesg HULK WOULD LIKE TO BELIEVE THERE IS ALWAYS TIME FOR POLITENESS

**Squirrel Girl!** @unbeatablesg
@HULKYSMASHY dude! you are blowing my mind here!! i had no idea you thought this way!

**Squirrel Girl!** @unbeatablesg
@HULKYSMASHY hulk smash...my prejudices against giant green rage monsters!!

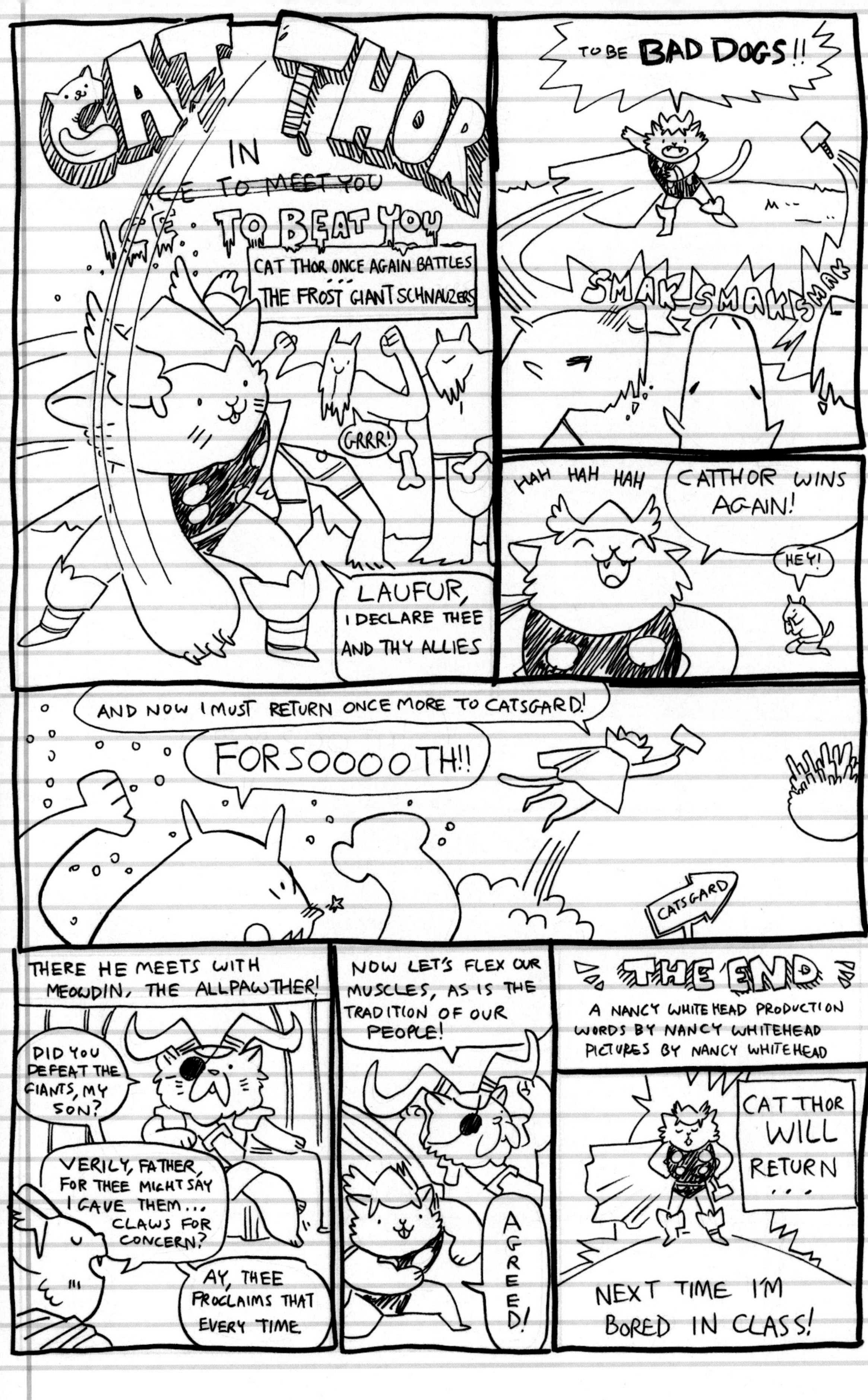
CAT THOR
IN
ICE TO MEET YOU
ICE TO BEAT YOU
CAT THOR ONCE AGAIN BATTLES THE FROST GIANT SCHNAUZERS
GRRR!
LAUFUR, I DECLARE THEE AND THY ALLIES
TO BE BAD DOGS!!
SMAK SMAK SMAK
HAH HAH HAH
CATTHOR WINS AGAIN!
HEY!
AND NOW I MUST RETURN ONCE MORE TO CATSGARD!
FORSOOOOTH!!
CATSGARD
THERE HE MEETS WITH MEOWDIN, THE ALLPAWTHER!
DID YOU DEFEAT THE GIANTS, MY SON?
VERILY, FATHER, FOR THEE MIGHT SAY I GAVE THEM... CLAWS FOR CONCERN?
AY, THEE PROCLAIMS THAT EVERY TIME.
NOW LET'S FLEX OUR MUSCLES, AS IS THE TRADITION OF OUR PEOPLE!
AGREED!
THE END
A NANCY WHITEHEAD PRODUCTION
WORDS BY NANCY WHITEHEAD
PICTURES BY NANCY WHITEHEAD
CAT THOR WILL RETURN...
NEXT TIME I'M BORED IN CLASS!

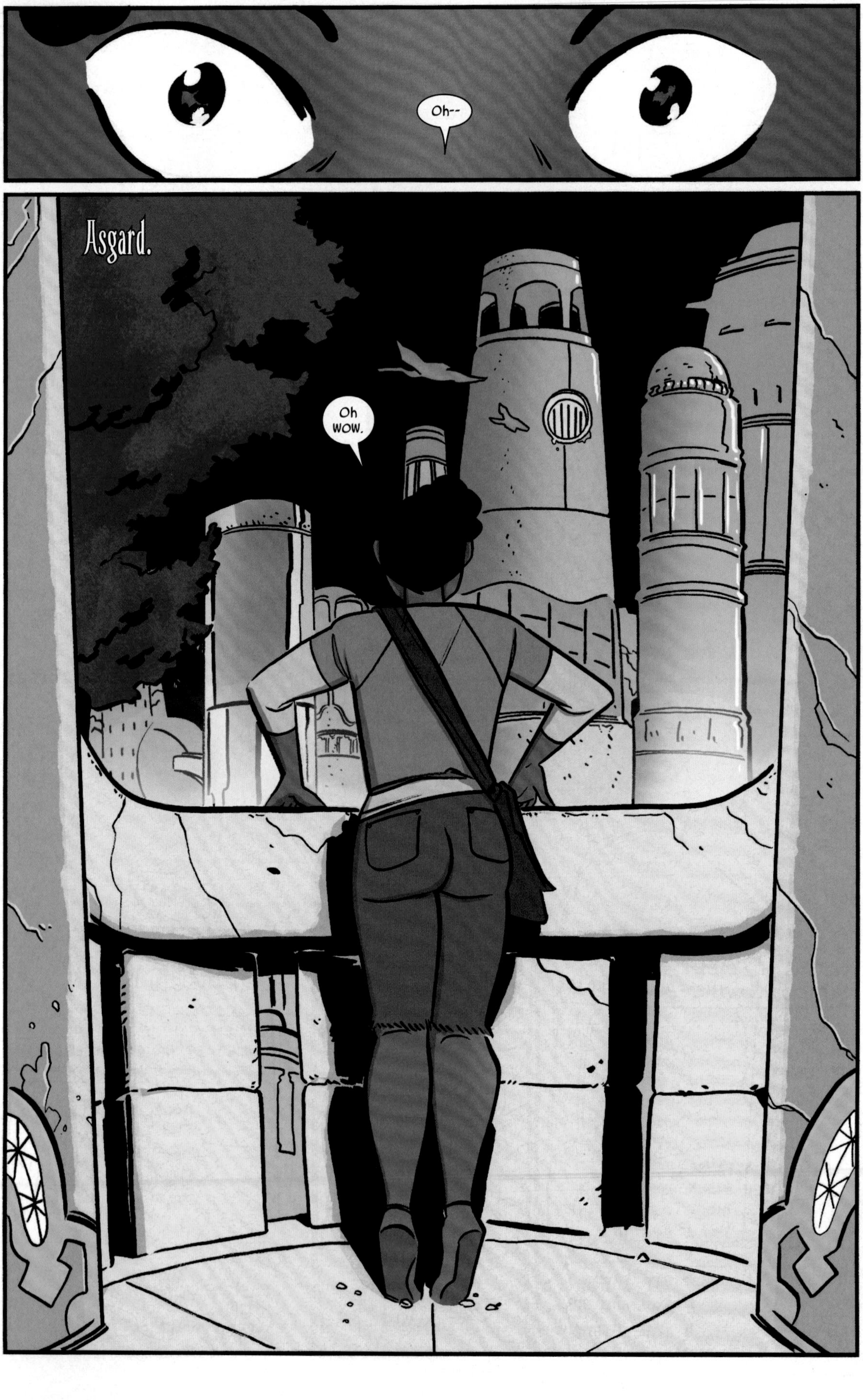
Oh--
Asgard.
Oh WOW.

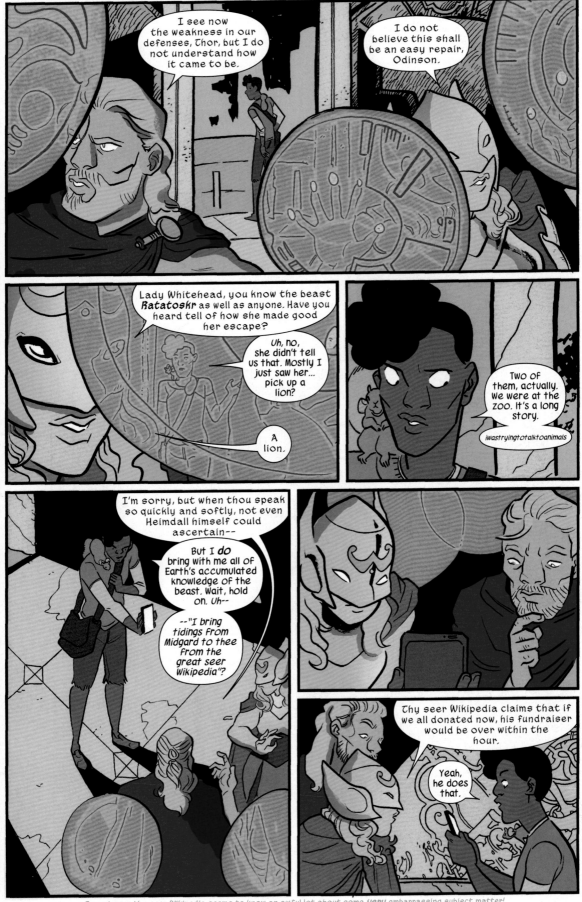

I see now the weakness in our defenses, Thor, but I do not understand how it came to be.

I do not believe this shall be an easy repair, Odinson.

Lady Whitehead, you know the beast *Ratatoskr* as well as anyone. Have you heard tell of how she made good her escape?

Uh, no, she didn't tell us that. Mostly I just saw her... pick up a lion?

A lion.

Two of them, actually. We were at the zoo. It's a long story.

*iwastryingtotalktoanimals*

I'm sorry, but when thou speak so quickly and softly, not even Heimdall himself could ascertain--

But I *do* bring with me all of Earth's accumulated knowledge of the beast. Wait, hold on. Uh--

--"I bring tidings from Midgard to thee from the great seer Wikipedia"?

Thy seer Wikipedia claims that if we all donated now, his fundraiser would be over within the hour.

Yeah, he does that.

I must say, thy seer Wikipedia seems to know an awful lot about some *very* embarrassing subject matter!

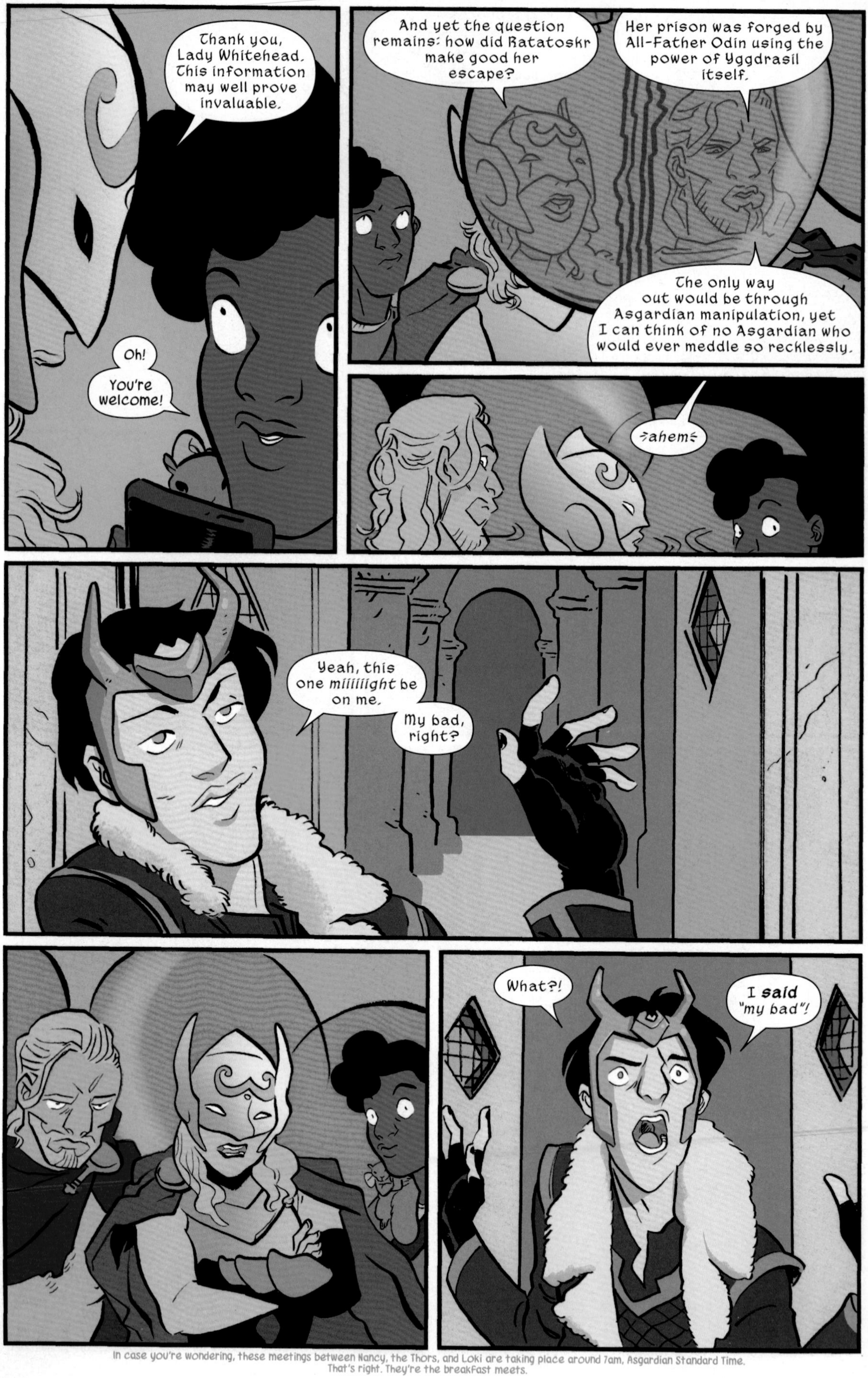
Thank you, Lady Whitehead. This information may well prove invaluable.
Oh!
You're welcome!
And yet the question remains: how did Ratatoskr make good her escape?
Her prison was forged by All-Father Odin using the power of Yggdrasil itself.
The only way out would be through Asgardian manipulation, yet I can think of no Asgardian who would ever meddle so recklessly.
ahem
Yeah, this one *miiiiiight* be on me.
My bad, right?
What?!
I **said** "my bad"!

In case you're wondering, these meetings between Nancy, the Thors, and Loki are taking place around 7am, Asgardian Standard Time.
That's right. They're the breakfast meets.

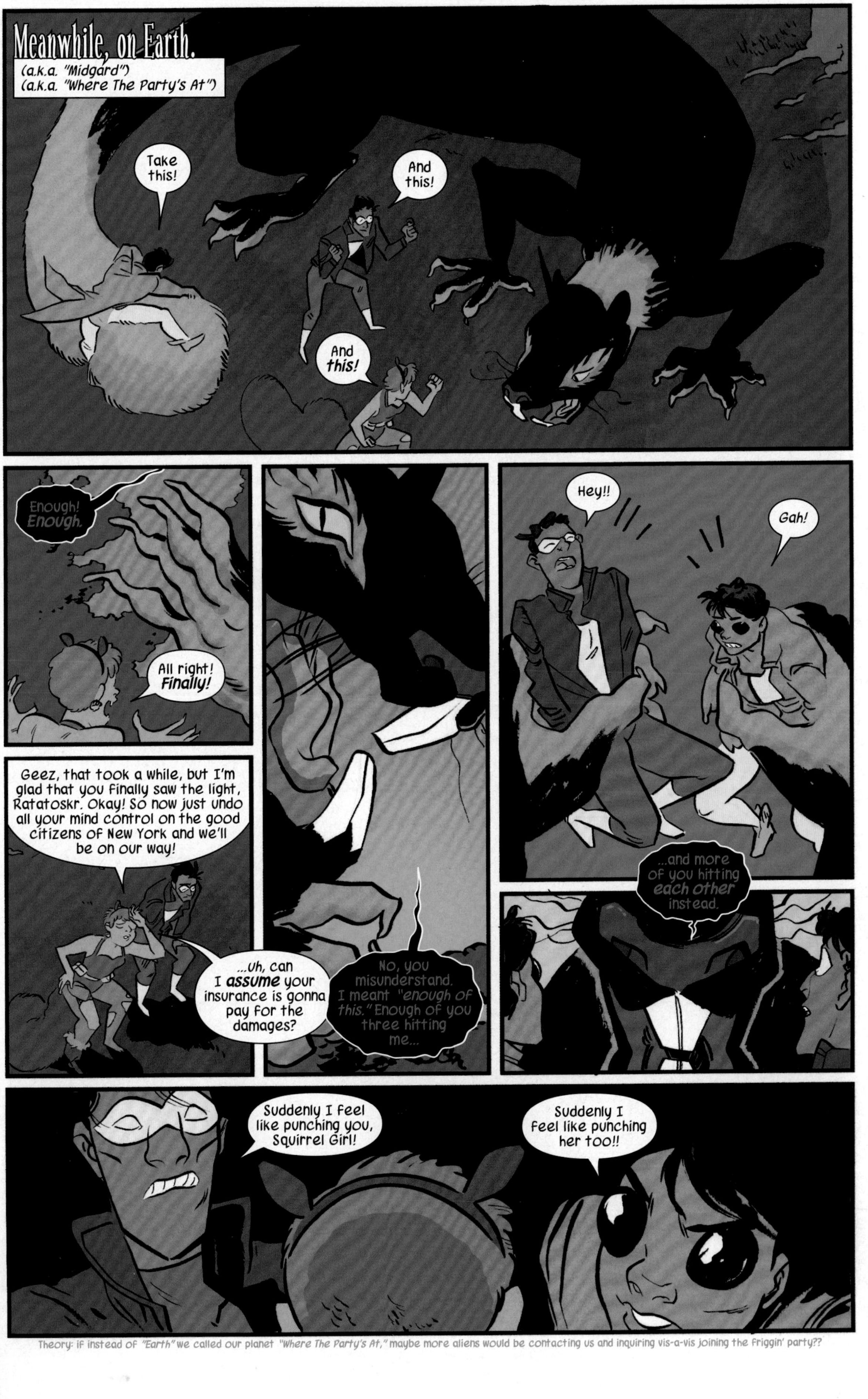
Meanwhile, on Earth.
(a.k.a. "Midgard")
(a.k.a. "Where The Party's At")
Take this!
And this!
And this!
Enough! Enough.
All right! Finally!
Geez, that took a while, but I'm glad that you finally saw the light, Ratatoskr. Okay! So now just undo all your mind control on the good citizens of New York and we'll be on our way!
...uh, can I assume your insurance is gonna pay for the damages?
No, you misunderstand. I meant "enough of this." Enough of you three hitting me...
Hey!!
Gah!
...and more of you hitting each other instead.
Suddenly I feel like punching you, Squirrel Girl!
Suddenly I feel like punching her too!!

Theory: if instead of "Earth" we called our planet "Where The Party's At," maybe more aliens would be contacting us and inquiring vis-a-vis joining the friggin' party??

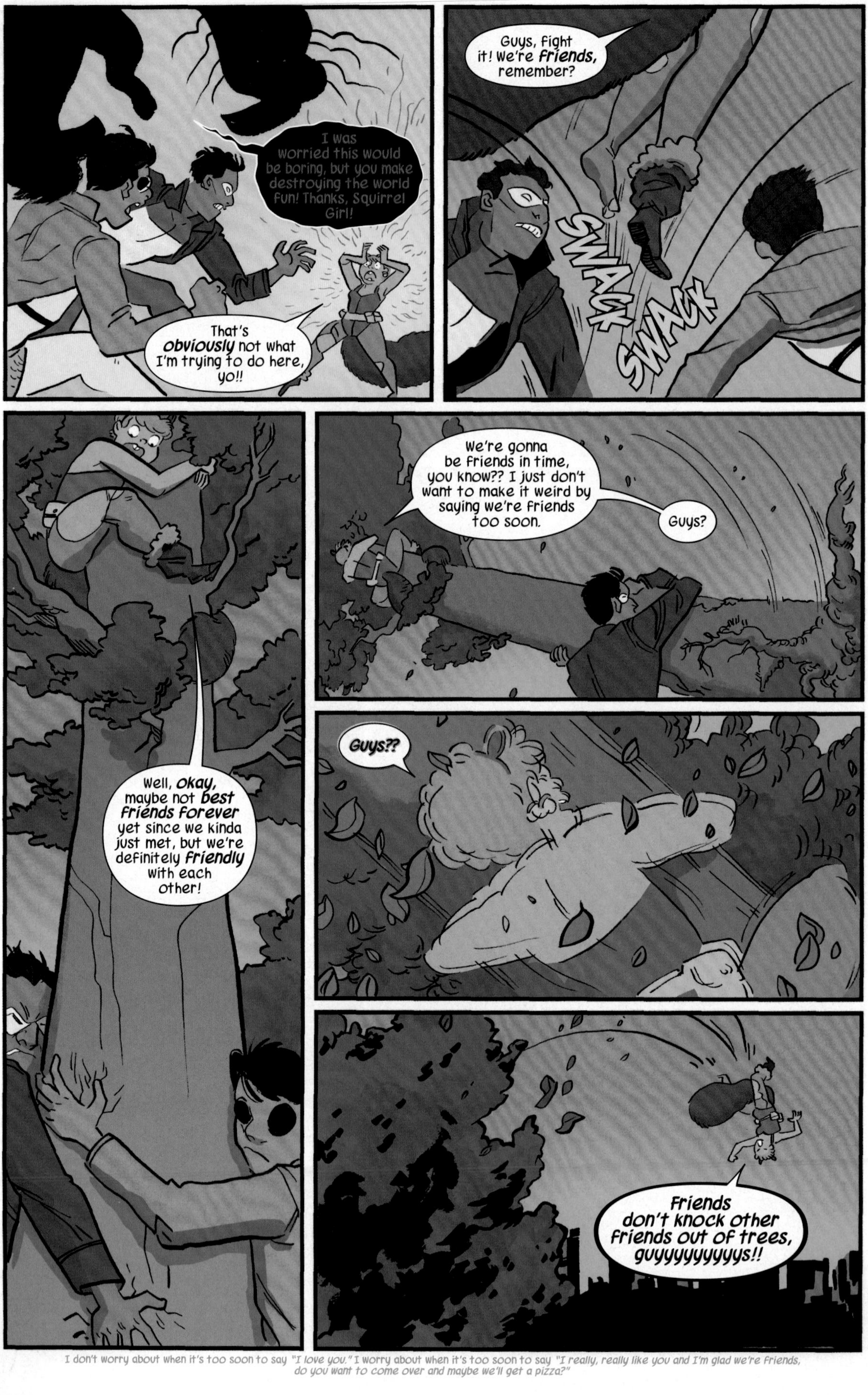
I was worried this would be boring, but you make destroying the world fun! Thanks, Squirrel Girl!
That's obviously not what I'm trying to do here, yo!!
Guys, fight it! We're friends, remember?
SWACK
SWACK
We're gonna be friends in time, you know?? I just don't want to make it weird by saying we're friends too soon.
Guys?
Well, okay, maybe not best friends forever yet since we kinda just met, but we're definitely friendly with each other!
Guys??
Friends don't knock other friends out of trees, guyyyyyyyyys!!

*I don't worry about when it's too soon to say "I love you." I worry about when it's too soon to say "I really, really like you and I'm glad we're friends, do you want to come over and maybe we'll get a pizza?"*

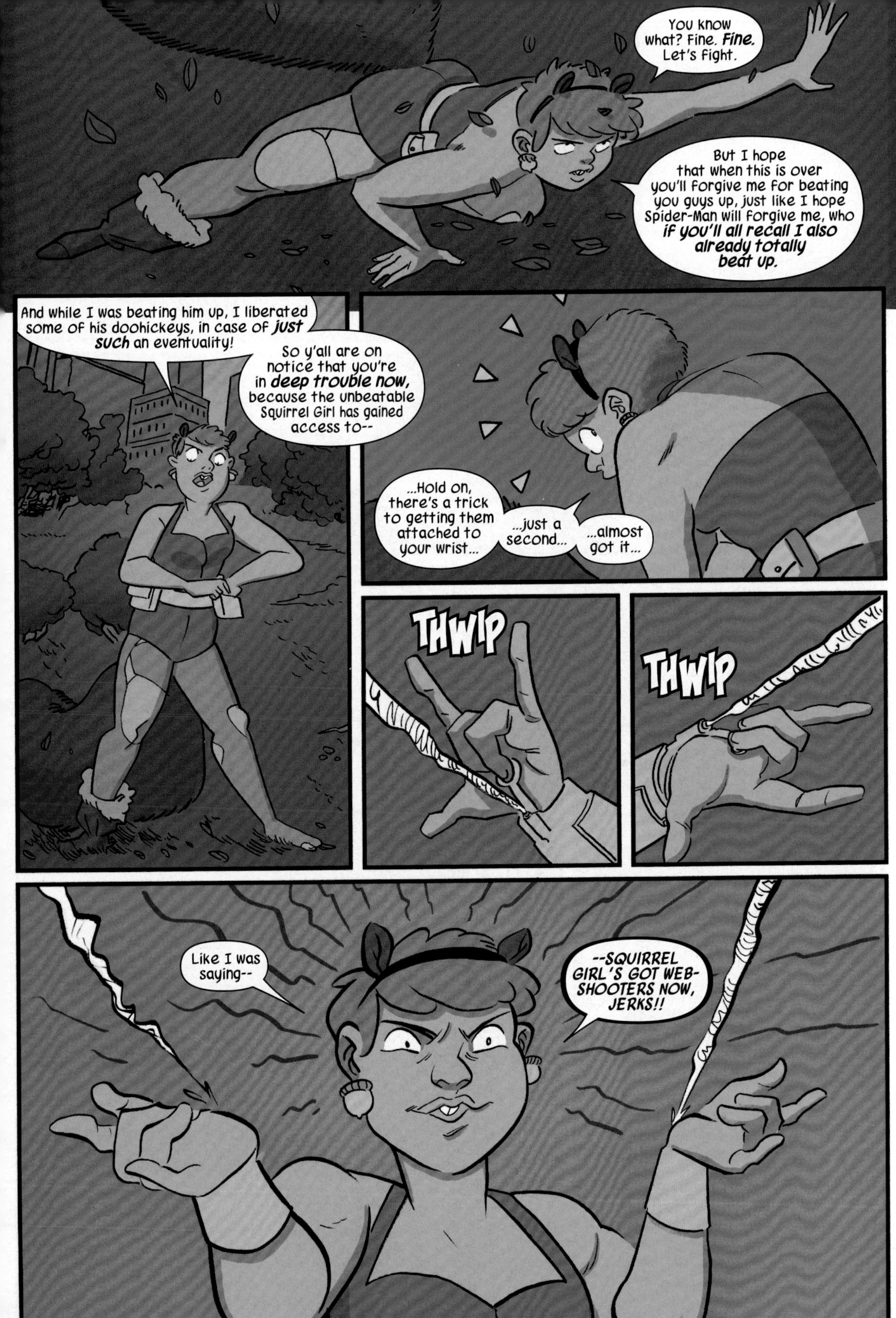
You know what? Fine. *Fine.* Let's fight.
But I hope that when this is over you'll forgive me for beating you guys up, just like I hope Spider-Man will forgive me, who *if you'll all recall I also already totally beat up.*
And while I was beating him up, I liberated some of his doohickeys, in case of *just such* an eventuality!
So y'all are on notice that you're in *deep trouble now,* because the unbeatable Squirrel Girl has gained access to--
...Hold on, there's a trick to getting them attached to your wrist...
...just a second...
...almost got it...
THWIP
THWIP
Like I was saying--
--SQUIRREL GIRL'S GOT WEB-SHOOTERS NOW, JERKS!!

Squirrel Girl's *also* got a liberal idea of personal property ownership, jerks!!

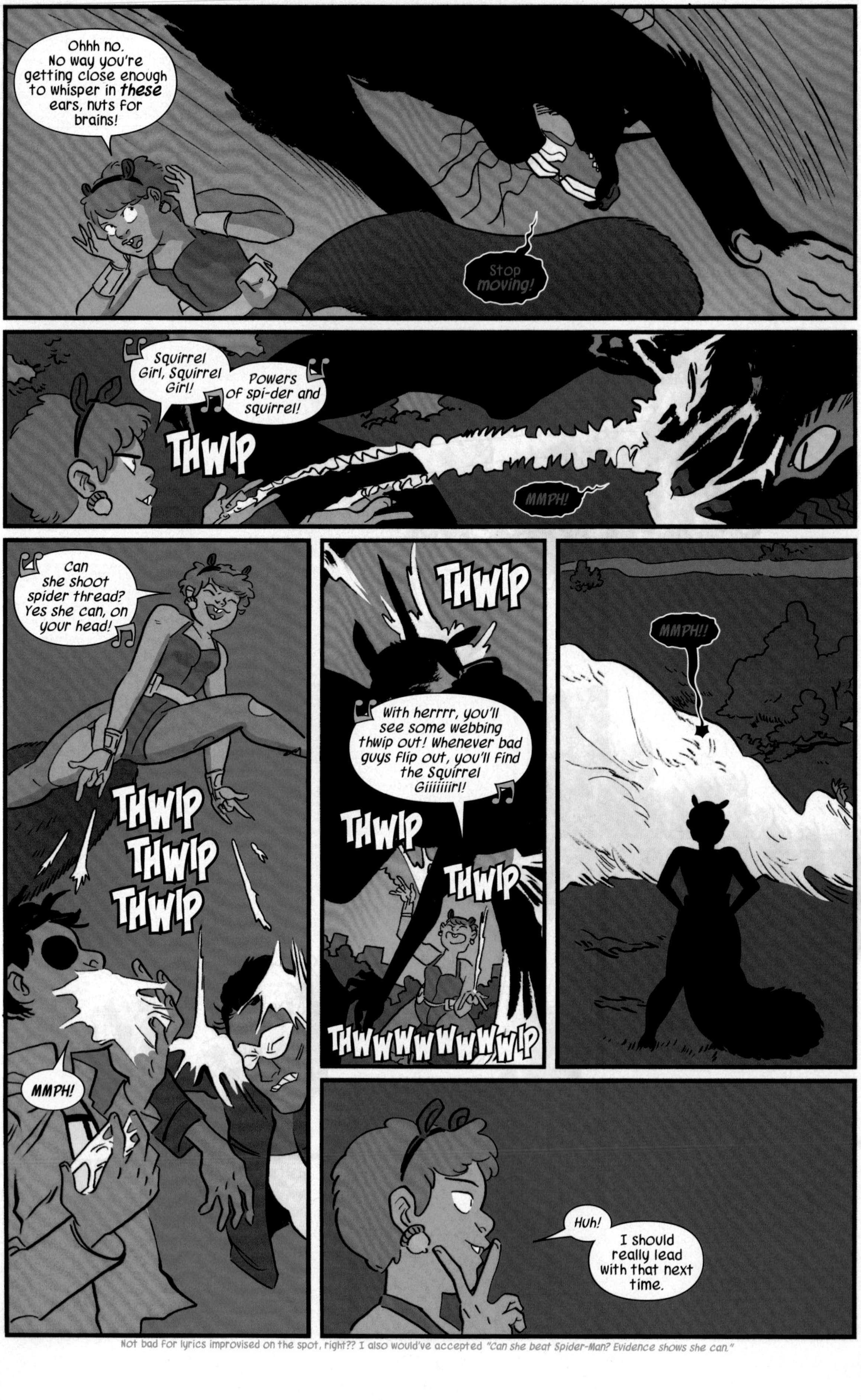
Ohhh no. No way you're getting close enough to whisper in *these* ears, nuts for brains!
Stop moving!
Squirrel Girl, Squirrel Girl!
Powers of spi-der and squirrel!
THWIP
MMPH!
Can she shoot spider thread? Yes she can, on your head!
THWIP
THWIP
THWIP
MMPH!
THWIP
With herrrr, you'll see some webbing thwip out! Whenever bad guys flip out, you'll find the Squirrel Giiiiiiirl!
THWIP
THWIP
THWWWWWWWWWIP
MMPH!!
Huh!
I should really lead with that next time.

Not bad for lyrics improvised on the spot, right?? I also would've accepted *"Can she beat Spider-Man? Evidence shows she can."*

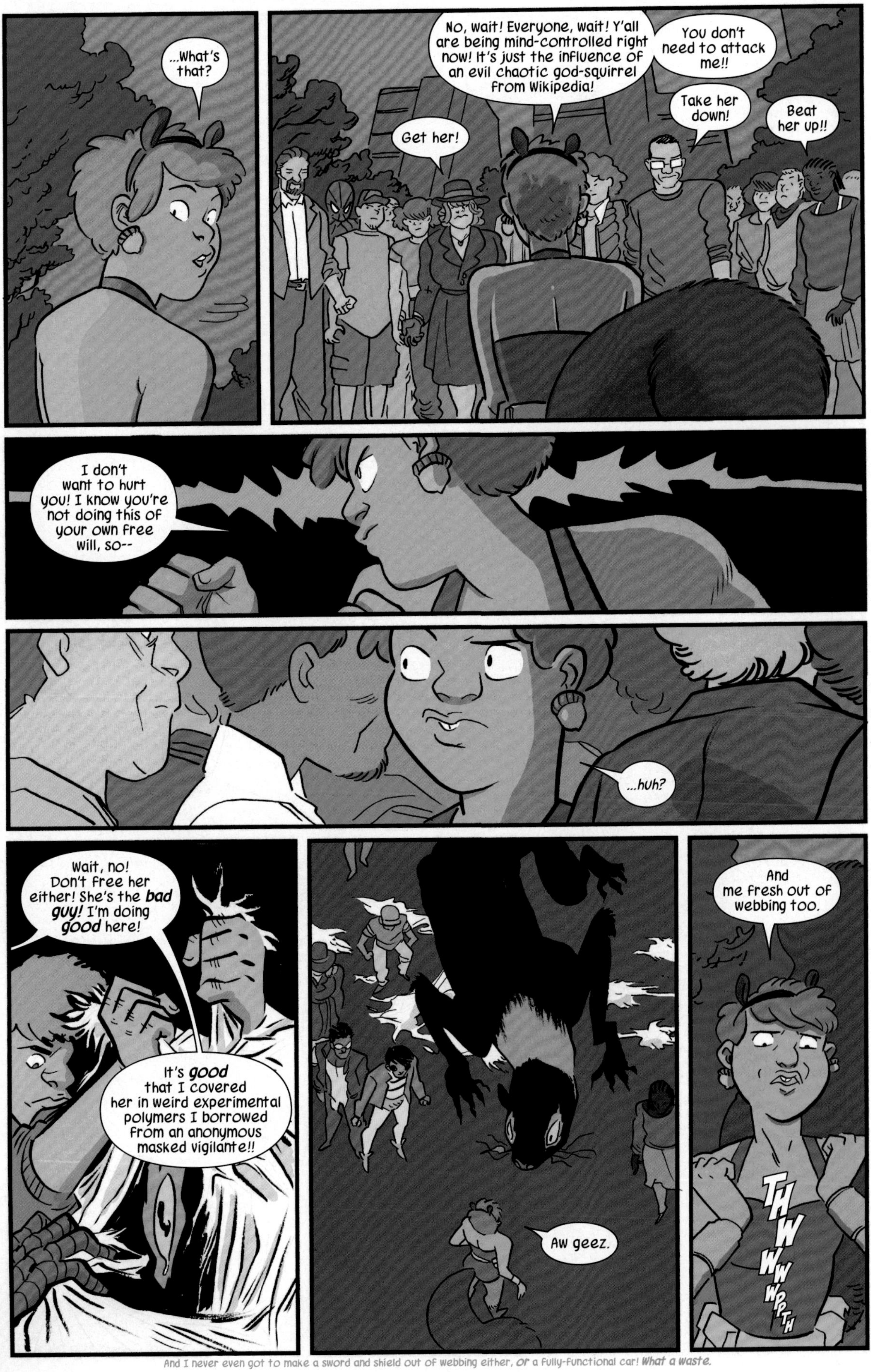
...What's that?
No, wait! Everyone, wait! Y'all are being mind-controlled right now! It's just the influence of an evil chaotic god-squirrel from Wikipedia!
You don't need to attack me!!
Get her!
Take her down!
Beat her up!!
I don't want to hurt you! I know you're not doing this of your own free will, so--
...huh?
Wait, no! Don't free her either! She's the *bad guy!* I'm doing *good* here!
It's *good* that I covered her in weird experimental polymers I borrowed from an anonymous masked vigilante!!
Aw geez.
And me fresh out of webbing too.
THWWWWPPTH

And I never even got to make a sword and shield out of webbing either, *or* a fully-functional car! ***What a waste.***

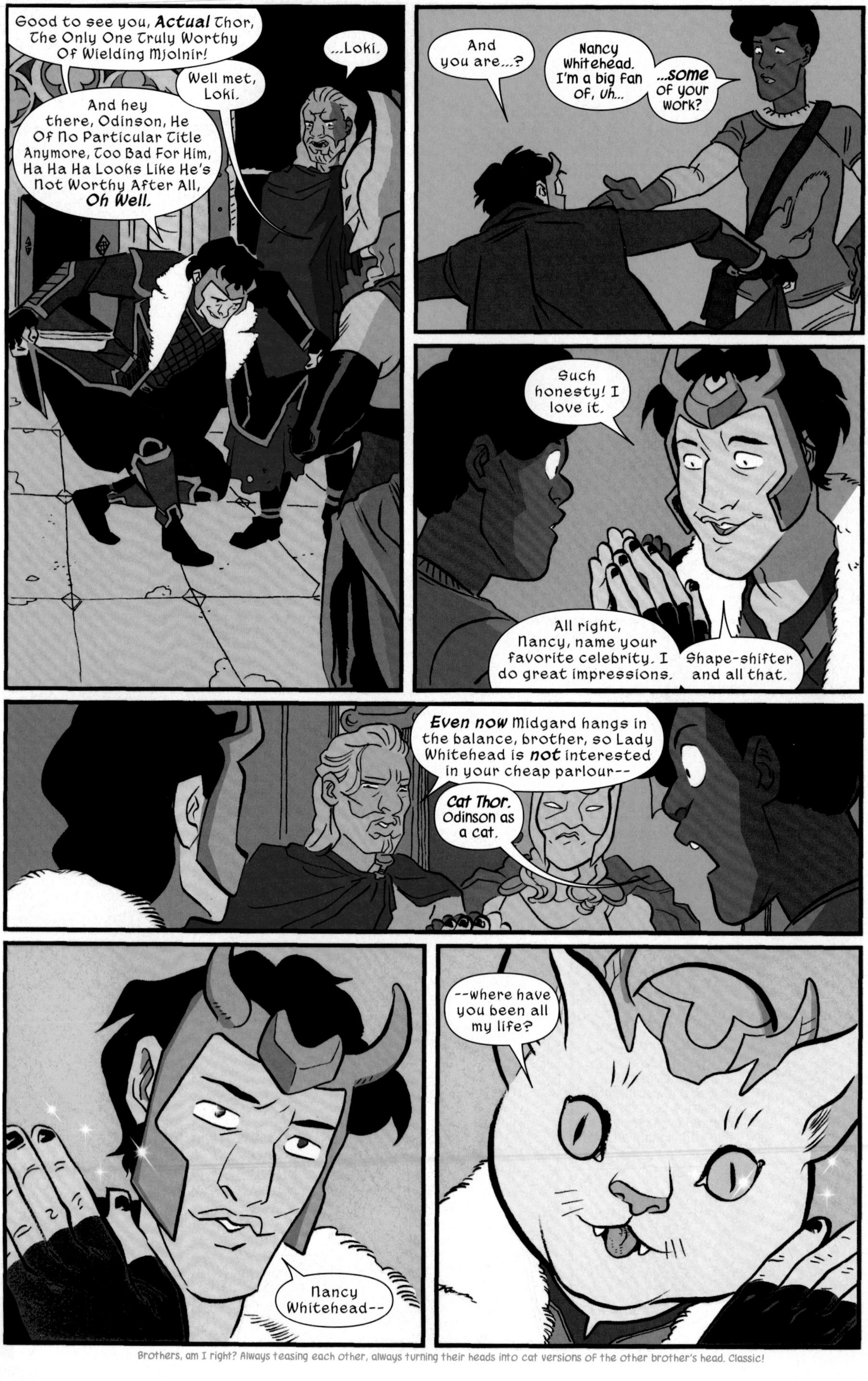
Good to see you, **Actual** Thor, The Only One Truly Worthy Of Wielding Mjolnir!
...Loki.
Well met, Loki.
And hey there, Odinson, He Of No Particular Title Anymore, Too Bad For Him, Ha Ha Ha Looks Like He's Not Worthy After All, **Oh Well.**
And you are...?
Nancy Whitehead. I'm a big fan of, uh...
**...some** of your work?
Such honesty! I love it.
All right, Nancy, name your favorite celebrity. I do great impressions.
Shape-shifter and all that.
**Even now** Midgard hangs in the balance, brother, so Lady Whitehead is **not** interested in your cheap parlour--
**Cat Thor.** Odinson as a cat.
Nancy Whitehead--
--where have you been all my life?

Brothers, am I right? Always teasing each other, always turning their heads into cat versions of the other brother's head. Classic!

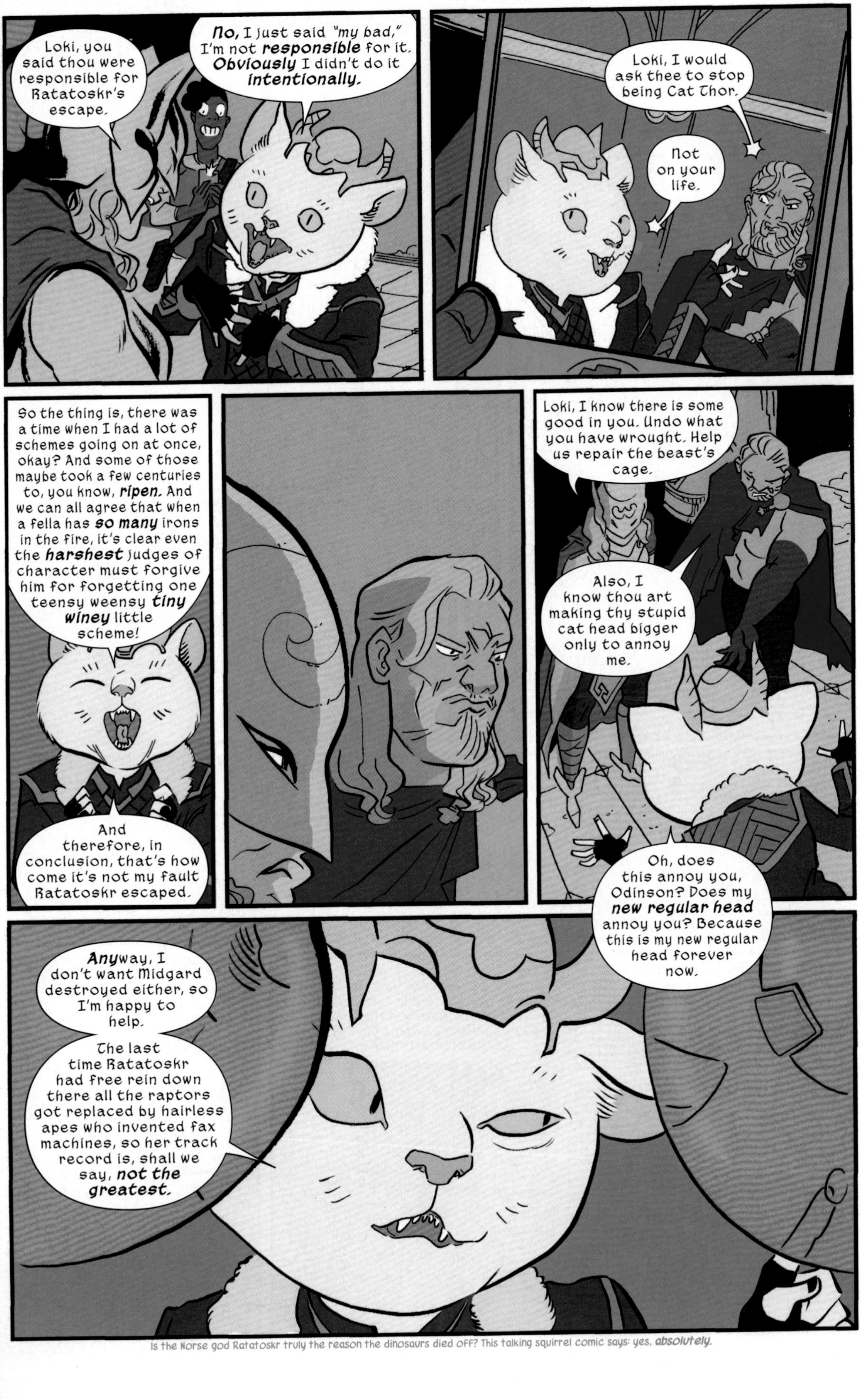
Loki, you said thou were responsible for Ratatoskr's escape.
No, I just said "my bad," I'm not responsible for it. Obviously I didn't do it intentionally.
Loki, I would ask thee to stop being Cat Thor.
Not on your life.
So the thing is, there was a time when I had a lot of schemes going on at once, okay? And some of those maybe took a few centuries to, you know, ripen. And we can all agree that when a fella has so many irons in the fire, it's clear even the harshest judges of character must forgive him for forgetting one teensy weensy tiny winey little scheme!
And therefore, in conclusion, that's how come it's not my fault Ratatoskr escaped.
Loki, I know there is some good in you. Undo what you have wrought. Help us repair the beast's cage.
Also, I know thou art making thy stupid cat head bigger only to annoy me.
Oh, does this annoy you, Odinson? Does my new regular head annoy you? Because this is my new regular head forever now.
Anyway, I don't want Midgard destroyed either, so I'm happy to help.
The last time Ratatoskr had free rein down there all the raptors got replaced by hairless apes who invented fax machines, so her track record is, shall we say, not the greatest.

Is the Norse god Ratatoskr truly the reason the dinosaurs died off? This talking squirrel comic says: yes, *absolutely.*

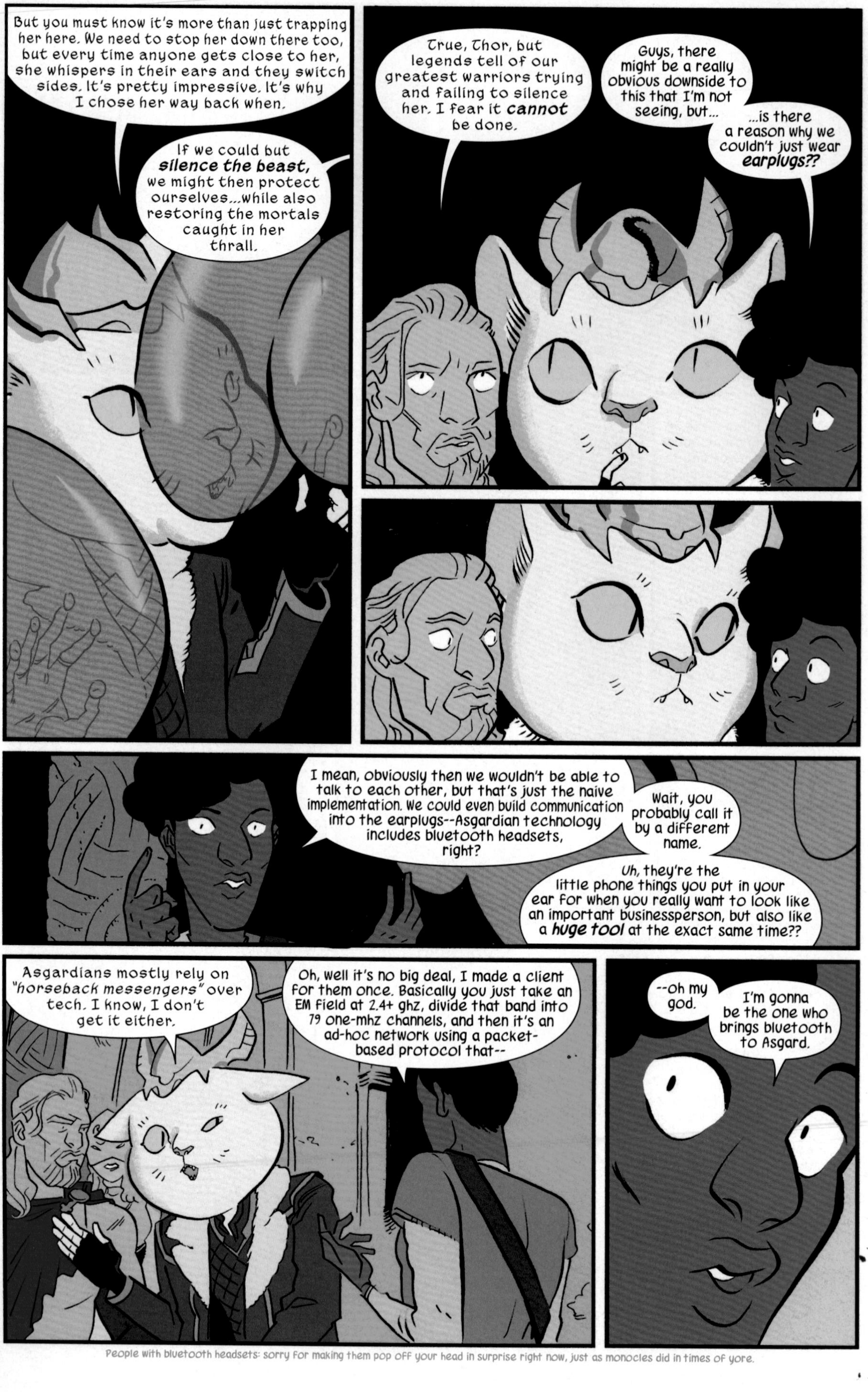
But you must know it's more than just trapping her here. We need to stop her down there too, but every time anyone gets close to her, she whispers in their ears and they switch sides. It's pretty impressive. It's why I chose her way back when.
If we could but *silence the beast*, we might then protect ourselves...while also restoring the mortals caught in her thrall.
True, Thor, but legends tell of our greatest warriors trying and failing to silence her. I fear it *cannot* be done.
Guys, there might be a really obvious downside to this that I'm not seeing, but...
...is there a reason why we couldn't just wear *earplugs??*
I mean, obviously then we wouldn't be able to talk to each other, but that's just the naive implementation. We could even build communication into the earplugs--Asgardian technology includes bluetooth headsets, right?
Wait, you probably call it by a different name.
*Uh*, they're the little phone things you put in your ear for when you really want to look like an important businessperson, but also like a *huge tool* at the exact same time??
Asgardians mostly rely on "*horseback messengers*" over tech. I know, I don't get it either.
Oh, well it's no big deal, I made a client for them once. Basically you just take an EM field at 2.4+ ghz, divide that band into 79 one-mhz channels, and then it's an ad-hoc network using a packet-based protocol that--
--oh my god.
I'm gonna be the one who brings bluetooth to Asgard.

People with bluetooth headsets: sorry for making them pop off your head in surprise right now, just as monocles did in times of yore.

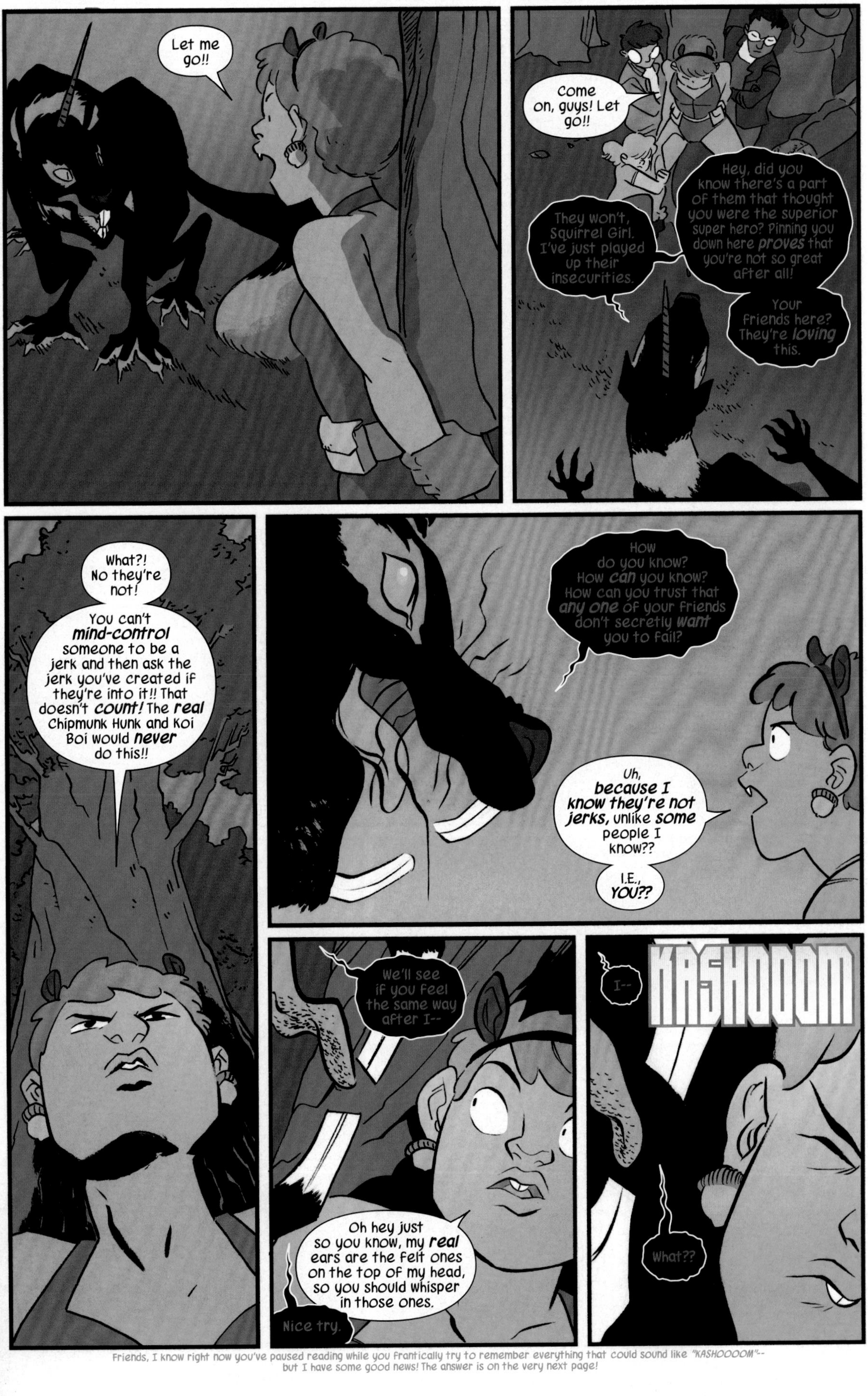
Let me go!!
Come on, guys! Let go!!
They won't, Squirrel Girl. I've just played up their insecurities.
Hey, did you know there's a part of them that thought you were the superior super hero? Pinning you down here *proves* that you're not so great after all!
Your friends here? They're *loving* this.
What?! No they're not!
You can't *mind-control* someone to be a jerk and then ask the jerk you've created if they're into it!! That doesn't *count!* The *real* Chipmunk Hunk and Koi Boi would *never* do this!!
How do you know? How *can* you know? How can you trust that *any one* of your friends don't secretly *want* you to fail?
Uh, *because I know they're not jerks,* unlike *some* people I know??
I.E., *YOU??*
We'll see if you feel the same way after I--
Oh hey just so you know, my *real* ears are the felt ones on the top of my head, so you should whisper in those ones.
Nice try.
KASHOOOM
I--
What??

Friends, I know right now you've paused reading while you frantically try to remember everything that could sound like *"KASHOOOM"*-- but I have some good news! The answer is on the very next page!

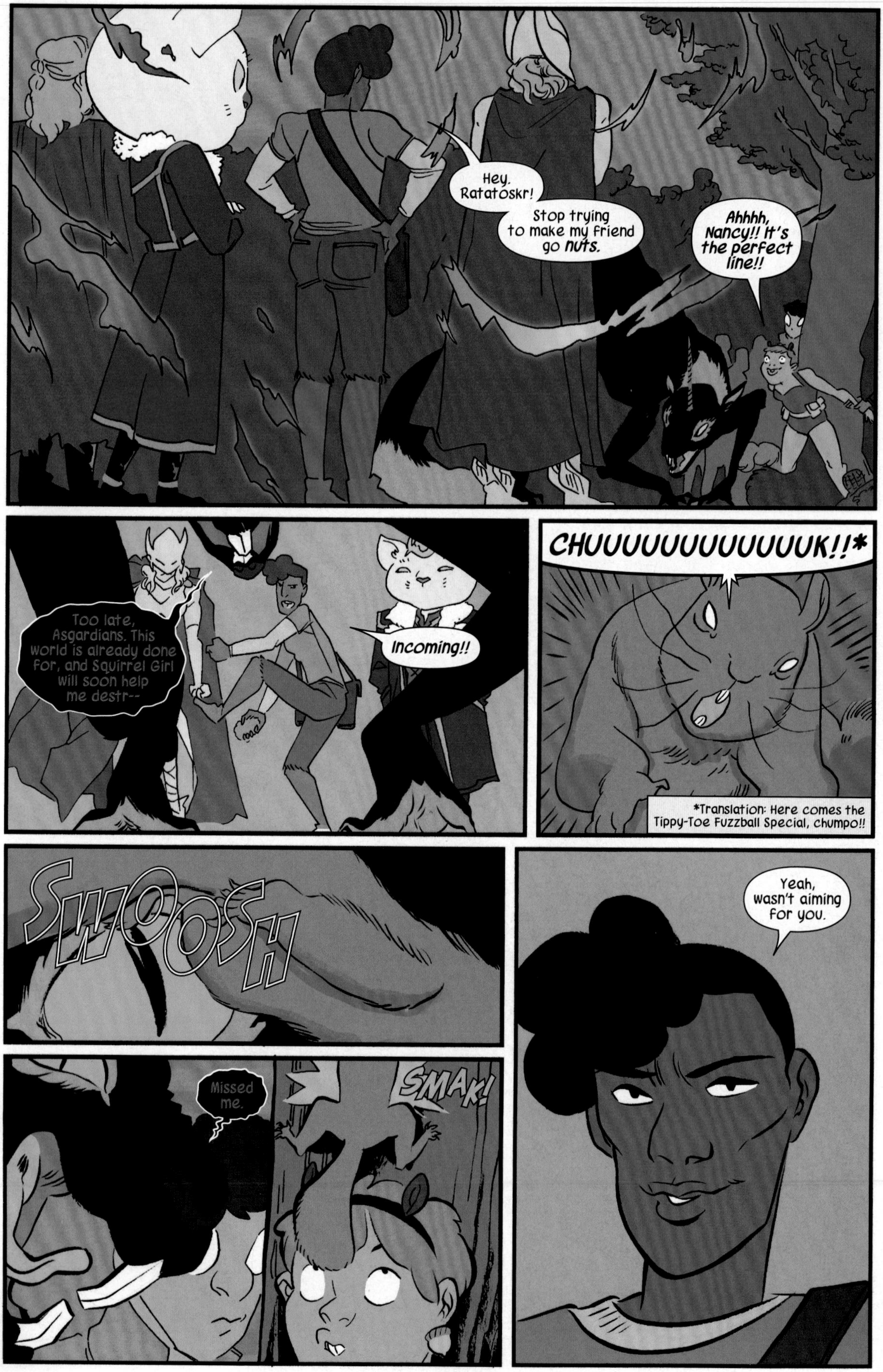
Hey. Ratatoskr!
Stop trying to make my friend go nuts.
Ahhhh, Nancy!! It's the perfect line!!
Too late, Asgardians. This world is already done for, and Squirrel Girl will soon help me destr--
Incoming!!
CHUUUUUUUUUUUUK!!*
*Translation: Here comes the Tippy-Toe Fuzzball Special, chumpo!!
SWOOSH
Yeah, wasn't aiming for you.
Missed me.
SMAK!

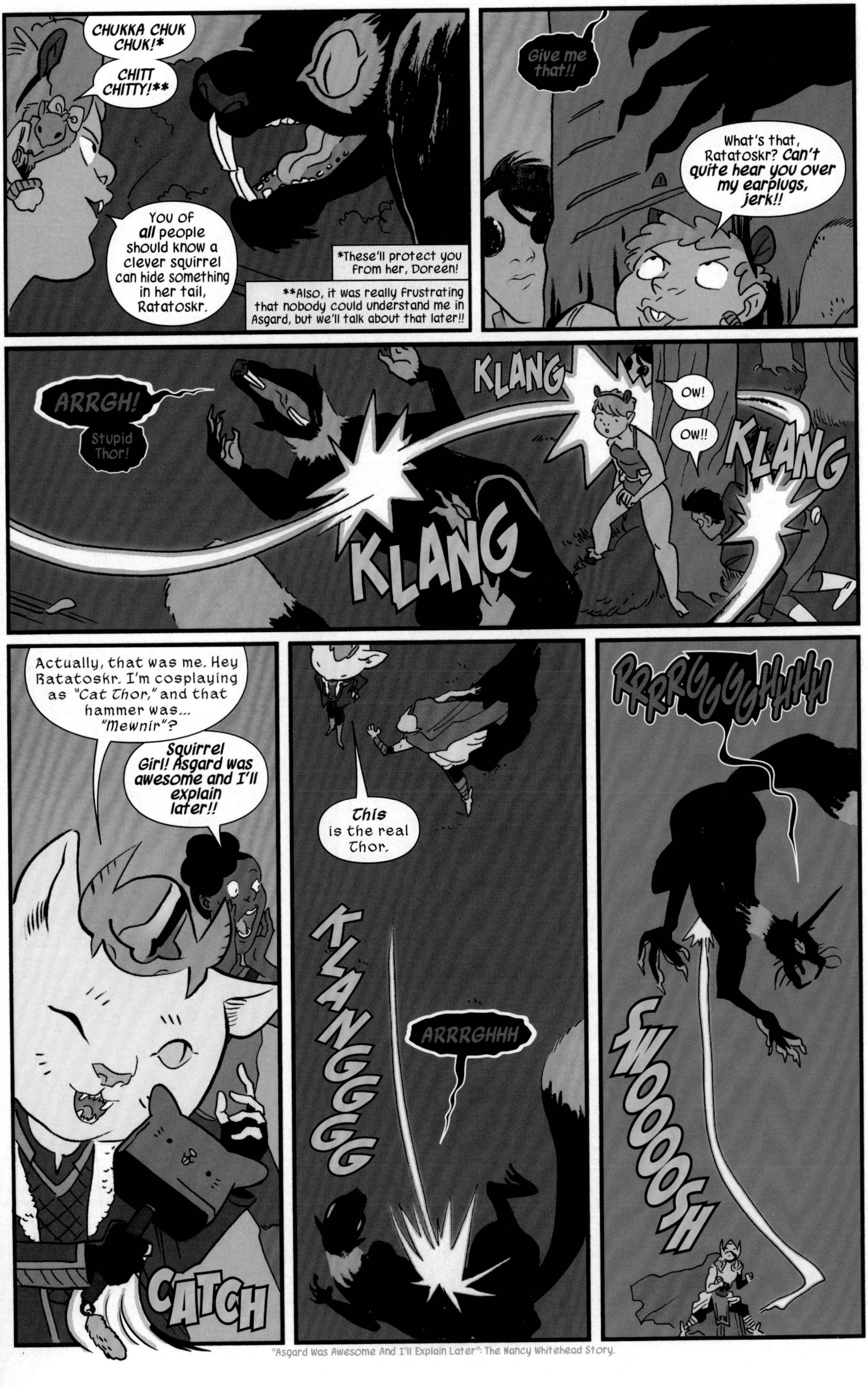

CHUKKA CHUK CHUK!*
CHITT CHITTY!**
You of all people should know a clever squirrel can hide something in her tail, Ratatoskr.
*These'll protect you from her, Doreen!
**Also, it was really frustrating that nobody could understand me in Asgard, but we'll talk about that later!!
Give me that!!
What's that, Ratatoskr? Can't quite hear you over my earplugs, jerk!!
ARRGH!
Stupid Thor!
KLANG
OW!
OW!!
KLANG
KLANG
Actually, that was me. Hey Ratatoskr. I'm cosplaying as "Cat Thor," and that hammer was... "Mewnir"?
Squirrel Girl! Asgard was awesome and I'll explain later!!
CATCH
This is the real Thor.
KLANNGGGG
ARRRGHHH
RRRRGGGHHHH
SWOOOOSH


"Asgard Was Awesome And I'll Explain Later": The Nancy Whitehead Story.

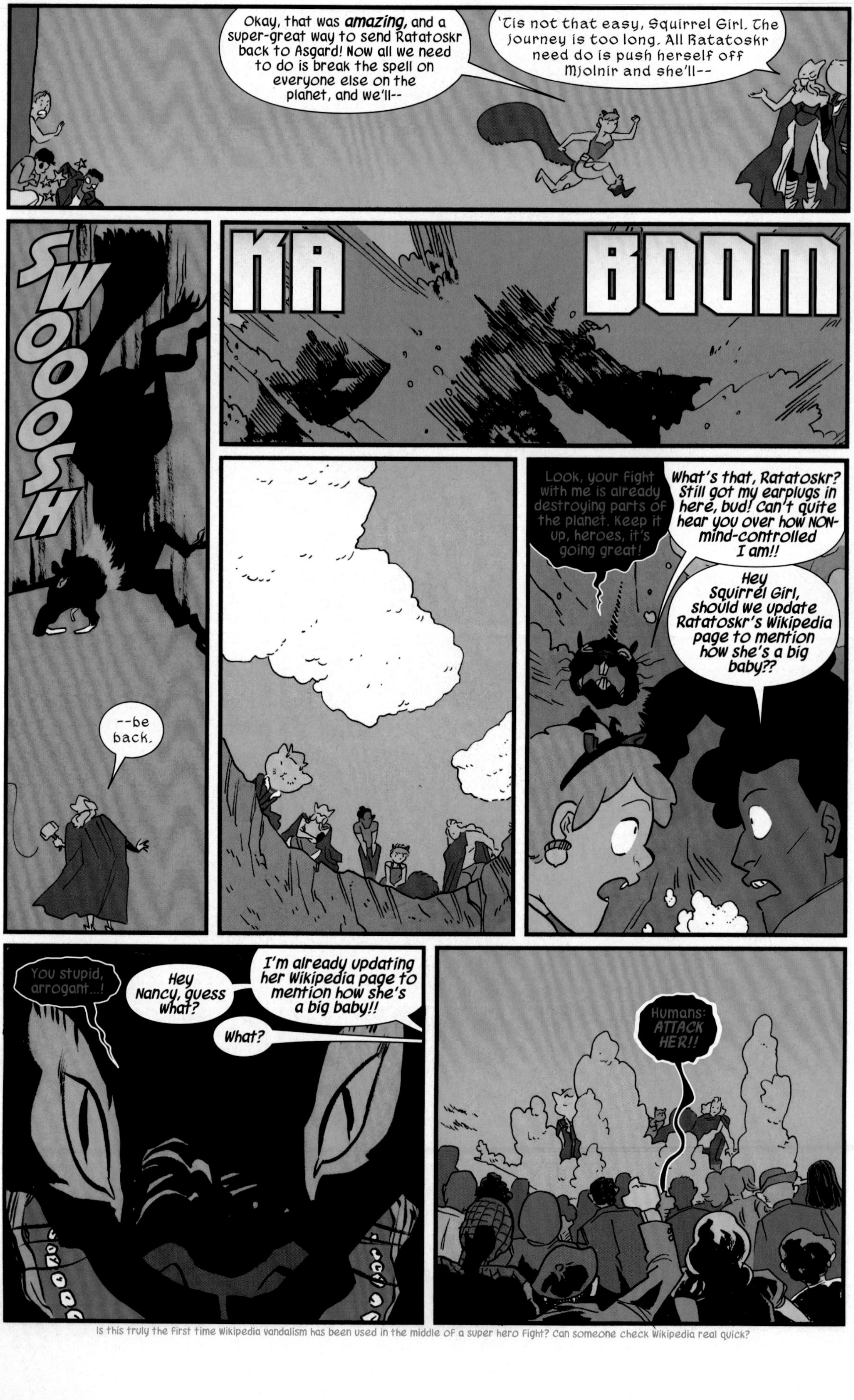
Okay, that was amazing, and a super-great way to send Ratatoskr back to Asgard! Now all we need to do is break the spell on everyone else on the planet, and we'll--
'Tis not that easy, Squirrel Girl. The journey is too long. All Ratatoskr need do is push herself off Mjolnir and she'll--
SWOOOOSH
KA
BOOM
--be back.
Look, your fight with me is already destroying parts of the planet. Keep it up, heroes, it's going great!
What's that, Ratatoskr? Still got my earplugs in here, bud! Can't quite hear you over how NON-mind-controlled I am!!
Hey Squirrel Girl, should we update Ratatoskr's Wikipedia page to mention how she's a big baby??
You stupid, arrogant...!
Hey Nancy, guess what?
What?
I'm already updating her Wikipedia page to mention how she's a big baby!!
Humans: ATTACK HER!!

Is this truly the first time Wikipedia vandalism has been used in the middle of a super hero fight? Can someone check Wikipedia real quick?

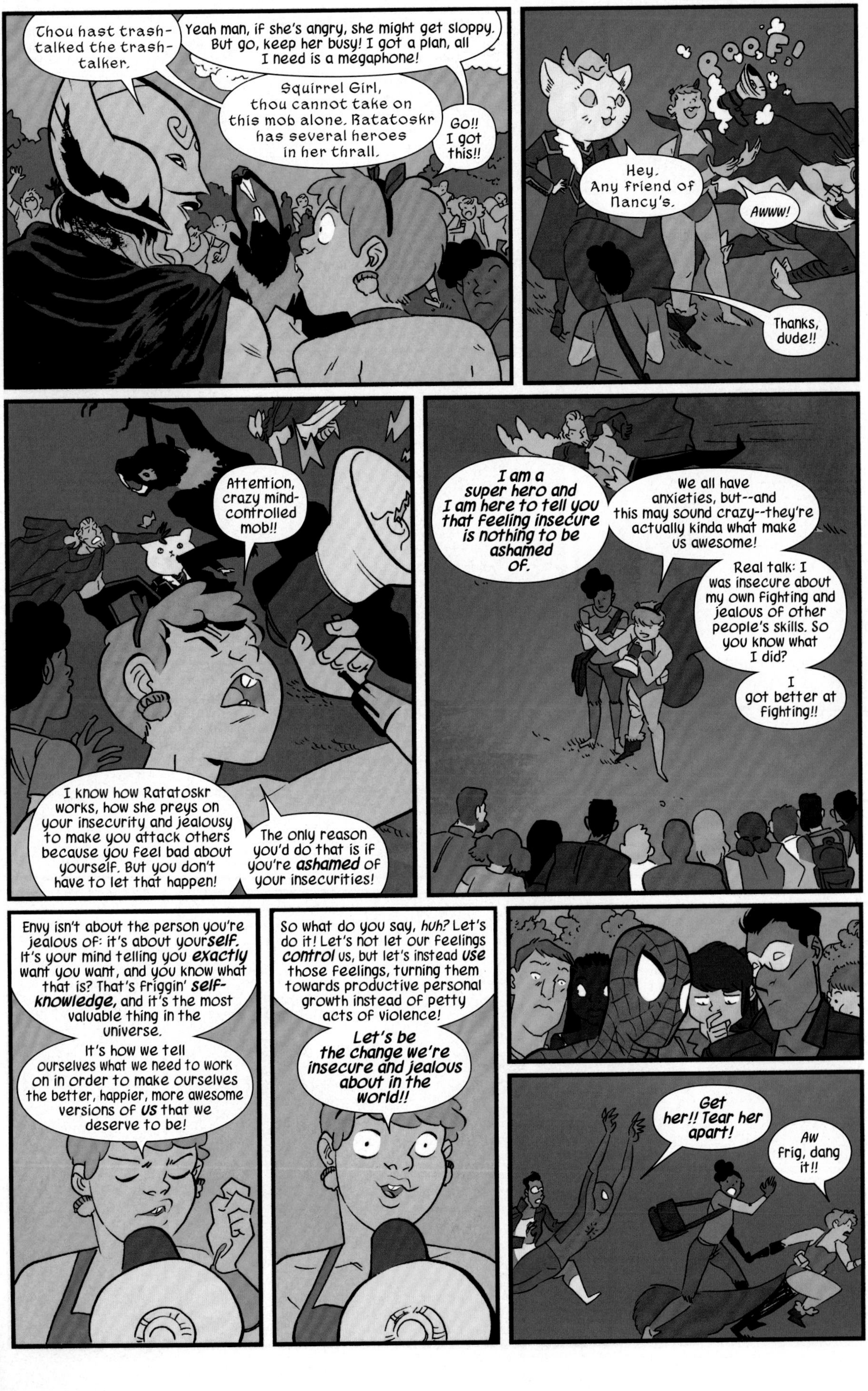
Thou hast trash-talked the trash-talker.
Yeah man, if she's angry, she might get sloppy. But go, keep her busy! I got a plan, all I need is a megaphone!
Squirrel Girl, thou cannot take on this mob alone. Ratatoskr has several heroes in her thrall.
Go!! I got this!!
POOF!
Hey. Any friend of Nancy's.
AWWW!
Thanks, dude!!
Attention, crazy mind-controlled mob!!
I know how Ratatoskr works, how she preys on your insecurity and jealousy to make you attack others because you feel bad about yourself. But you don't have to let that happen!
The only reason you'd do that is if you're ashamed of your insecurities!
I am a super hero and I am here to tell you that feeling insecure is nothing to be ashamed of.
We all have anxieties, but--and this may sound crazy--they're actually kinda what make us awesome!
Real talk: I was insecure about my own fighting and jealous of other people's skills. So you know what I did?
I got better at fighting!!
Envy isn't about the person you're jealous of: it's about yourself. It's your mind telling you exactly want you want, and you know what that is? That's friggin' self-knowledge, and it's the most valuable thing in the universe.
It's how we tell ourselves what we need to work on in order to make ourselves the better, happier, more awesome versions of us that we deserve to be!
So what do you say, huh? Let's do it! Let's not let our feelings control us, but let's instead use those feelings, turning them towards productive personal growth instead of petty acts of violence!
Let's be the change we're insecure and jealous about in the world!!
Get her!! Tear her apart!
Aw frig, dang it!!

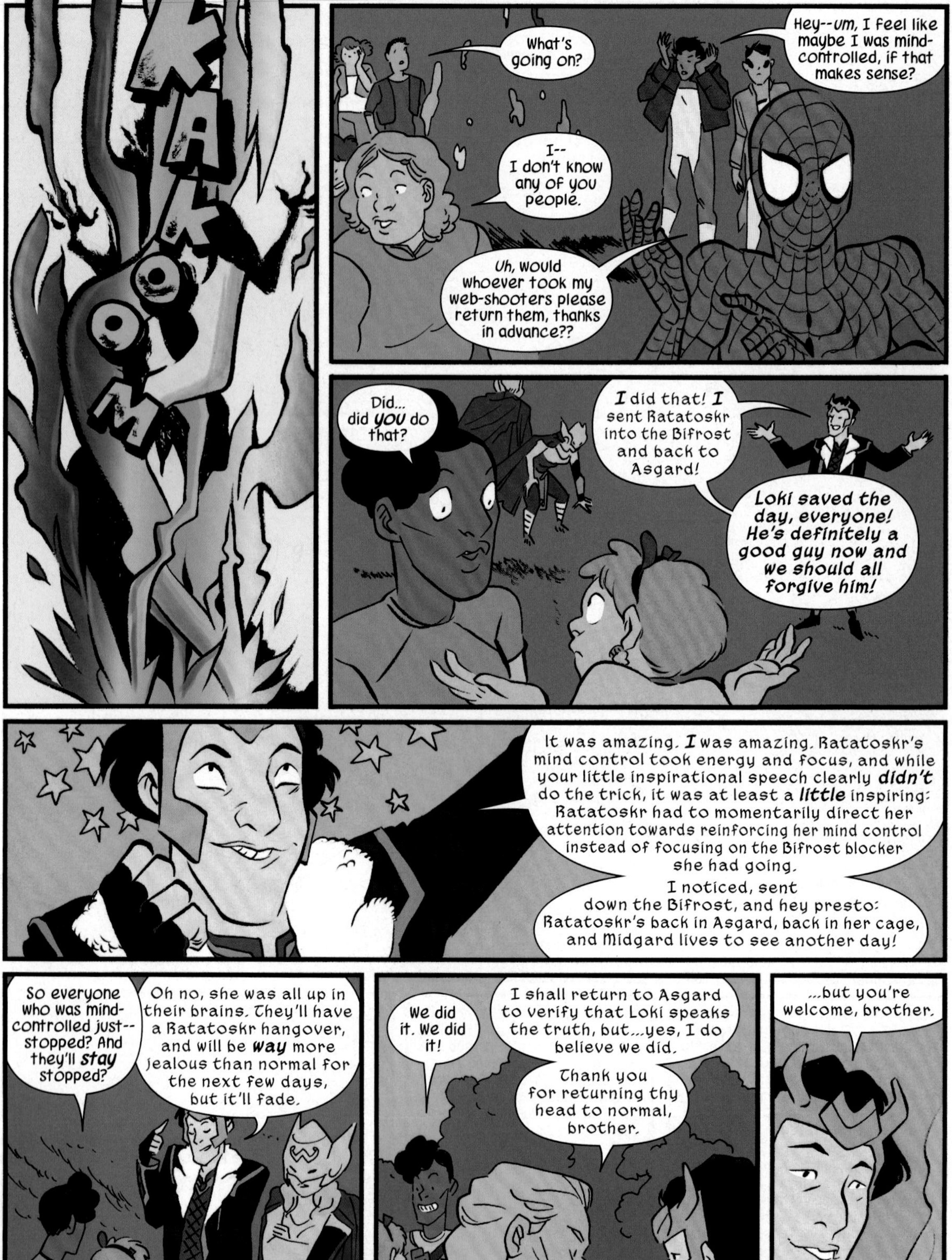
KAKOOM
What's going on?
Hey--*um*, I feel like maybe I was mind-controlled, if that makes sense?
I-- I don't know any of you people.
Uh, would whoever took my web-shooters please return them, thanks in advance??
Did... did ***you*** do that?
***I*** did that! ***I*** sent Ratatoskr into the Bifrost and back to Asgard!
***Loki saved the day, everyone! He's definitely a good guy now and we should all forgive him!***
It was amazing. ***I*** was amazing. Ratatoskr's mind control took energy and focus, and while your little inspirational speech clearly ***didn't*** do the trick, it was at least a ***little*** inspiring: Ratatoskr had to momentarily direct her attention towards reinforcing her mind control instead of focusing on the Bifrost blocker she had going.
I noticed, sent down the Bifrost, and hey presto: Ratatoskr's back in Asgard, back in her cage, and Midgard lives to see another day!
So everyone who was mind-controlled just--stopped? And they'll ***stay*** stopped?
Oh no, she was all up in their brains. They'll have a Ratatoskr hangover, and will be ***way*** more jealous than normal for the next few days, but it'll fade.
Of course. That rage we saw: that's what required her reinforcement.
Great anger requires great energy. No one can stay angry all the time.
We did it. We did it!
I shall return to Asgard to verify that Loki speaks the truth, but...yes, I do believe we did.
Thank you for returning thy head to normal, brother.
Oh, I just needed to be sure Heimdall would recognize me to send down the Bifrost. You know...not a second to lose and all that.
But...
...but you're welcome, brother.

*Aw, pals! And a happy ending for the two brothers! Now as long as you don't read Loki: Agent of Asgard #10, this happy feeling can last **forever!!***

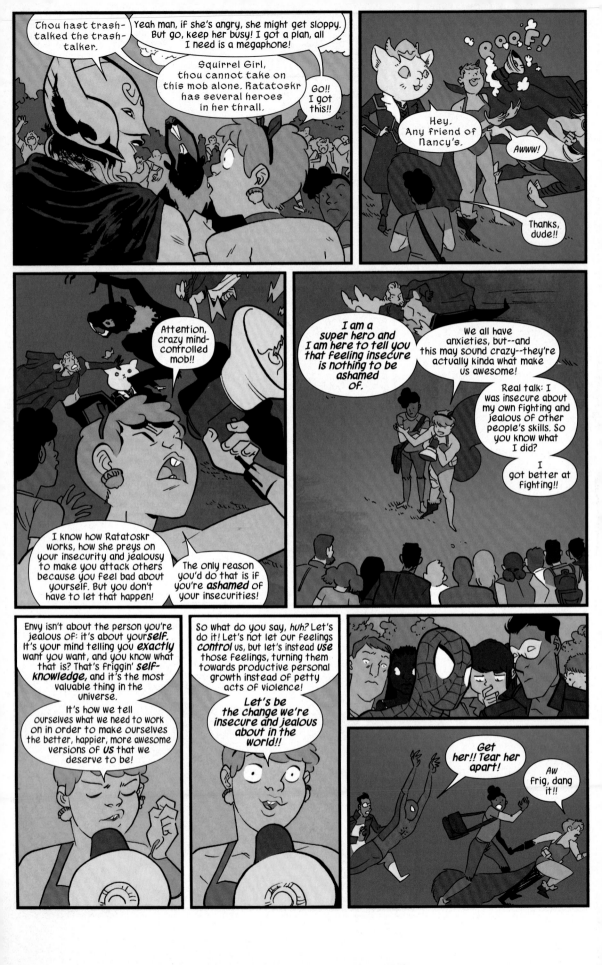

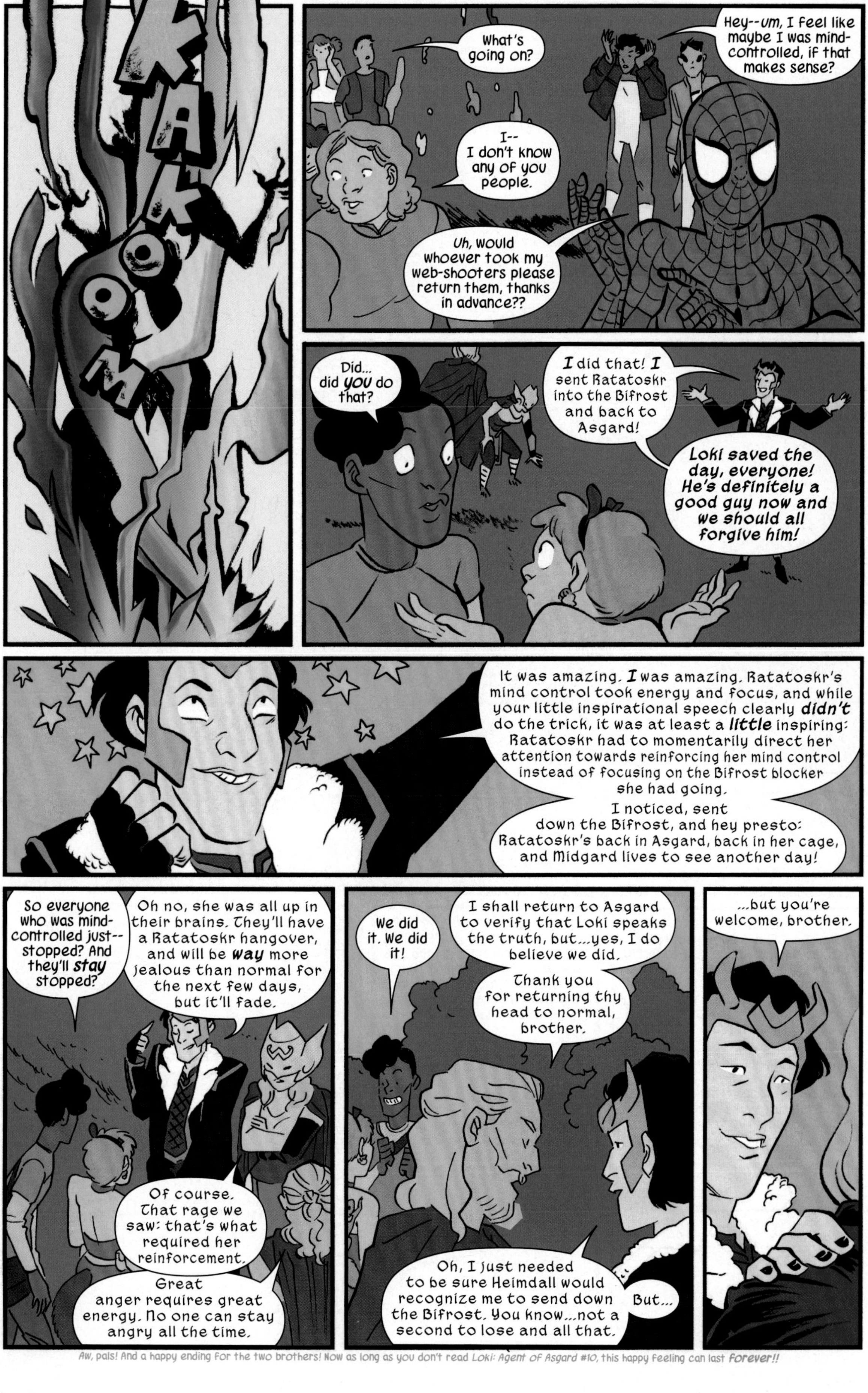
KAKOOM
What's going on?
Hey--um, I feel like maybe I was mind-controlled, if that makes sense?
I-- I don't know any of you people.
Uh, would whoever took my web-shooters please return them, thanks in advance??
Did... did you do that?
I did that! I sent Ratatoskr into the Bifrost and back to Asgard!
Loki saved the day, everyone! He's definitely a good guy now and we should all forgive him!
It was amazing. I was amazing. Ratatoskr's mind control took energy and focus, and while your little inspirational speech clearly didn't do the trick, it was at least a little inspiring: Ratatoskr had to momentarily direct her attention towards reinforcing her mind control instead of focusing on the Bifrost blocker she had going.
I noticed, sent down the Bifrost, and hey presto: Ratatoskr's back in Asgard, back in her cage, and Midgard lives to see another day!
So everyone who was mind-controlled just--stopped? And they'll stay stopped?
Oh no, she was all up in their brains. They'll have a Ratatoskr hangover, and will be way more jealous than normal for the next few days, but it'll fade.
Of course. That rage we saw: that's what required her reinforcement.
Great anger requires great energy. No one can stay angry all the time.
We did it. We did it!
I shall return to Asgard to verify that Loki speaks the truth, but...yes, I do believe we did.
Thank you for returning thy head to normal, brother.
Oh, I just needed to be sure Heimdall would recognize me to send down the Bifrost. You know...not a second to lose and all that.
But...
...but you're welcome, brother.

*Aw, pals! And a happy ending for the two brothers! Now as long as you don't read Loki: Agent of Asgard #10, this happy feeling can last **Forever!!***

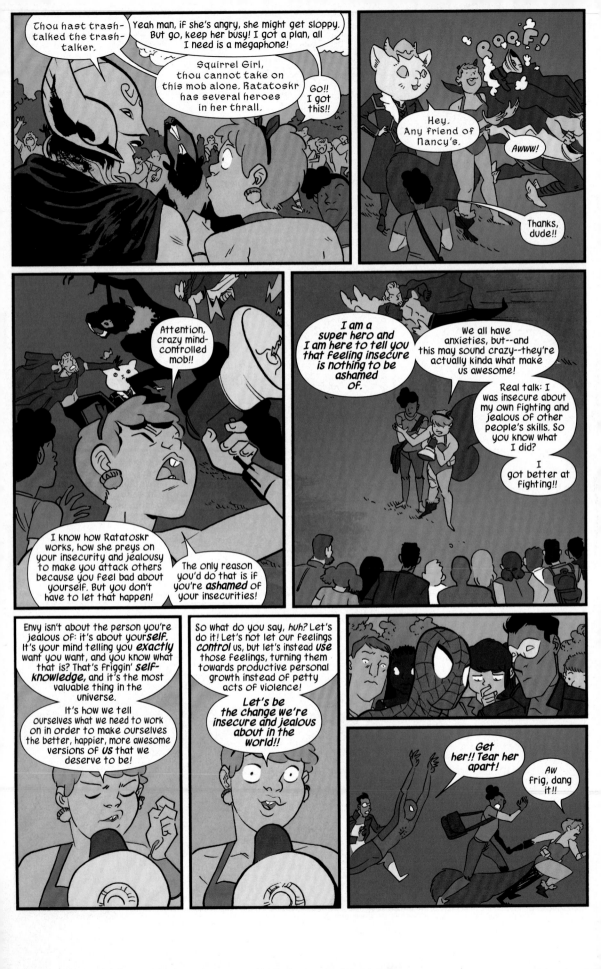

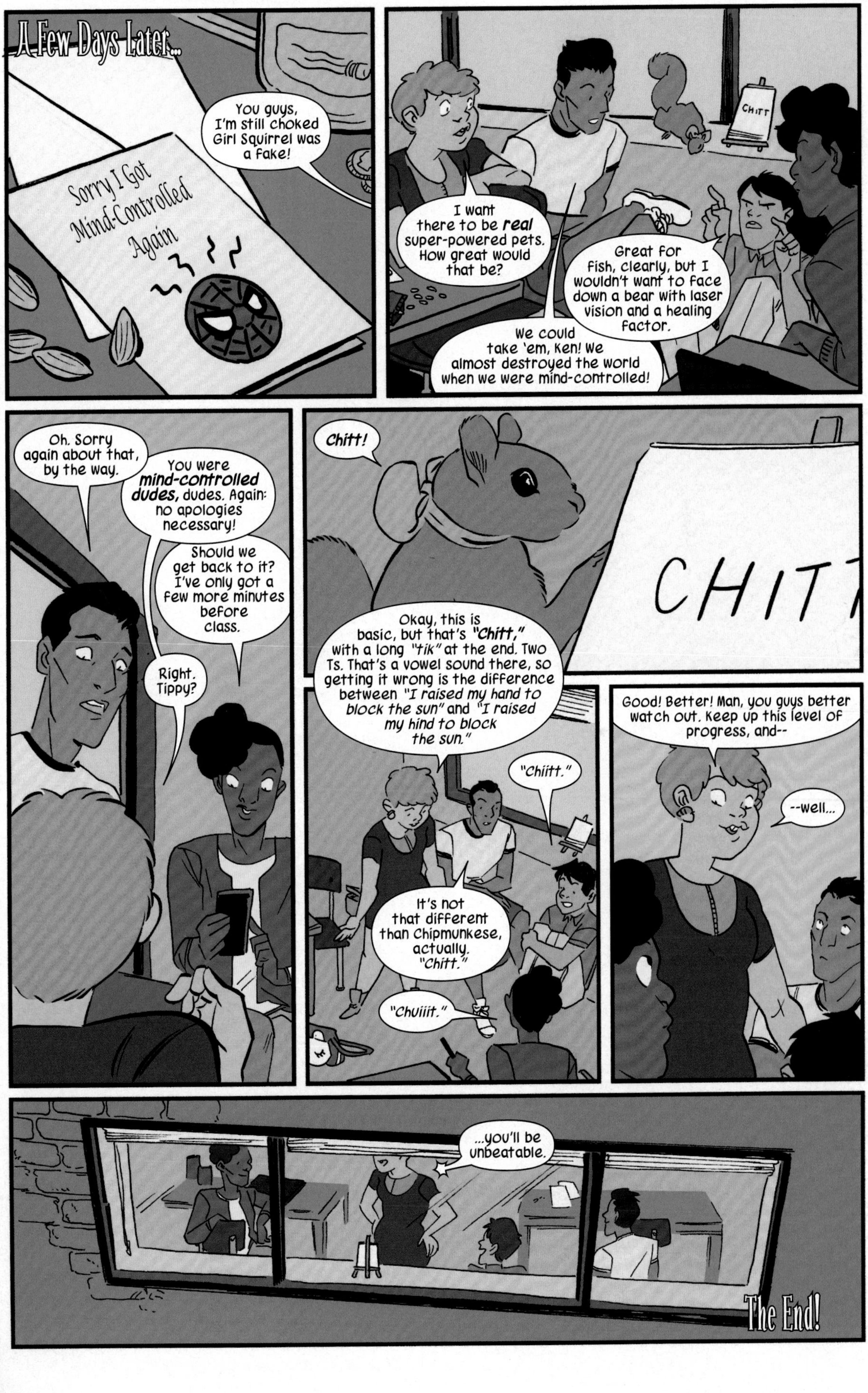
A Few Days Later...
Sorry I Got Mind-Controlled Again
You guys, I'm still choked Girl Squirrel was a fake!
I want there to be **real** super-powered pets. How great would that be?
CHITT
Great for fish, clearly, but I wouldn't want to face down a bear with laser vision and a healing factor.
We could take 'em, Ken! We almost destroyed the world when we were mind-controlled!
Oh. Sorry again about that, by the way.
You were ***mind-controlled dudes,*** dudes. Again: no apologies necessary!
Should we get back to it? I've only got a few more minutes before class.
Right. Tippy?
*Chitt!*
CHITT
Okay, this is basic, but that's ***"Chitt,"*** with a long *"tik"* at the end. Two Ts. That's a vowel sound there, so getting it wrong is the difference between *"I raised my hand to block the sun"* and *"I raised my hind to block the sun."*
*"Chiitt."*
It's not that different than Chipmunkese, actually. *"Chitt."*
*"Chuiiit."*
Good! Better! Man, you guys better watch out. Keep up this level of progress, and--
--well...
...you'll be unbeatable.
The End!

# the unbeatable Squirrel Girl #8!

Written by
Ryan North

Art by
Erica Henderson

Color Art by
Rico Renzi

Lettering and Production by
VC's Clayton Cowles

| | |
|---|---|
| Cover Artist | Erica Henderson |
| Assistant Editor | Jon Moisan |
| Editor | Wil Moss |
| Executive Editor | Tom Brevoort |
| Editor in Chief | Axel Alonso |
| Chief Creative Officer | Joe Quesada |
| Publisher | Dan Buckley |
| Executive Producer | Alan Fine |

Squirrel Girl will return...
...in our second #1 issue this year because SHE'S JUST THAT GOOD.

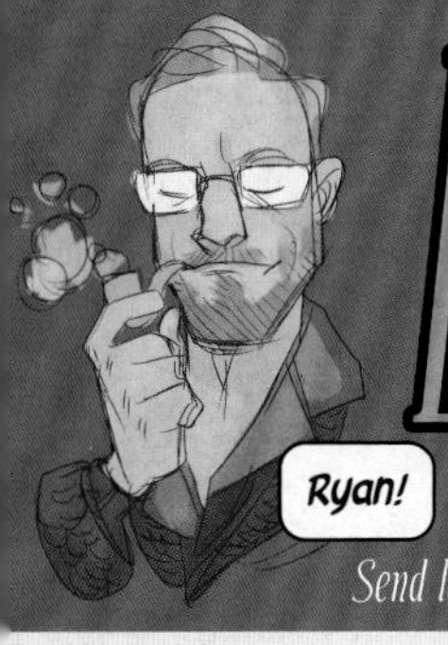
Ryan!

# Letters From Nuts

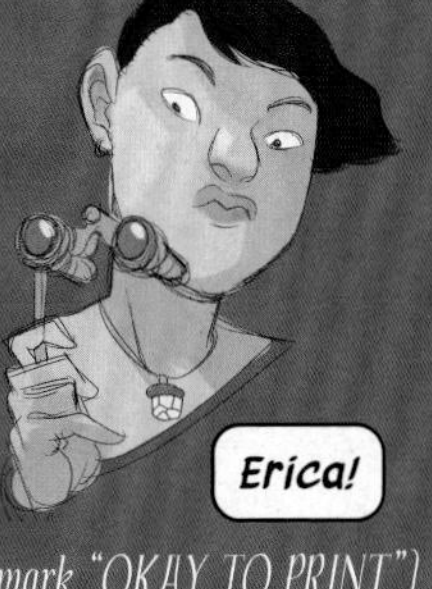
Erica!

*Send letters to mheroes@marvel.com or 135 W 50th St, 7th Floor, New York, NY 10020 (Please mark "OKAY TO PRINT")*

Dear Ryan and Erica,

I am the paleontologist boyfriend that Amanda the squirrel biologist mentioned when she wrote to you back in issue #5. I study predator-prey arms races in tyrannosaurs and duckbills. Thanks for responding to Amanda's letter. She is now totally obsessed with your comic (which I also think is delightful). Although, I am worried that I should start being a little jealous of that Chipmunk Hunk fellow. I notice that, unlike Doreen, he doesn't have a utility belt. I assume this means that, much like a real chipmunk, he carries all his hero gear in his cheek pouches, which is gross. Yeah, Chipmunk Hunk is gross. Why don't you go ahead and make that canon? Also, is it possible to get any of that sweet "Eat Nuts and Kick Butts" merchandise?

Anyway, I am glad to see you haven't taken Amanda up on her suggestion to introduce a paleontological comic foil who is dreadfully boring in comparison with Squirrel Girl and her other friends. But I do have an alternative suggestion for you. Amanda never told you about her squirrel research. She studies how the personalities of little squirrels relate to their siblings and how their personalities change as the squirrels mature. She does that by catching squirrels (which are complete suckers for peanut butter) and recording their behaviors when placed in a white-walled glass-roofed contraption filled with fake tunnel entrances and mirrors. It's all totally humane, but doesn't that sound like a premise for one of those alien-psychological-observer or hypno/illusionist super villains? Chew it over, and thanks again.

W. Scott Persons, IV

P.S. Erica, thanks for giving your tyrannosaur some protofeathers and for getting your pterosaur's wing membrane attachments right back in issue #5. Yours are much better than in that recently sequeled popular dinosaur movie franchise (the name escapes me, but you know the one I mean).

P.P.S. Attached is a photo of me visiting with one of Amanda's research subjects and also a photo of Amanda and me together, so you'll know that I am who I say I am and not just some nut . . . errr you get the point.

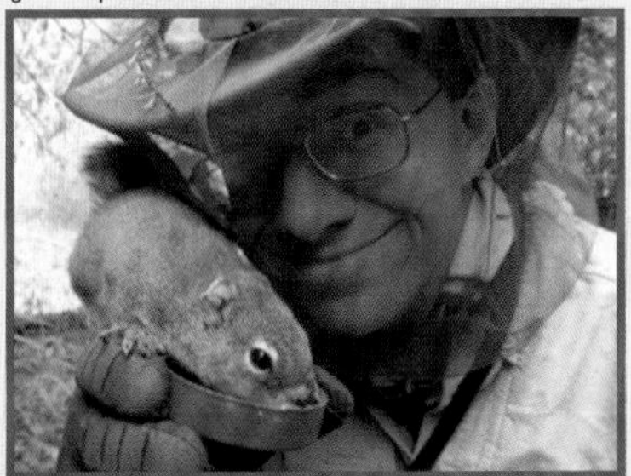

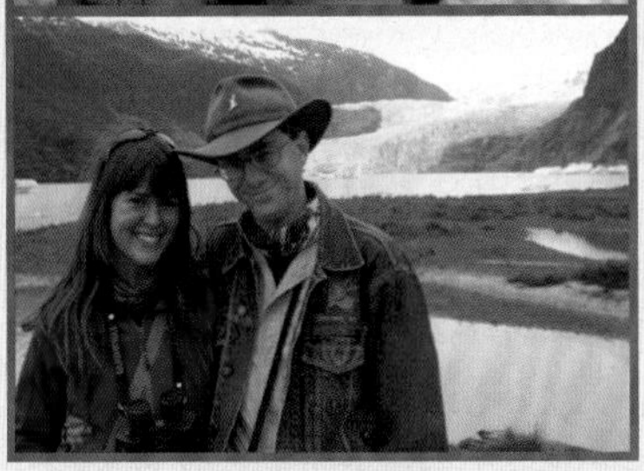

**RYAN: Okay this is the best letter ever, and everyone else is now on notice: your letters have to be at LEAST as awesome as this, so please feature a) squirrels b) love and c) interesting squirrel facts in all future letters. I personally just started reading a book about squirrel facts, and did you know there are squirrels on five different continents? They're so widespread that THE SUN NEVER SETS ON SQUIRRELS. There is no way this fact is not making it into a future comic, so uh, when you read it later on try to act surprised.**

**ERICA: TAKE THAT, HOLLYWOOD. SOME PEOPLE care about being up to date on the latest scientific knowledge on dinosaurs. Listen, we all like Charles Knight, but the golden age of paleontology is over, guys.**

**P.S. I hope you guys keep writing in.**

**P.P.S. Now that I know their weakness I'm going to lure in ALL THE SQUIRRELS.**

**P.P.S. Oh god, are we those people that nobody wants to see movies with because we're going to go on about how Ron Silver being defeated at the end of *Time Cop* makes no scientific sense?**

**P.P.P.S. Don't watch *Time Cop.***

Dear lovely Erica and Ryan,

Thank you, thank you, thank you for UNBEATABLE SQUIRREL GIRL! With your super-powers combined, you have brought Doreen Green to life in the absolute best way! I love your comic so much, I threw a Marvel themed party for my 30th birthday JUST so I could be Squirrel Girl. And the best part? My best friend Jack surprised me with a squirrel battle against one of Doreen's greatest adversaries...Doctor Doom! Take a look for yourself! #SquirrelSelfie! Thanks Erica and Ryan for doing what you do! Long live Squirrel Girl!

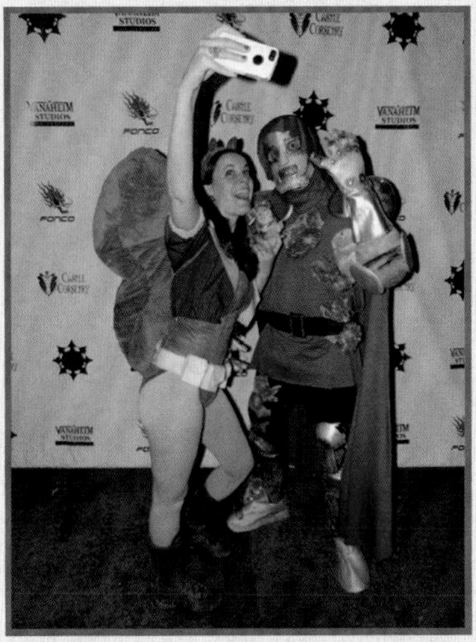

Brittany

**R: This is amazing, and I've got to go to way better parties! Great costumes too. I notice Doom's covered in squirrels: confound those wretched rodents!!**

**E: HM. Next year is my 30th. I may need to steal some ideas from you. PLUS my boyfriend LOVES Doom and does have a couple of teeny scars on his face to make the whole thing even more accurate. HMMMMMMMMMMMMM.**

Dear Erica and Ryan,

My dad and I have been reading this awesome comic, and I love it! For this year's Comic-Con in San Diego I tried to get my sister to come dressed as Tippy Toe, but she wouldn't! I have a question though, if Squirrel Girl was in a big crowd of people in her costume, wouldn't her tail keep hitting people in the face? Or would she have to flatten her tail across her back?

Your Inquisitive Fan,
Neva Devine, Age 12

**R: I have paid a lot of attention to our cosplaying fans (on account of how they are the best) and most attach the tail via a concealed hook at the back of the vest, which means the tail always stays in place. It shouldn't be hitting people in the face that way, but will still look great! We've reblogged a couple of tutorials, which you can find on the cosplay tag of our unbeatablesquirrelgirl.tumblr.com site!**

**Anyway, to answer your actual question, yes absolutely Squirrel Girl would hit people in the face with her tail, but only those that deserved it.**

**E: In a crowd situation I think it would be easier to wrap the tail around herself like in the laser defense system scene in issue #2.**

Dear USG team, makers of sheer delight,

I don't have an adorable baby squirrel to send you a photo of, but I do have the second printing of USG #4, which is almost as good, and coincidentally has become my all-time favorite comic issue ever. Of all the times. How will I ever beat that? It's impossible! I really liked how you had Doreen handle Galactus--getting him take-out--Beautiful. I love you crazy nuts for doing this comic. It's uproarious, and I keep getting people to read it. I just finished reading #6, and I can't wait for the next issue. If Squirrel Girl and Magneto form a road-trip duo, I think I'll pop from sheer giggles. Everything about this comic is delightful, and in the midst of the super-serious SECRET WARS and Mister Fantastic's moody melodrama, sheer delight is such a great change of tone. It's immensely needed, and positively needed.

John Polkowske

**R: Aw thanks! That's super sweet. I like the idea of Squirrel Girl and Magneto going on a road-trip and the car runs out of gas and Doreen makes Magneto "push" the car with his powers the rest of the way. That's my pitch: a put-upon Magneto and carefree Squirrel Girl discover America, and also...friendship. Marvel, you read your own letters pages, right?? [Ed. note: Only the ones that bag on *Time Cop.*]**

**E: Hey, he should push the car the whole way. We're not in a place where we should be wasting fuel when we don't have to! Plus, that way, they can tool around in a really sweet vintage ride without worrying about it breaking down all the time.**

Hey Squirrel Girl team,

A lot of my friends who are ladies often talk

about their crushes on fictional characters, and it has been something I respected but never really "got." But now that I may or may not have a crush on Squirrel Girl, it's possible that I maaaay see their points. I mean, it is likely that Doreen is super passionate about her interests and would probably have great conversations about squirrels, computer science and squirrel computer science on dates. Plus there is a possibility that she's a super caring, sweet person that would make anyone super happy. It also may be true that she's super cute and strong and awkward in an adorable way? But none of this is, of course, confirmed. Just like my crush on Squirrel Girl. Which is totally up for debate and not confirmed in any way.

(Possibly?) JD Boucher

**R: I have a big crush on Commander Data from *Star Trek,* so I understand you. It's more of a friendship crush though. I just want to hang out with robots and the robot-adjacent!**

**E: I'm pretty sure my first crush ever was on Race Bannon. I totally get it.**

Hi Ryan! Hi Erica!

SQUIRREL GIRL is a grand book, yielding laughs and thoughts and an appreciation of pictures. I like it and buy it often.

But I'm afraid there's a bug in your sixth comic. In the front menu, I (naturally) picked Dazzler and Devil Dinosaur as the newest friends of the unbeatable Squirrel Girl, but the "Answer Inside" gave Chipmunk Hunk and Koi Boi. It's 100% reproducible. It even lets me select zero characters but then presents these two.

In case anyone else is facing this issue, I've attached a fix:

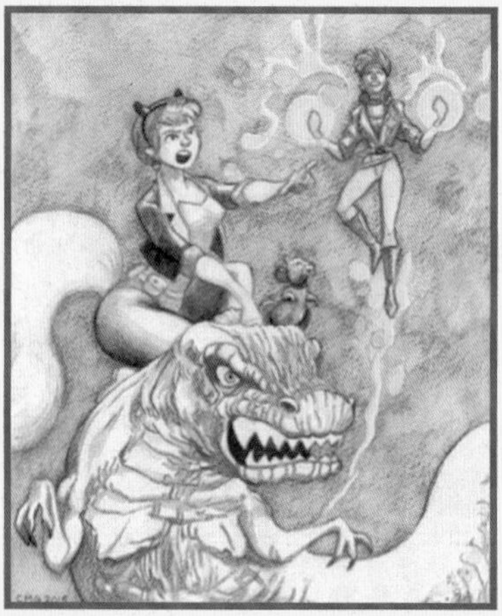

Up with squirrels!
Cheston

**R: Cheston, I love this. Also: Thank you for the bug report; it has been confirmed on our end and will hopefully be corrected in a future team-up.**

**E: Marvel IS restarting WHAT IF? Man, I also hope that Marvel reads its own letter columns. [Ed. note: Only the ones with embarrassing *Star Trek* crush revelations.]**

Good day, fine folks at Squirrel Girl's headquarters!

This comic brings me more joy than I know what to do with! It's the funniest comic and my absolute favorite. Doreen is my kind of hero--she's so positive, tough, way cool and a total sweetheart. The artwork is endearing, the writing is hilarious, and the animal rhyming names are the best. Thank you so much for this book. You guys are super awesome. My life is better for having read it.

Will you be restarting the series this fall after SECRET WARS ends?? I just looked through the All-New All-Different Marvel Previews and it wasn't in there. I'm worried, to say the least. Are you planning for Superior Squirrel Girl? All-New Squirrel Girl? Old Gal Doreen? Squirrel-Verse event? Squirrel Wars?? I'll take any Doreen Green you wanna serve up.

I've never written in to a comic before, but this book is so great that getting my picture in an issue of SQUIRREL GIRL is now on my bucket list. Here I am reading my books in a tree, so as to be closer to Tippy Toe and Doreen:

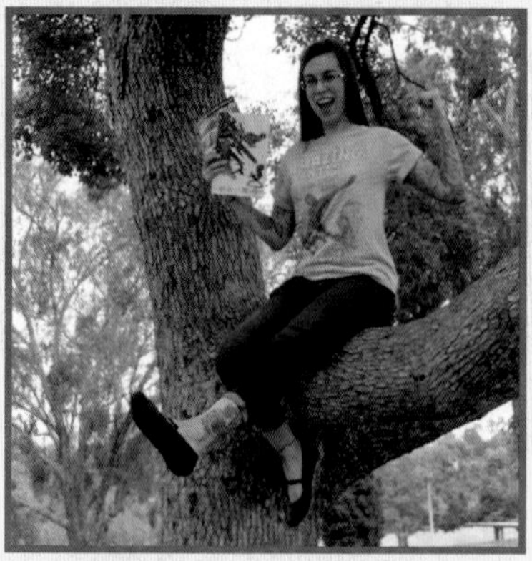

Making Mine Marvel, and wishing you all the nuts,
Molly J. Santa Maria
San Diego, CA

**R: This is ALSO amazing. Thank you, Molly! And I have good news: we ARE continuing after SECRET WARS! We're taking a (short!) break, but then we'll be restarting with a new #1 in October. Same characters! Same creative team! Just a new story that builds on everything here. Also, while it's not "Old Man Doreen," you'll be able to get even more Squirrel Girl then, as she'll be in the NEW AVENGERS book too!**

**E: "Old Man Doreen" is another one for WHAT IF. Also, consider that photo PRINTED.**

Erica and Ryan,

Forget all other work commitments, social obligations and personal hobbies, okay? I'm going to need this series to go on FOREVER. Will you accept haikus as a form of reimbursement? Here's a small down payment:

Chik chukka chut chut
Chit chit chukka chitty chut
Chut chitty chukka

Brittany Meredith

**R: Ran that by Tippy and she said it was FLATTERING and SAUCY, so thank you!**

**E: WHAT MAKES YOU THINK WE MIGHT WANT TO STOP?**

Erica, Ryan, and Rico,

Hi! I love SQUIRREL GIRL, I've been reading since issue #1, and the story has gotten better and better with each book -- which seems impossible because it's already so amazing. I loved the inclusion of the Avengers in #7. Black Widow and Squirrel Girl in the same panel was like a most wonderful dream... That quickly came to end end because... well...insert spoiler here.I'm really looking forward to the next issue, especially because Ratatoskr is an extremely-scary-looking squirrel with unicorn qualities. An evil unicorn. And I didn't know those types existed.

So yeah, you're all amazing and I love your book and Doreen and Tippy-Toe. Thanks for a great comic book! (:

Brake for squirrels!
Erin

PS: Way back in February when someone at the comic book store told me the person who did the coloring for SQUIRREL GIRL worked at the store, I was blown away and totally geeked out. Thanks Rico!

**E: Haha. I liked Black Widow better in #5 because she wasn't mind-controlled into being a jerk. She's so much fun either way though. Ratatoskr is great. I haven't had a chance to draw monsters for a while so it's been a treat!**

Friends,

I'm a teacher in North Carolina and picked up the first issues of UNBEATABLE SQUIRREL GIRL for our after school comic club. After reading the first two comics, SQUIRREL GIRL became a part of my personal pull-list, as well as a title the kids couldn't wait for more of. Thanks for such a fun, positive book!

Additionally, around issue #4 our daughter Penelope was born. I'm pretty sure she's a huge fan because between naps she has been fighting crime under the guise of "Sugar Glider":

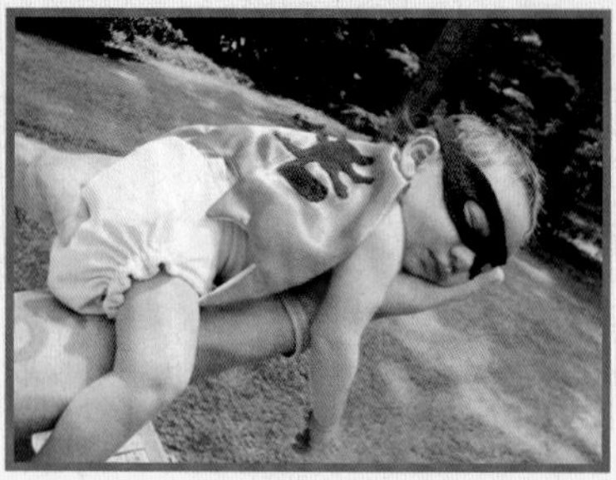

Does Squirrel Girl need a sidekick? Keep up the great work.

Joel Richardson,
Washington, NC

**R: Can we just turn this letters page into an "adorable pictures of fans" page instead? I am so into this. Welcome to the world, Penelope! I had to wait until I was actually writing a book to be published in a letters page; you've got a huge head start (and awesome costume!).**

**E: Did you make that or is there a store that sells tiny super hero apparel for babies? Is it in North Carolina? I'm amazed it took this long to break into this untapped market!**

Hi Erica and Ryan,

I've been picking up UNBEATABLE SQUIRREL GIRL since the beginning, and it's just terrific (although it takes twice as long to read because of the tiny type at the bottom of the pages). That said, why I'm writing is to thank you on behalf of my five-year-old daughter, Thessaly. She loves comics, and we always read SQUIRREL GIRL together so she can find out what's happening with Tippy-Toe.

A while ago, we played through *Lego Marvel Heroes* together, and after beating the end boss, Galactus, she developed a persistent fear that he was coming to eat her. That same week, SQUIRREL GIRL #4 came out, and as soon as I got home, I handed it to her to read. No more Galactus fears --she even wrote him a note telling him she loved him! Thanks a lot, guys (not only for helping out my girl, but for advancing a plausible theory of just why Galactus can never manage to devour Earth)-- you've earned these two readers.

Bob Britten (and Thessaly)

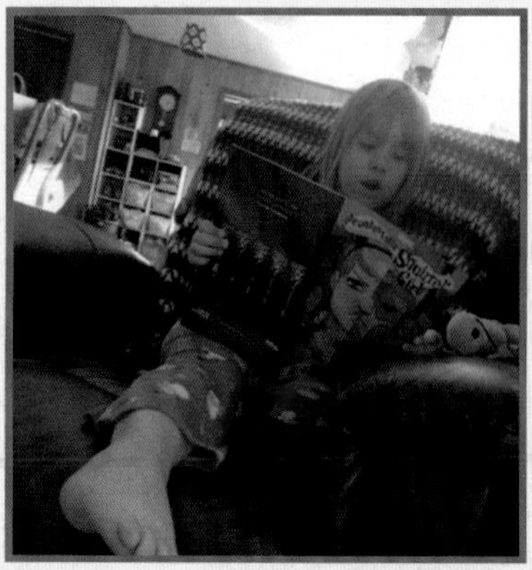

**R: Terrific! And tell Thessaly that when I wrote the story it was after playing that very same game! I took a photo of Galactus and Squirrel Girl together (you can unlock her, she's by the dockyard!) and sent it to my wife with the subject line "story idea."**

**E: Oh my god, everything about that story is great and I can't even.**

# New Series. New Avenger (!).
# Still Eats Nuts and Kicks Butts!

See you in October!
(And keep the letters coming in the meantime!)
- Ryan, Erica, Rico, Clayton, Jon and Wil!

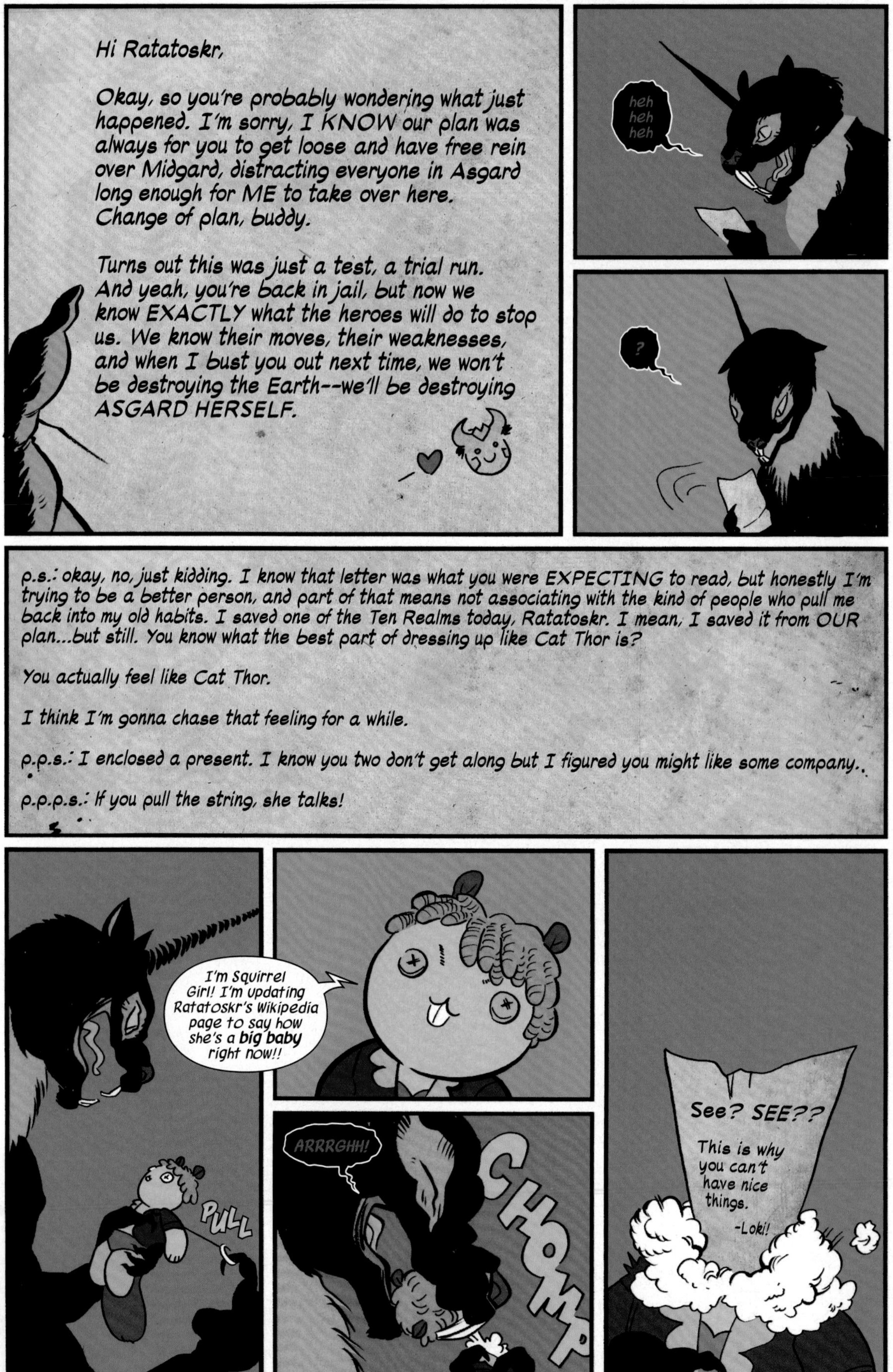
Hi Ratatoskr,
Okay, so you're probably wondering what just happened. I'm sorry, I KNOW our plan was always for you to get loose and have free rein over Midgard, distracting everyone in Asgard long enough for ME to take over here. Change of plan, buddy.
Turns out this was just a test, a trial run. And yeah, you're back in jail, but now we know EXACTLY what the heroes will do to stop us. We know their moves, their weaknesses, and when I bust you out next time, we won't be destroying the Earth--we'll be destroying ASGARD HERSELF.
heh heh heh
?
p.s.: okay, no, just kidding. I know that letter was what you were EXPECTING to read, but honestly I'm trying to be a better person, and part of that means not associating with the kind of people who pull me back into my old habits. I saved one of the Ten Realms today, Ratatoskr. I mean, I saved it from OUR plan...but still. You know what the best part of dressing up like Cat Thor is?
You actually feel like Cat Thor.
I think I'm gonna chase that feeling for a while.
p.p.s.: I enclosed a present. I know you two don't get along but I figured you might like some company.
p.p.p.s.: If you pull the string, she talks!
PULL
I'm Squirrel Girl! I'm updating Ratatoskr's Wikipedia page to say how she's a **big baby** right now!!
ARRRGHH!
CHOMP
See? SEE??
This is why you can't have nice things.
-Loki!

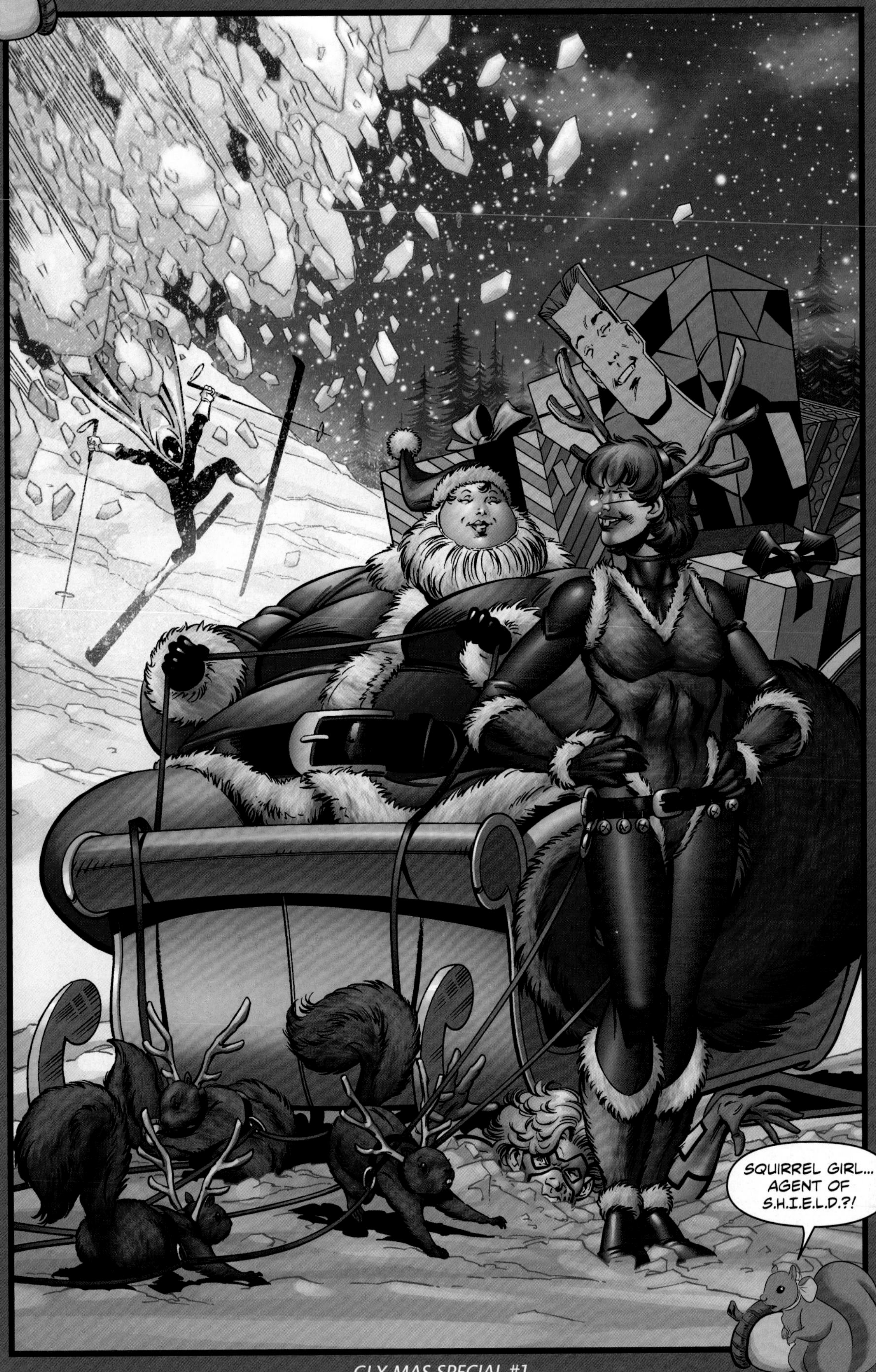
SQUIRREL GIRL... AGENT OF S.H.I.E.L.D.?!

GLX-MAS SPECIAL #1

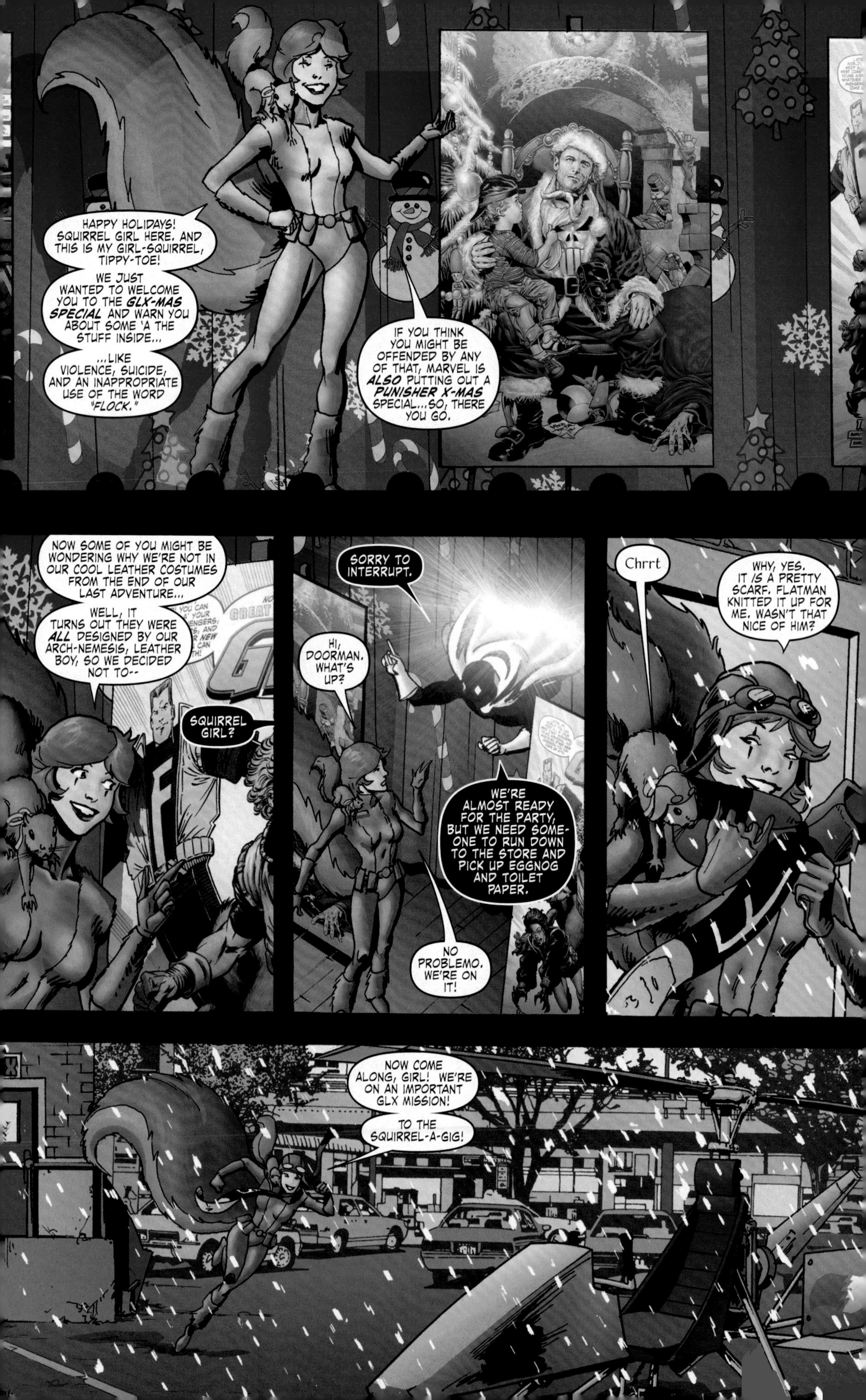
HAPPY HOLIDAYS! SQUIRREL GIRL HERE. AND THIS IS MY GIRL-SQUIRREL, TIPPY-TOE!
WE JUST WANTED TO WELCOME YOU TO THE GLX-MAS SPECIAL AND WARN YOU ABOUT SOME 'A THE STUFF INSIDE...
...LIKE VIOLENCE, SUICIDE, AND AN INAPPROPRIATE USE OF THE WORD "FLOCK."
IF YOU THINK YOU MIGHT BE OFFENDED BY ANY OF THAT, MARVEL IS ALSO PUTTING OUT A PUNISHER X-MAS SPECIAL...SO, THERE YOU GO.
NOW SOME OF YOU MIGHT BE WONDERING WHY WE'RE NOT IN OUR COOL LEATHER COSTUMES FROM THE END OF OUR LAST ADVENTURE...
WELL, IT TURNS OUT THEY WERE ALL DESIGNED BY OUR ARCH-NEMESIS, LEATHER BOY, SO WE DECIDED NOT TO--
SQUIRREL GIRL?
SORRY TO INTERRUPT.
HI, DOORMAN. WHAT'S UP?
WE'RE ALMOST READY FOR THE PARTY, BUT WE NEED SOME-ONE TO RUN DOWN TO THE STORE AND PICK UP EGGNOG AND TOILET PAPER.
NO PROBLEMO. WE'RE ON IT!
Chrrt
WHY, YES. IT IS A PRETTY SCARF. FLATMAN KNITTED IT UP FOR ME. WASN'T THAT NICE OF HIM?
NOW COME ALONG, GIRL! WE'RE ON AN IMPORTANT GLX MISSION!
TO THE SQUIRREL-A-GIG!

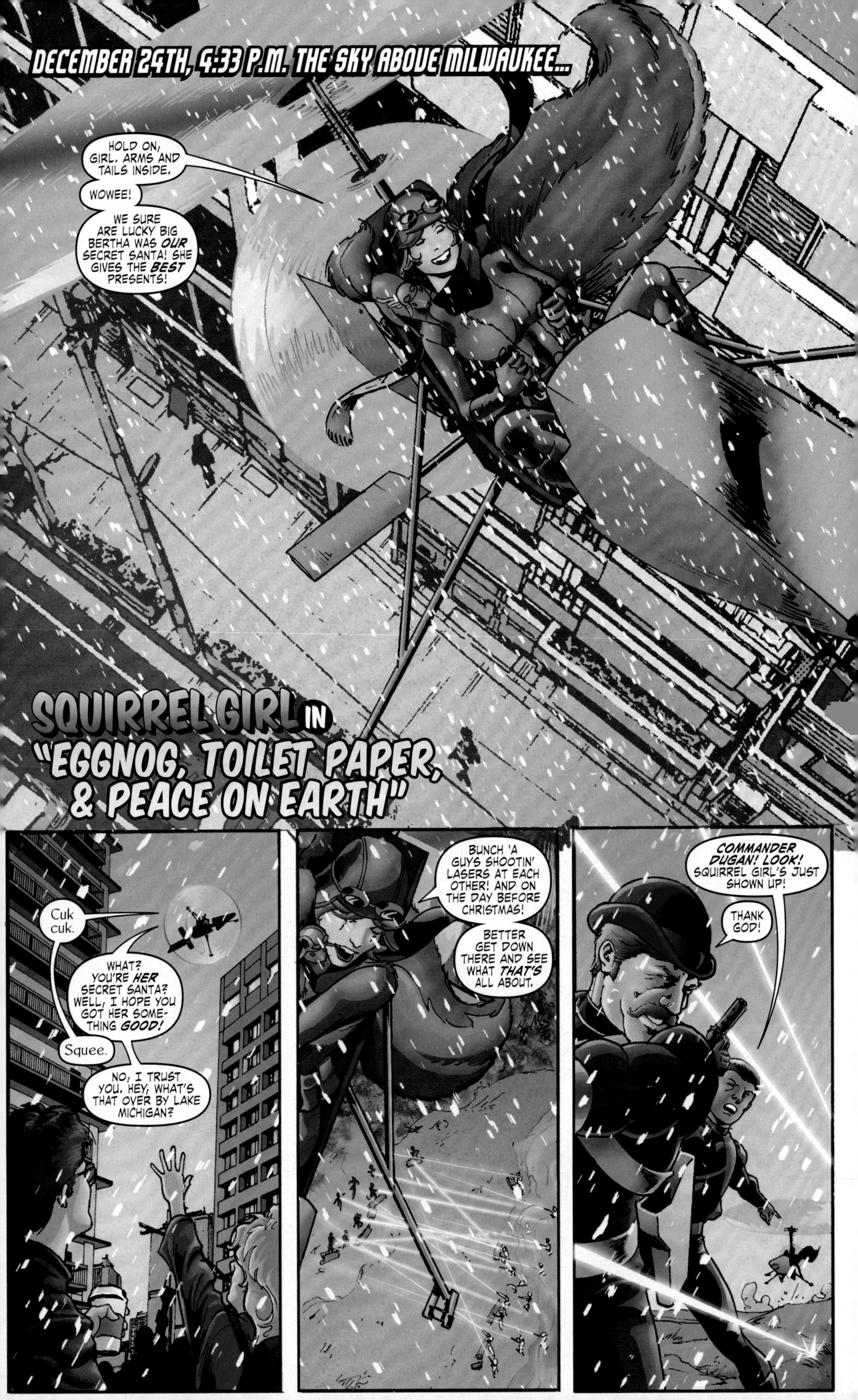
DECEMBER 24TH, 4:33 P.M. THE SKY ABOVE MILWAUKEE...
HOLD ON, GIRL. ARMS AND TAILS INSIDE.
WOWEE!
WE SURE ARE LUCKY BIG BERTHA WAS OUR SECRET SANTA! SHE GIVES THE BEST PRESENTS!
SQUIRREL GIRL IN
"EGGNOG, TOILET PAPER, & PEACE ON EARTH"
Cuk cuk.
WHAT? YOU'RE HER SECRET SANTA? WELL, I HOPE YOU GOT HER SOME-THING GOOD!
Squee.
NO, I TRUST YOU. HEY, WHAT'S THAT OVER BY LAKE MICHIGAN?
BUNCH 'A GUYS SHOOTIN' LASERS AT EACH OTHER! AND ON THE DAY BEFORE CHRISTMAS!
BETTER GET DOWN THERE AND SEE WHAT THAT'S ALL ABOUT.
COMMANDER DUGAN! LOOK! SQUIRREL GIRL'S JUST SHOWN UP!
THANK GOD!

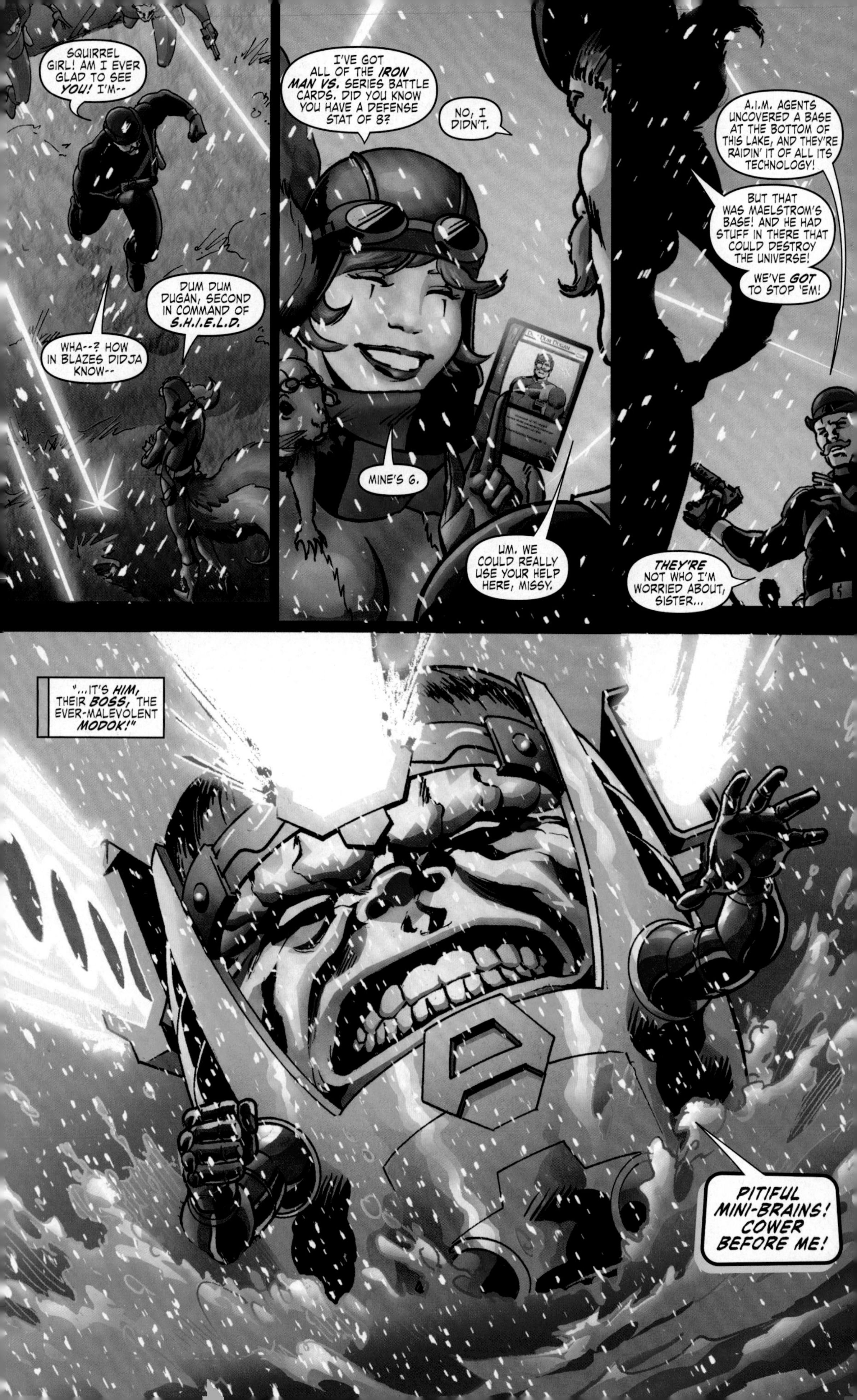
SQUIRREL GIRL! AM I EVER GLAD TO SEE YOU! I'M--
WHA--? HOW IN BLAZES DIDJA KNOW--
DUM DUM DUGAN, SECOND IN COMMAND OF S.H.I.E.L.D.
I'VE GOT ALL OF THE IRON MAN VS. SERIES BATTLE CARDS. DID YOU KNOW YOU HAVE A DEFENSE STAT OF 8?
NO, I DIDN'T.
MINE'S 6.
UM. WE COULD REALLY USE YOUR HELP HERE, MISSY.
A.I.M. AGENTS UNCOVERED A BASE AT THE BOTTOM OF THIS LAKE, AND THEY'RE RAIDIN' IT OF ALL ITS TECHNOLOGY!
BUT THAT WAS MAELSTROM'S BASE! AND HE HAD STUFF IN THERE THAT COULD DESTROY THE UNIVERSE!
WE'VE GOT TO STOP 'EM!
THEY'RE NOT WHO I'M WORRIED ABOUT, SISTER...
"...IT'S HIM, THEIR BOSS, THE EVER-MALEVOLENT MODOK!"
PITIFUL MINI-BRAINS! COWER BEFORE ME!

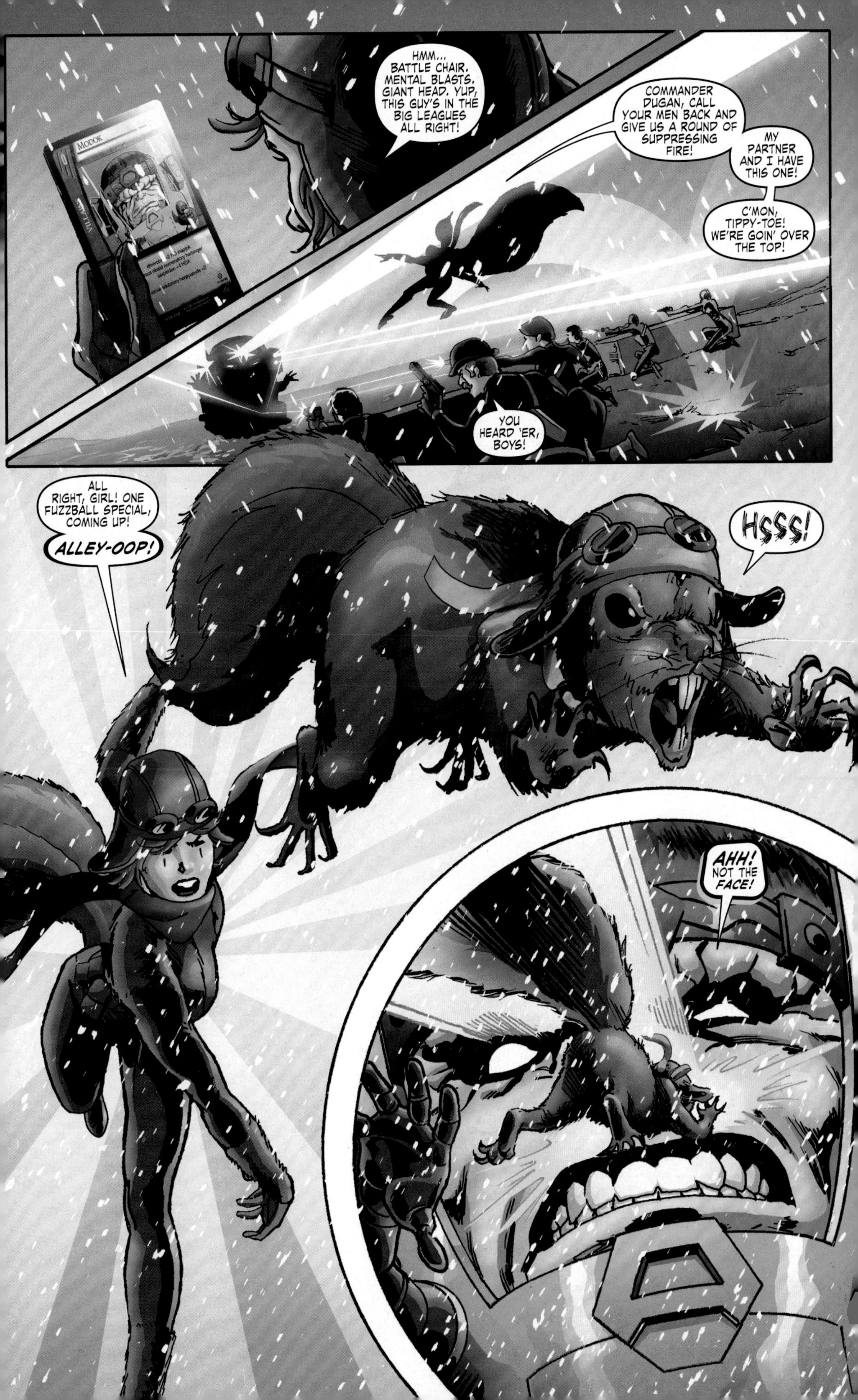
HMM... BATTLE CHAIR. MENTAL BLASTS. GIANT HEAD. YUP, THIS GUY'S IN THE BIG LEAGUES ALL RIGHT!
COMMANDER DUGAN, CALL YOUR MEN BACK AND GIVE US A ROUND OF SUPPRESSING FIRE!
MY PARTNER AND I HAVE THIS ONE!
C'MON, TIPPY-TOE! WE'RE GOIN' OVER THE TOP!
YOU HEARD 'ER, BOYS!
ALL RIGHT, GIRL! ONE FUZZBALL SPECIAL, COMING UP!
ALLEY-OOP!
HSSS!
AHH! NOT THE FACE!

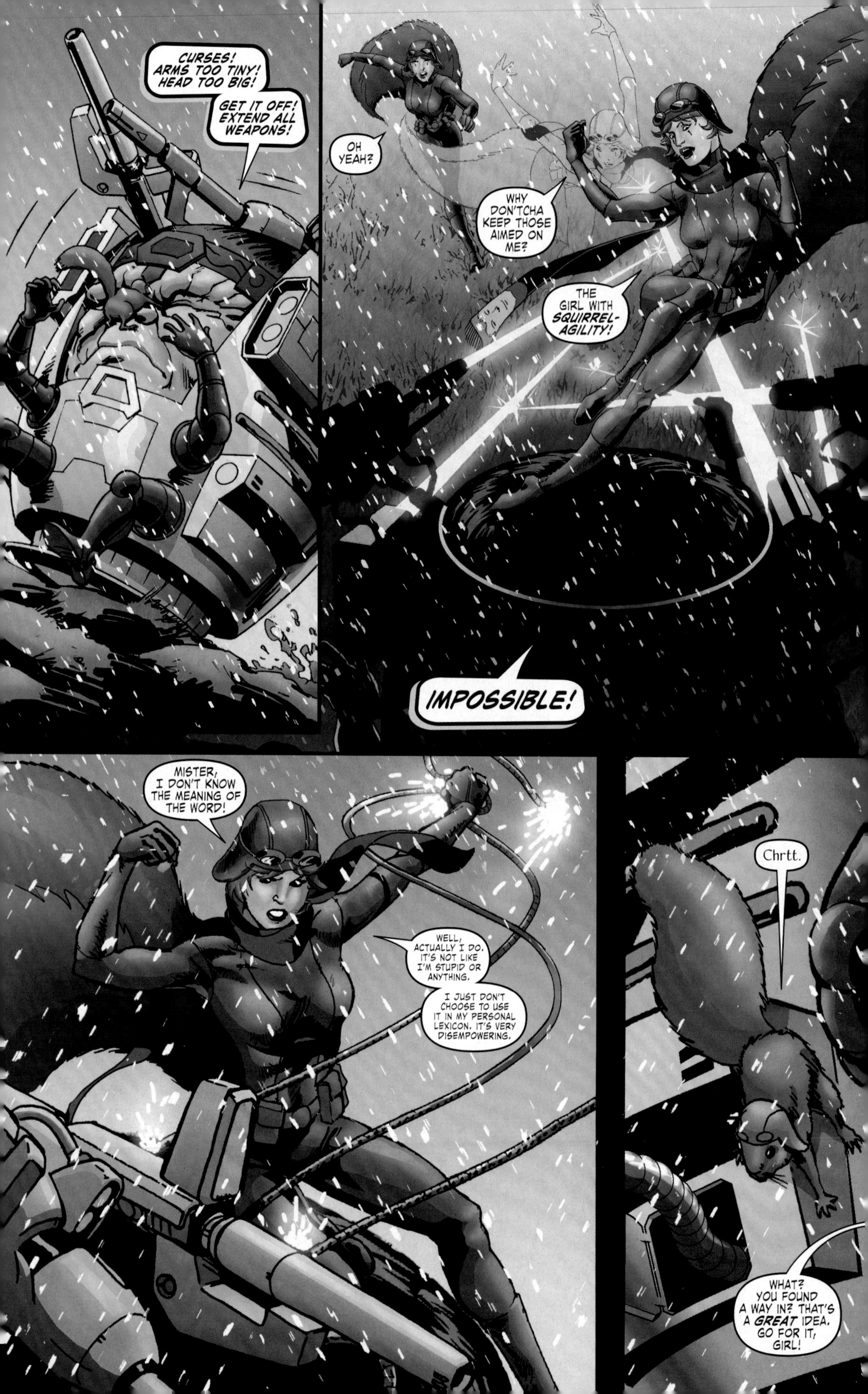
CURSES! ARMS TOO TINY! HEAD TOO BIG!
GET IT OFF! EXTEND ALL WEAPONS!
OH YEAH?
WHY DON'TCHA KEEP THOSE AIMED ON ME?
THE GIRL WITH SQUIRREL-AGILITY!
IMPOSSIBLE!
MISTER, I DON'T KNOW THE MEANING OF THE WORD!
WELL, ACTUALLY I DO. IT'S NOT LIKE I'M STUPID OR ANYTHING.
I JUST DON'T CHOOSE TO USE IT IN MY PERSONAL LEXICON. IT'S VERY DISEMPOWERING.
Chrtt.
WHAT? YOU FOUND A WAY IN? THAT'S A GREAT IDEA. GO FOR IT, GIRL!

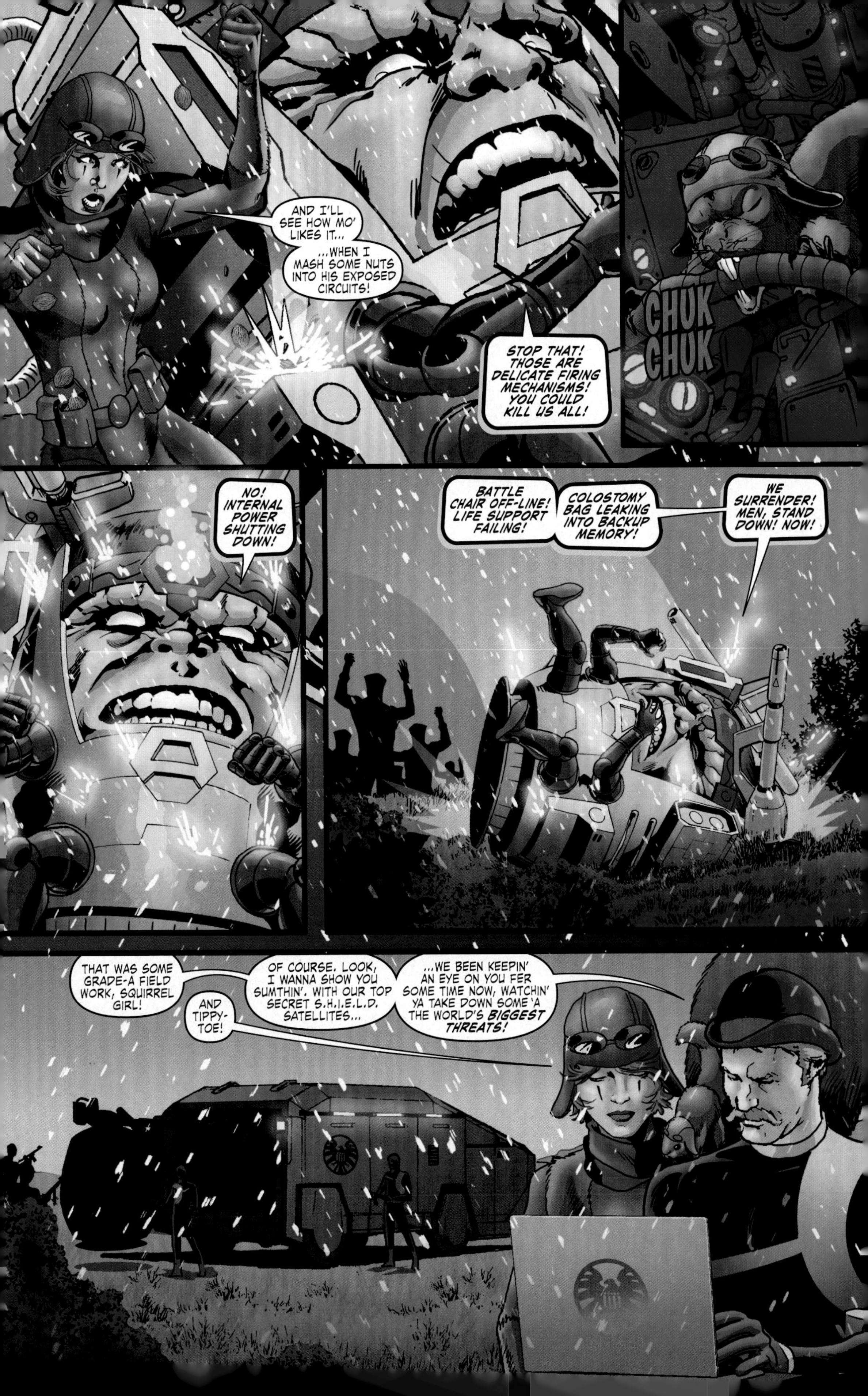
AND I'LL SEE HOW MO' LIKES IT...
...WHEN I MASH SOME NUTS INTO HIS EXPOSED CIRCUITS!
STOP THAT! THOSE ARE DELICATE FIRING MECHANISMS! YOU COULD KILL US ALL!
CHUK CHUK
NO! INTERNAL POWER SHUTTING DOWN!
BATTLE CHAIR OFF-LINE! LIFE SUPPORT FAILING!
COLOSTOMY BAG LEAKING INTO BACKUP MEMORY!
WE SURRENDER! MEN, STAND DOWN! NOW!
THAT WAS SOME GRADE-A FIELD WORK, SQUIRREL GIRL!
AND TIPPY-TOE!
OF COURSE. LOOK, I WANNA SHOW YOU SUMTHIN'. WITH OUR TOP SECRET S.H.I.E.L.D. SATELLITES...
...WE BEEN KEEPIN' AN EYE ON YOU FER SOME TIME NOW, WATCHIN' YA TAKE DOWN SOME 'A THE WORLD'S BIGGEST THREATS!

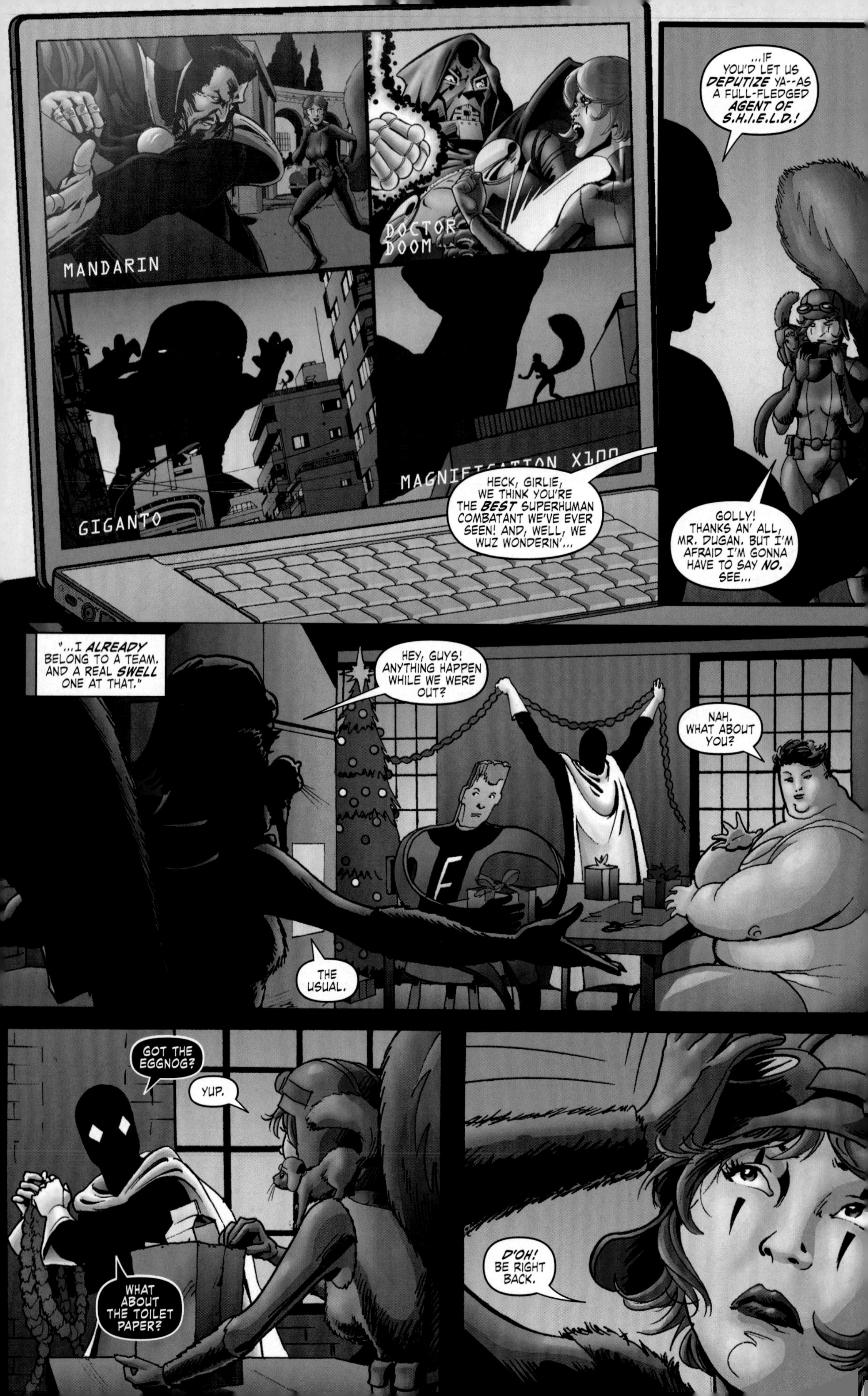
MANDARIN
DOCTOR DOOM
GIGANTO
MAGNIFICATION X100
HECK, GIRLIE, WE THINK YOU'RE THE BEST SUPERHUMAN COMBATANT WE'VE EVER SEEN! AND, WELL, WE WUZ WONDERIN'...
...IF YOU'D LET US DEPUTIZE YA--AS A FULL-FLEDGED AGENT OF S.H.I.E.L.D.!
GOLLY! THANKS AN' ALL, MR. DUGAN. BUT I'M AFRAID I'M GONNA HAVE TO SAY NO. SEE...
"...I ALREADY BELONG TO A TEAM. AND A REAL SWELL ONE AT THAT."
HEY, GUYS! ANYTHING HAPPEN WHILE WE WERE OUT?
NAH. WHAT ABOUT YOU?
THE USUAL.
GOT THE EGGNOG?
YUP.
WHAT ABOUT THE TOILET PAPER?
D'OH! BE RIGHT BACK.

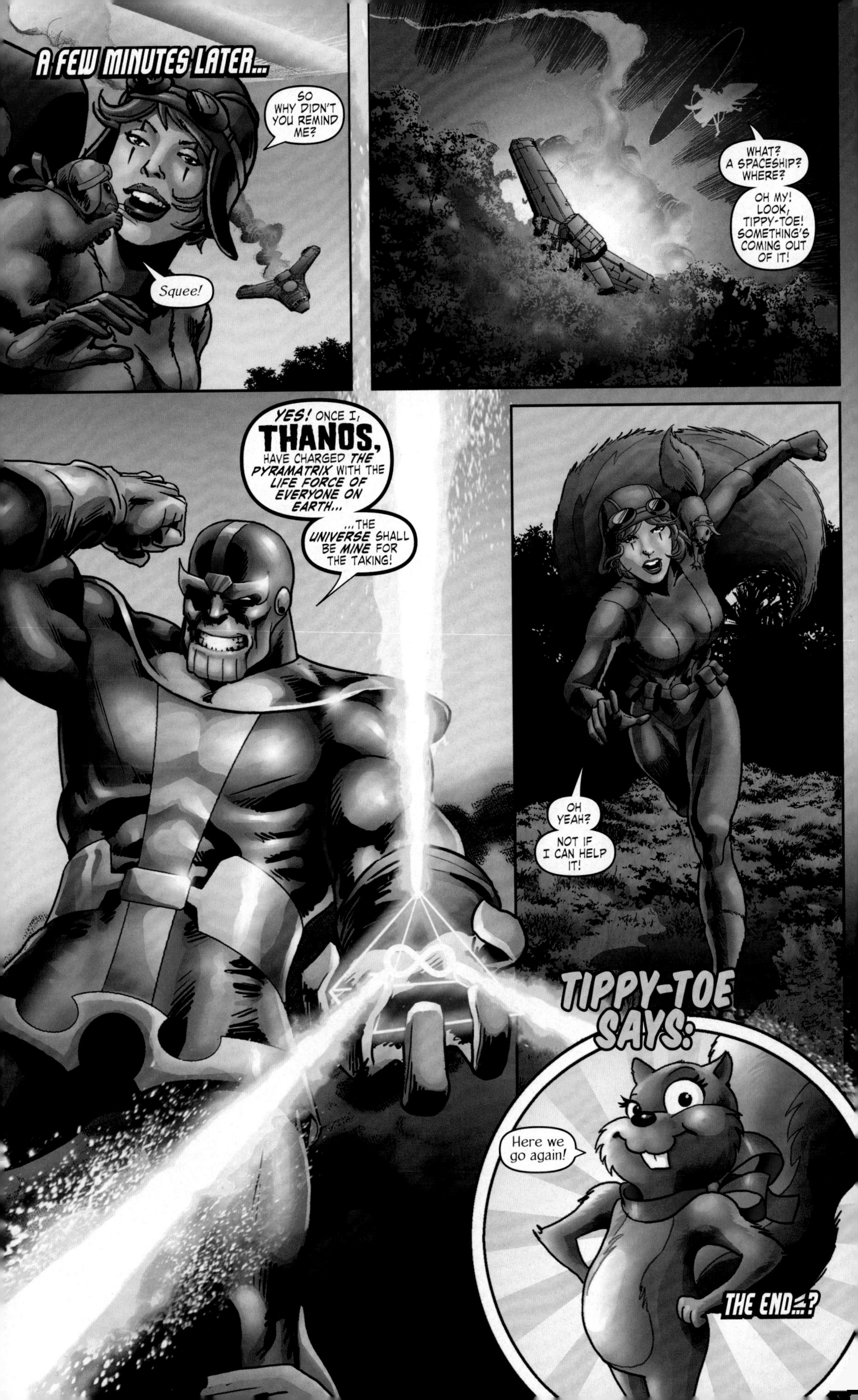
A FEW MINUTES LATER...
SO WHY DIDN'T YOU REMIND ME?
Squee!
WHAT? A SPACESHIP? WHERE?
OH MY! LOOK, TIPPY-TOE! SOMETHING'S COMING OUT OF IT!
YES! ONCE I, THANOS, HAVE CHARGED THE PYRAMATRIX WITH THE LIFE FORCE OF EVERYONE ON EARTH...
...THE UNIVERSE SHALL BE MINE FOR THE TAKING!
OH YEAH?
NOT IF I CAN HELP IT!
TIPPY-TOE SAYS:
Here we go again!
THE END...?

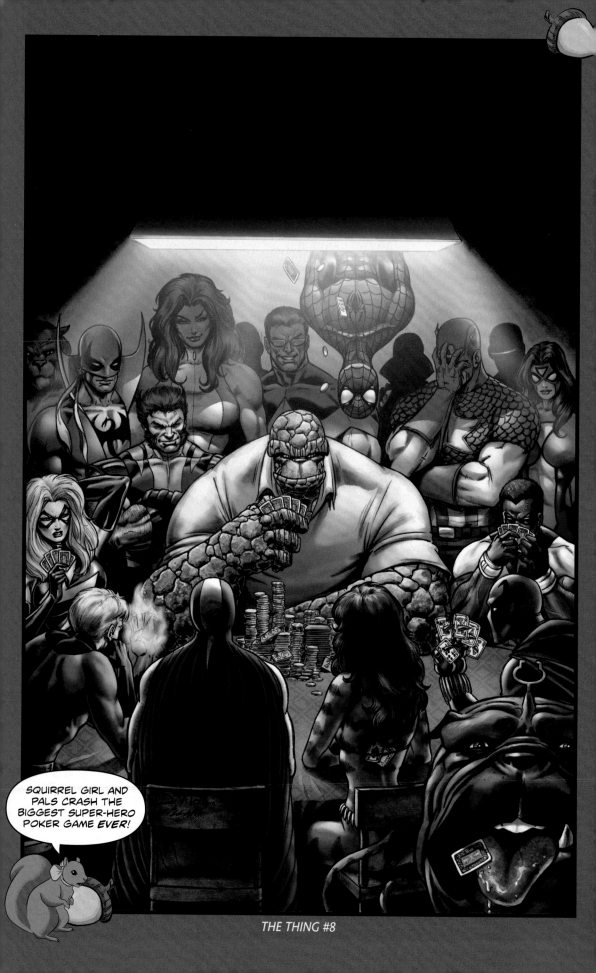

SQUIRREL GIRL AND PALS CRASH THE BIGGEST SUPER-HERO POKER GAME *EVER!*

*THE THING #8*

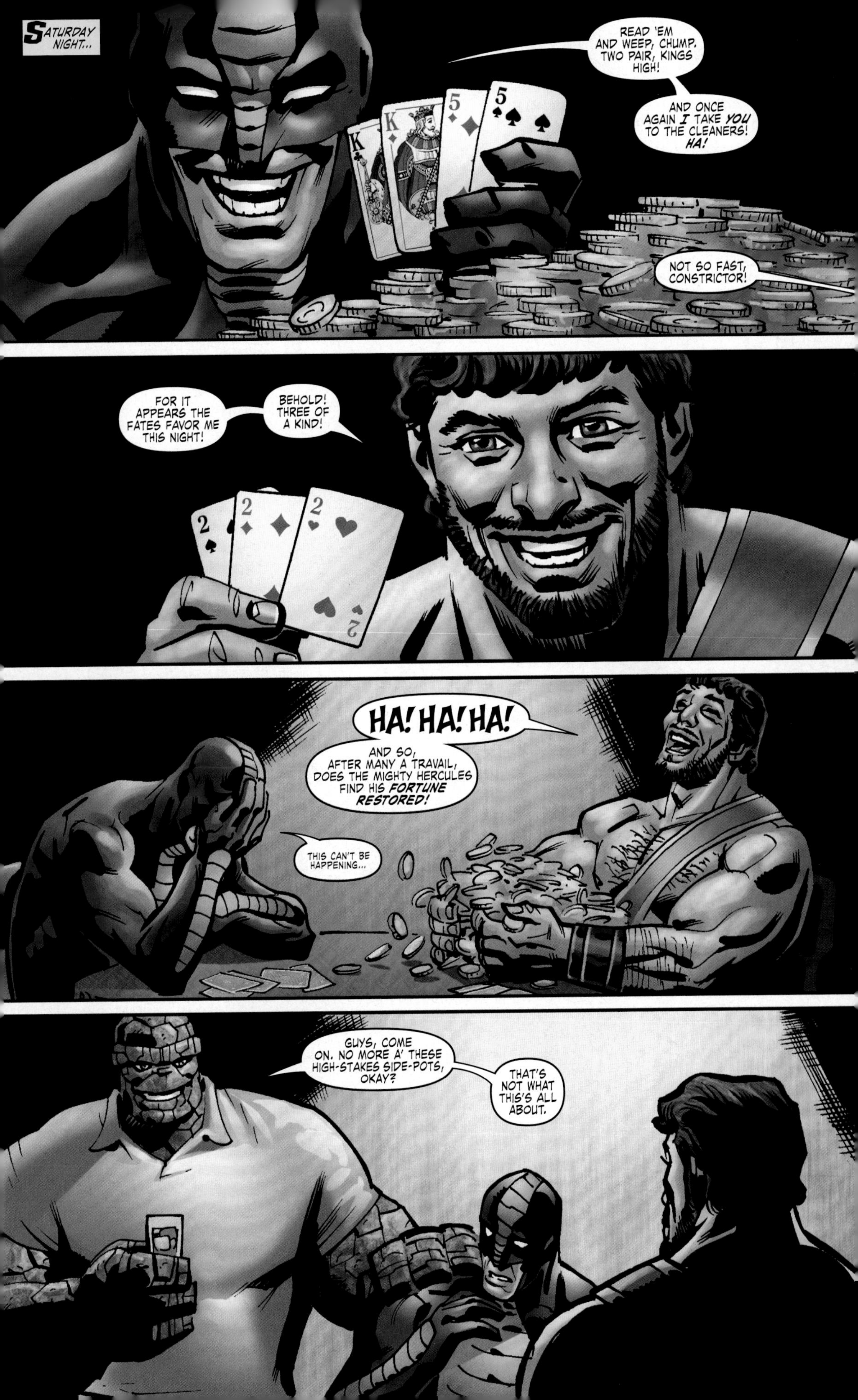
SATURDAY NIGHT...
READ 'EM AND WEEP, CHUMP. TWO PAIR, KINGS HIGH!
AND ONCE AGAIN I TAKE YOU TO THE CLEANERS! HA!
NOT SO FAST, CONSTRICTOR!
BEHOLD! THREE OF A KIND!
FOR IT APPEARS THE FATES FAVOR ME THIS NIGHT!
HA! HA! HA!
AND SO, AFTER MANY A TRAVAIL, DOES THE MIGHTY HERCULES FIND HIS FORTUNE RESTORED!
THIS CAN'T BE HAPPENING...
GUYS, COME ON. NO MORE A' THESE HIGH-STAKES SIDE-POTS, OKAY?
THAT'S NOT WHAT THIS'S ALL ABOUT.

# LAST HAND

DAN SLOTT STORY
KIERON DWYER ARTIST
LAURA VILLARI COLORS
DAVE LANPHEAR LETTERS
SCHMIDT, LAZER & SITTERSON ASSISTANT EDITORS
TOM BREVOORT EDITOR
JOE QUESADA EDITOR IN CHIEF
DAN BUCKLEY PUBLISHER

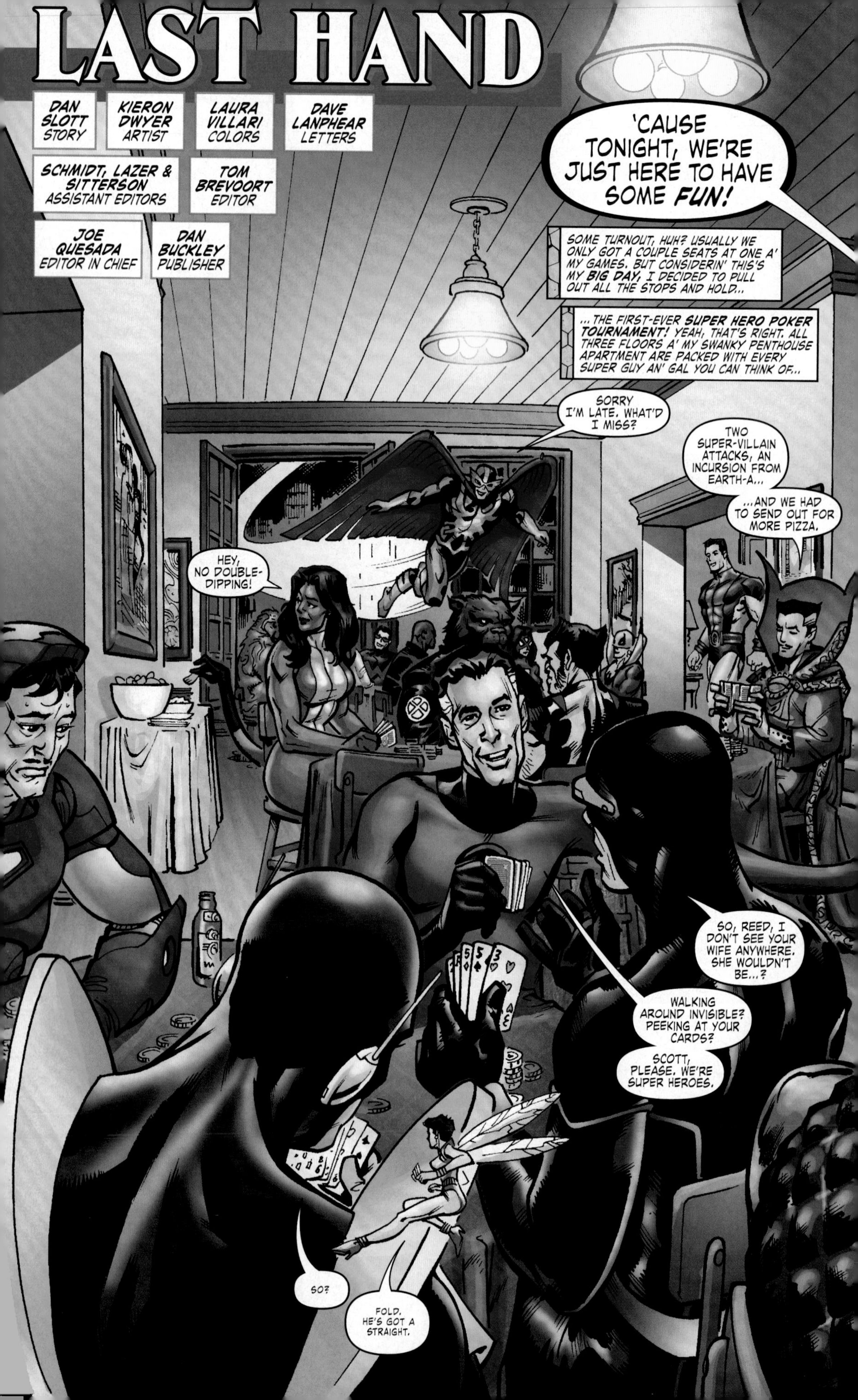

'CAUSE TONIGHT, WE'RE JUST HERE TO HAVE SOME FUN!
SOME TURNOUT, HUH? USUALLY WE ONLY GOT A COUPLE SEATS AT ONE A' MY GAMES. BUT CONSIDERIN' THIS'S MY BIG DAY, I DECIDED TO PULL OUT ALL THE STOPS AND HOLD...
...THE FIRST-EVER SUPER HERO POKER TOURNAMENT! YEAH, THAT'S RIGHT. ALL THREE FLOORS A' MY SWANKY PENTHOUSE APARTMENT ARE PACKED WITH EVERY SUPER GUY AN' GAL YOU CAN THINK OF...
SORRY I'M LATE. WHAT'D I MISS?
TWO SUPER-VILLAIN ATTACKS, AN INCURSION FROM EARTH-A...
...AND WE HAD TO SEND OUT FOR MORE PIZZA.
HEY, NO DOUBLE-DIPPING!
SO, REED, I DON'T SEE YOUR WIFE ANYWHERE. SHE WOULDN'T BE...?
WALKING AROUND INVISIBLE? PEEKING AT YOUR CARDS?
SCOTT, PLEASE. WE'RE SUPER HEROES.
SO?
FOLD. HE'S GOT A STRAIGHT.

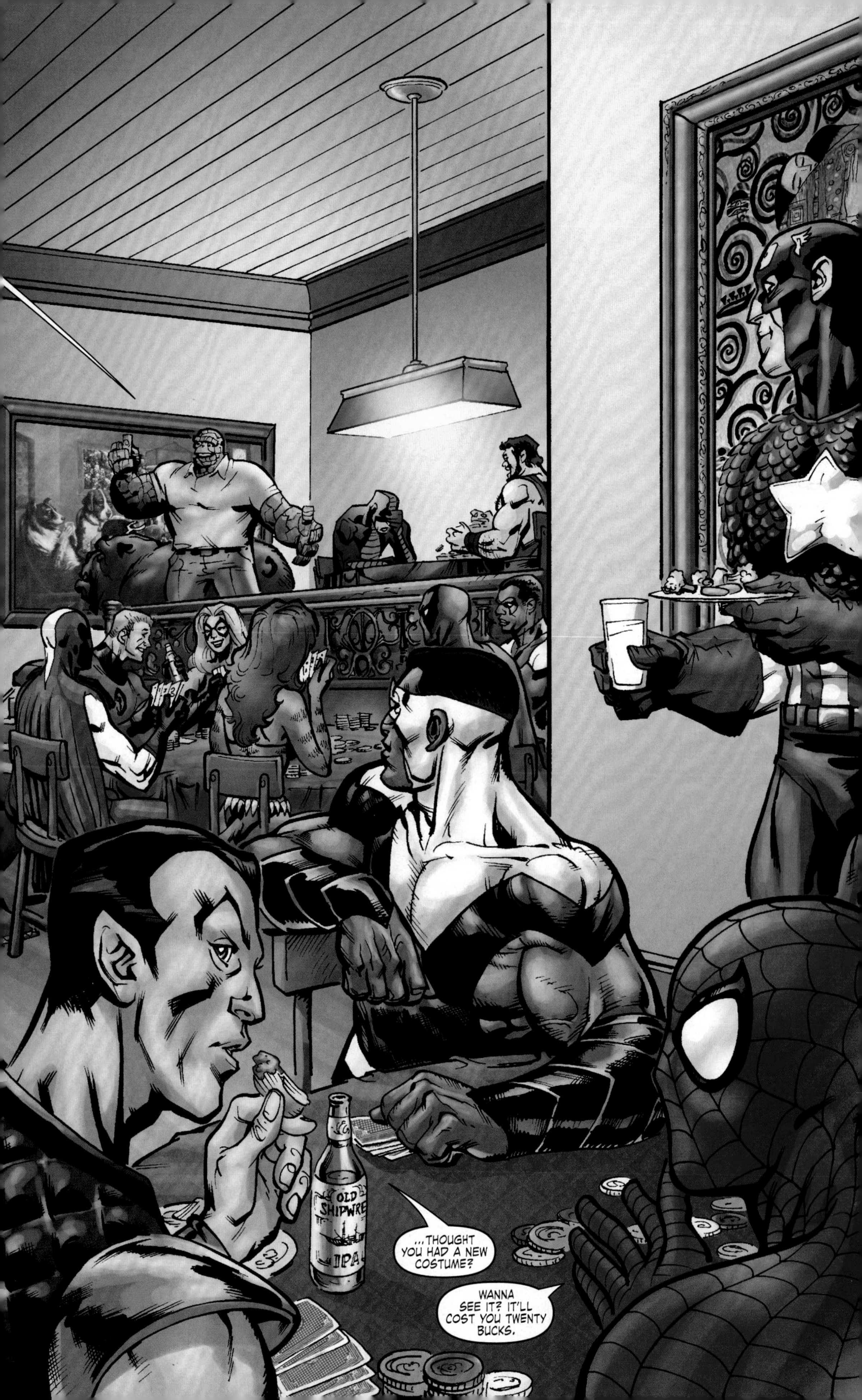
...THOUGHT YOU HAD A NEW COSTUME?
WANNA SEE IT? IT'LL COST YOU TWENTY BUCKS.
OLD SHIPWRE
IPA

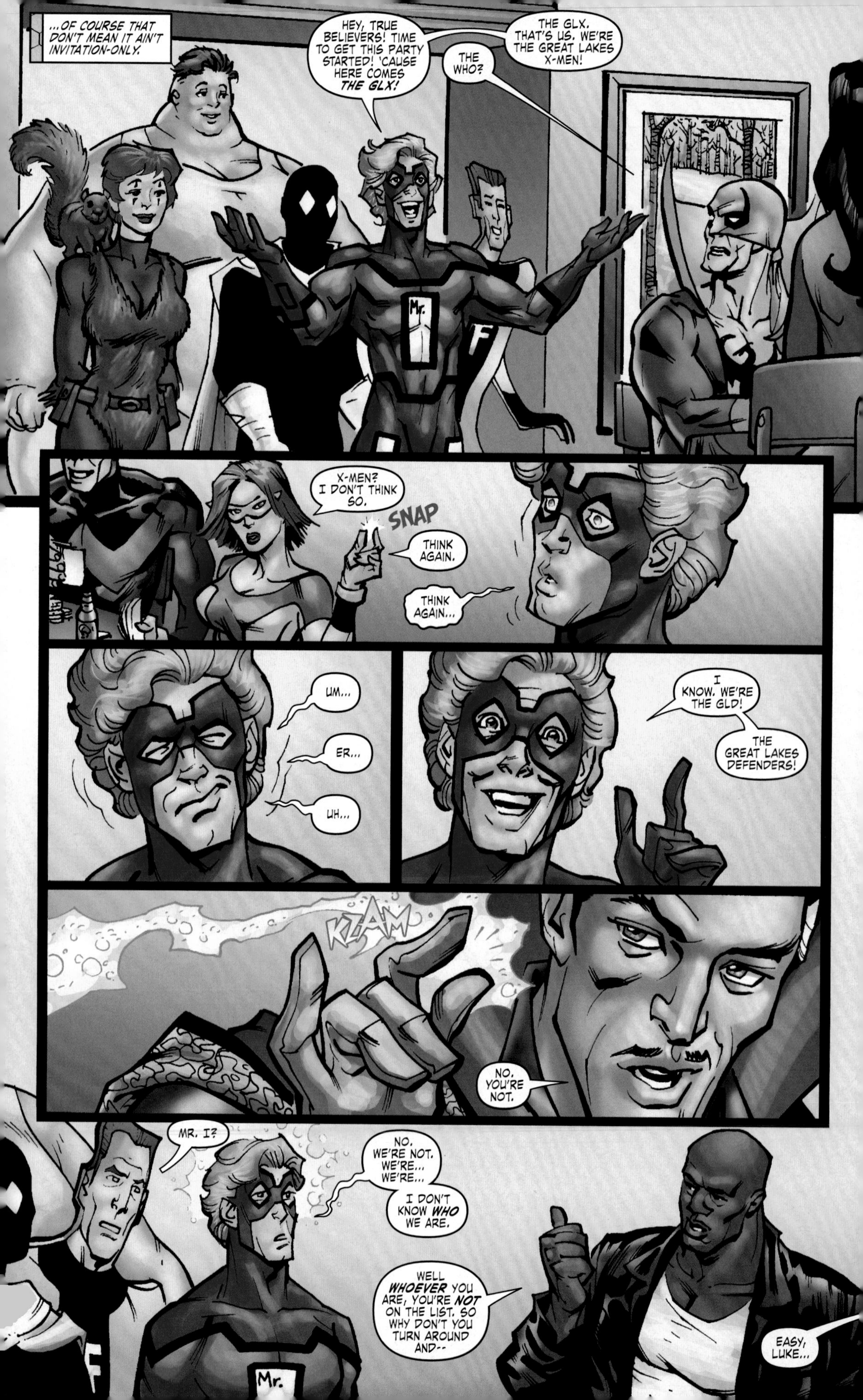
...OF COURSE THAT DON'T MEAN IT AIN'T INVITATION-ONLY.
HEY, TRUE BELIEVERS! TIME TO GET THIS PARTY STARTED! 'CAUSE HERE COMES THE GLX!
THE WHO?
THE GLX. THAT'S US. WE'RE THE GREAT LAKES X-MEN!
X-MEN? I DON'T THINK SO.
SNAP
THINK AGAIN.
THINK AGAIN...
UM...
ER...
UH...
I KNOW. WE'RE THE GLD!
THE GREAT LAKES DEFENDERS!
KZAM
NO, YOU'RE NOT.
MR. I?
NO, WE'RE NOT. WE'RE... WE'RE...
I DON'T KNOW WHO WE ARE.
WELL WHOEVER YOU ARE, YOU'RE NOT ON THE LIST. SO WHY DON'T YOU TURN AROUND AND--
EASY, LUKE...

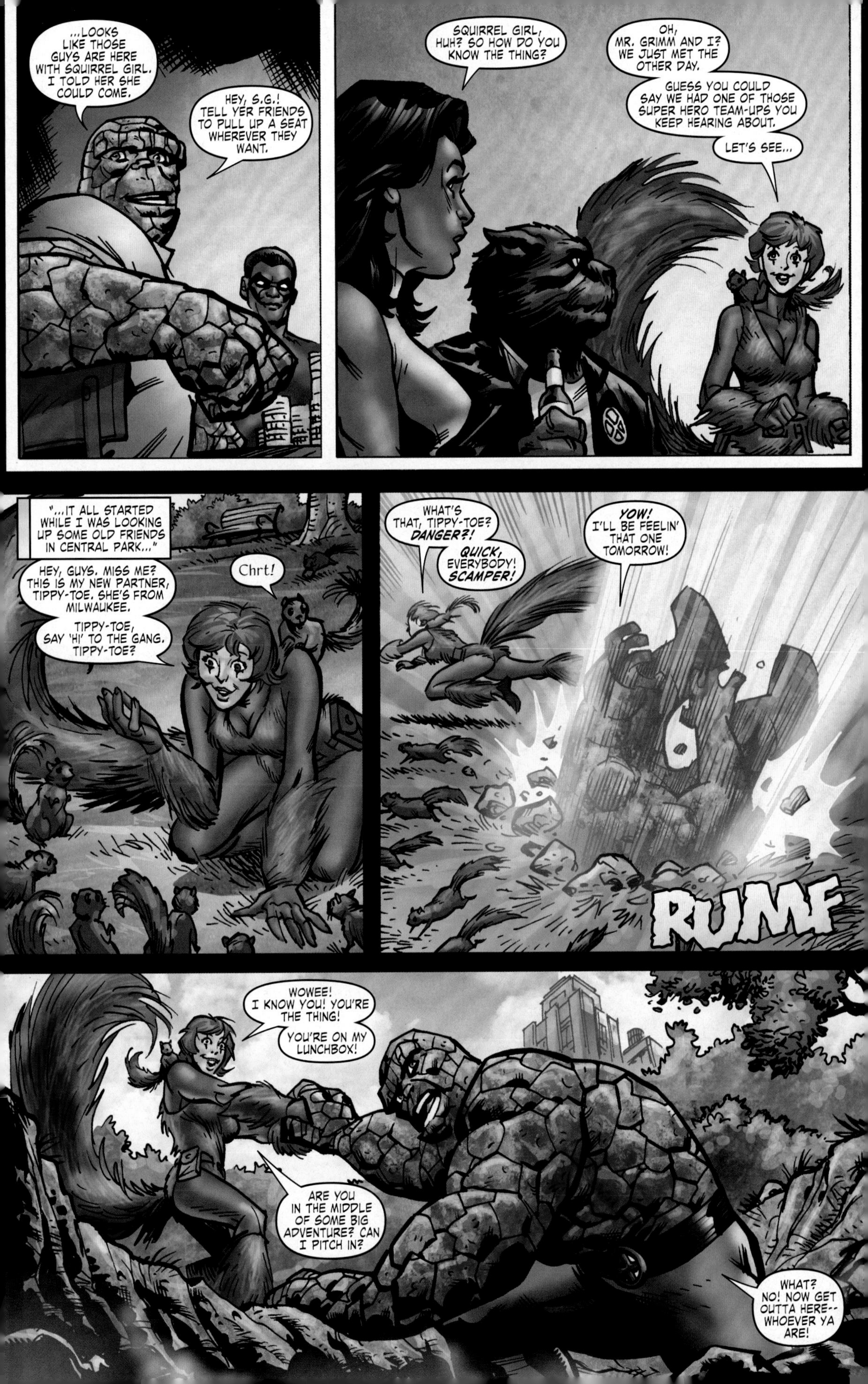
...LOOKS LIKE THOSE GUYS ARE HERE WITH SQUIRREL GIRL. I TOLD HER SHE COULD COME.
HEY, S.G.! TELL YER FRIENDS TO PULL UP A SEAT WHEREVER THEY WANT.
SQUIRREL GIRL, HUH? SO HOW DO YOU KNOW THE THING?
OH, MR. GRIMM AND I? WE JUST MET THE OTHER DAY.
GUESS YOU COULD SAY WE HAD ONE OF THOSE SUPER HERO TEAM-UPS YOU KEEP HEARING ABOUT.
LET'S SEE...
"...IT ALL STARTED WHILE I WAS LOOKING UP SOME OLD FRIENDS IN CENTRAL PARK..."
HEY, GUYS. MISS ME? THIS IS MY NEW PARTNER, TIPPY-TOE. SHE'S FROM MILWAUKEE.
TIPPY-TOE, SAY 'HI' TO THE GANG. TIPPY-TOE?
Chrt!
WHAT'S THAT, TIPPY-TOE? DANGER?!
QUICK, EVERYBODY! SCAMPER!
YOW! I'LL BE FEELIN' THAT ONE TOMORROW!
RUMF
WOWEE! I KNOW YOU! YOU'RE THE THING!
YOU'RE ON MY LUNCHBOX!
ARE YOU IN THE MIDDLE OF SOME BIG ADVENTURE? CAN I PITCH IN?
WHAT? NO! NOW GET OUTTA HERE-- WHOEVER YA ARE!

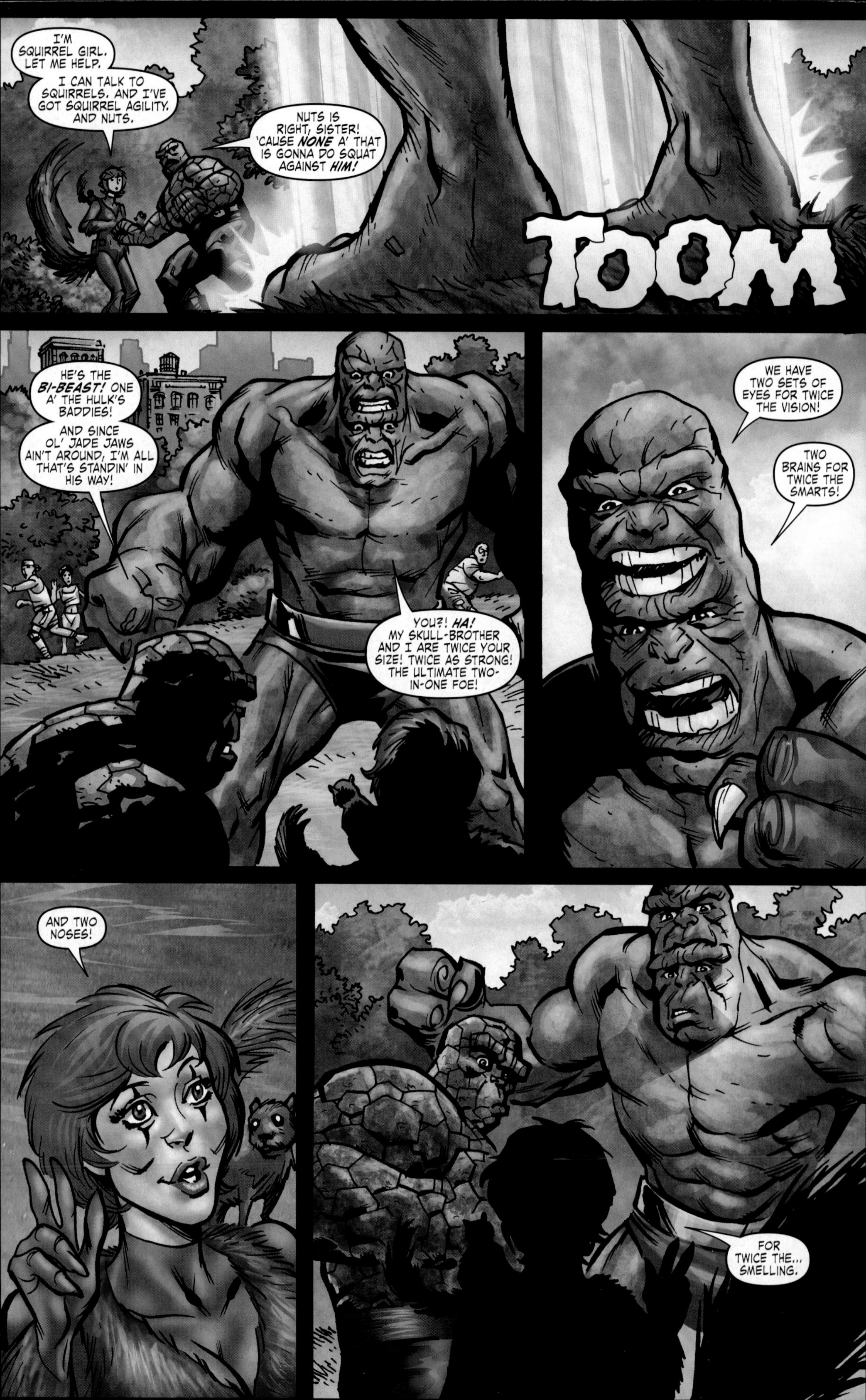
I'M SQUIRREL GIRL. LET ME HELP.
I CAN TALK TO SQUIRRELS. AND I'VE GOT SQUIRREL AGILITY. AND NUTS.
NUTS IS RIGHT, SISTER! 'CAUSE NONE A' THAT IS GONNA DO SQUAT AGAINST HIM!
TOOM
HE'S THE BI-BEAST! ONE A' THE HULK'S BADDIES!
AND SINCE OL' JADE JAWS AIN'T AROUND, I'M ALL THAT'S STANDIN' IN HIS WAY!
YOU?! HA! MY SKULL-BROTHER AND I ARE TWICE YOUR SIZE! TWICE AS STRONG! THE ULTIMATE TWO-IN-ONE FOE!
WE HAVE TWO SETS OF EYES FOR TWICE THE VISION!
TWO BRAINS FOR TWICE THE SMARTS!
AND TWO NOSES!
FOR TWICE THE... SMELLING.

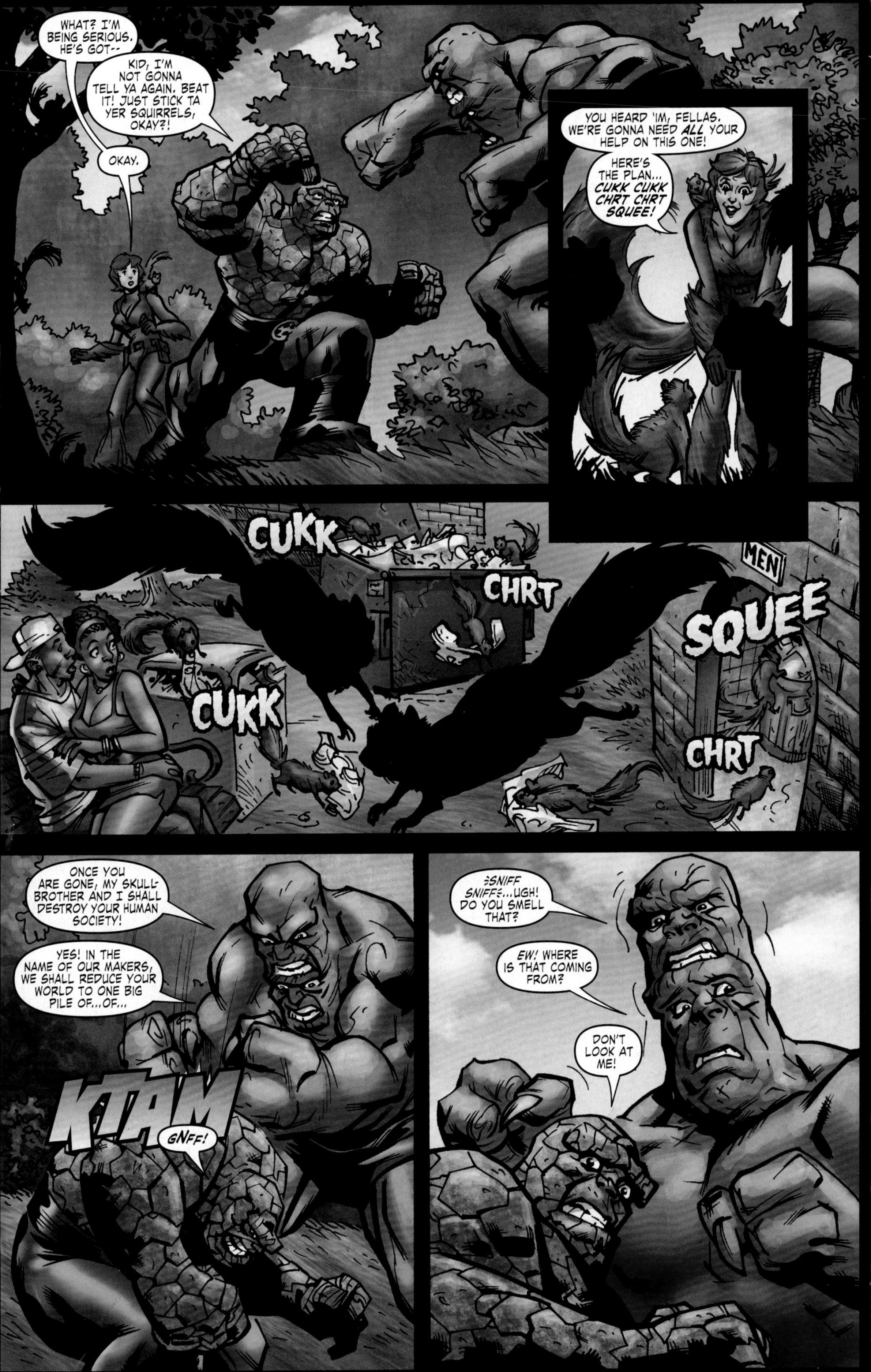
WHAT? I'M BEING SERIOUS. HE'S GOT--
KID, I'M NOT GONNA TELL YA AGAIN. BEAT IT! JUST STICK TA YER SQUIRRELS, OKAY?!
OKAY.
YOU HEARD 'IM, FELLAS. WE'RE GONNA NEED ALL YOUR HELP ON THIS ONE!
HERE'S THE PLAN... CUKK CUKK CHRT CHRT SQUEE!
CUKK
CHRT
MEN
SQUEE
CUKK
CHRT
ONCE YOU ARE GONE, MY SKULL-BROTHER AND I SHALL DESTROY YOUR HUMAN SOCIETY!
YES! IN THE NAME OF OUR MAKERS, WE SHALL REDUCE YOUR WORLD TO ONE BIG PILE OF...OF...
KTAM
GNFF!
SNIFF SNIFF...UGH! DO YOU SMELL THAT?
EW! WHERE IS THAT COMING FROM?
DON'T LOOK AT ME!

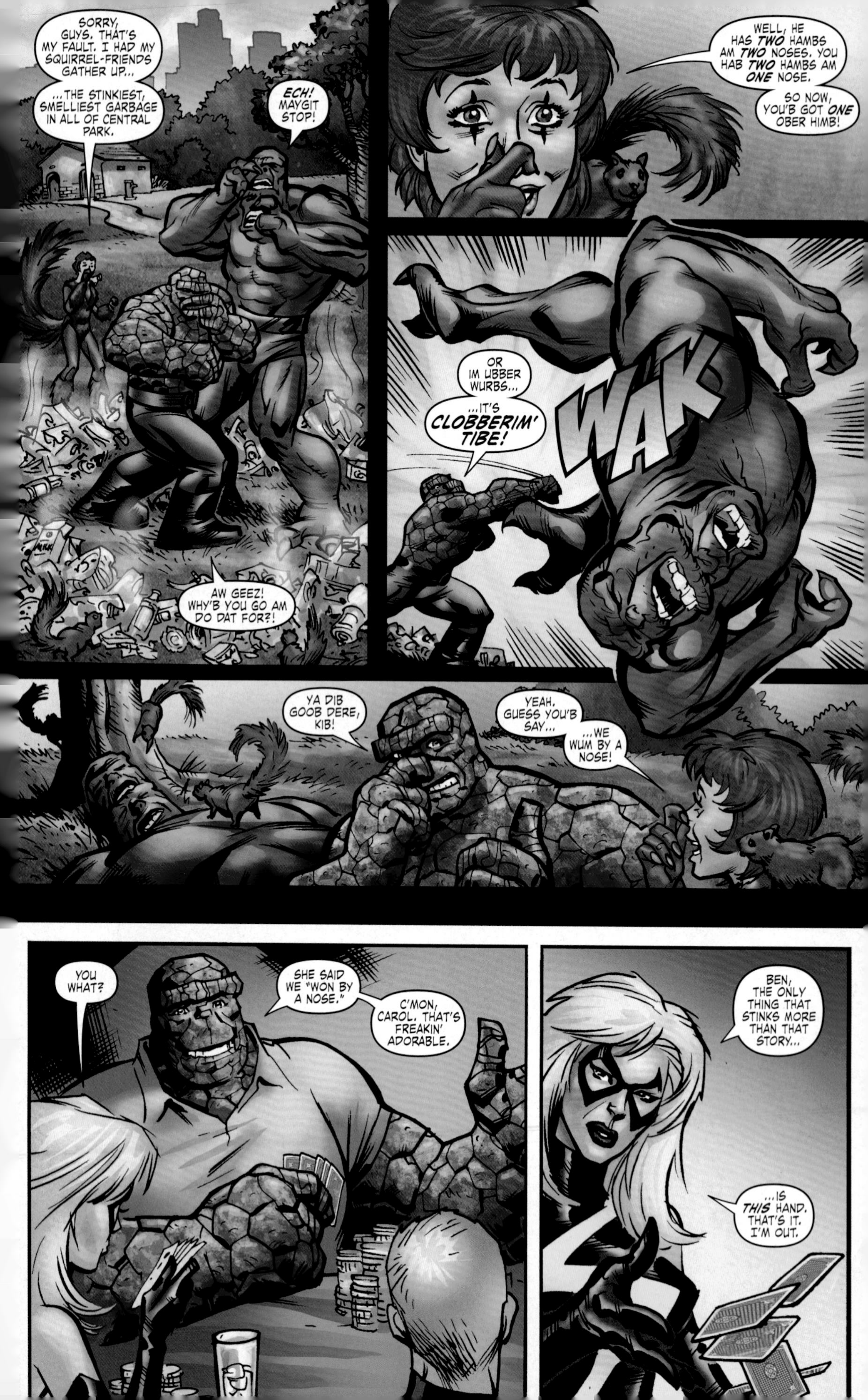
SORRY, GUYS. THAT'S MY FAULT. I HAD MY SQUIRREL-FRIENDS GATHER UP...
...THE STINKIEST, SMELLIEST GARBAGE IN ALL OF CENTRAL PARK.
ECH! MAYGIT STOP!
AW GEEZ! WHY'B YOU GO AM DO DAT FOR?!
WELL, HE HAS TWO HAMBS AM TWO NOSES. YOU HAB TWO HAMBS AM ONE NOSE.
SO NOW, YOU'B GOT ONE OBER HIMB!
OR IM UBBER WURBS...
...IT'S CLOBBERIM' TIBE!
WAK
YA DIB GOOB DERE, KIB!
YEAH. GUESS YOU'B SAY...
...WE WUM BY A NOSE!
YOU WHAT?
SHE SAID WE "WON BY A NOSE."
C'MON, CAROL. THAT'S FREAKIN' ADORABLE.
BEN, THE ONLY THING THAT STINKS MORE THAN THAT STORY...
...IS THIS HAND. THAT'S IT. I'M OUT.

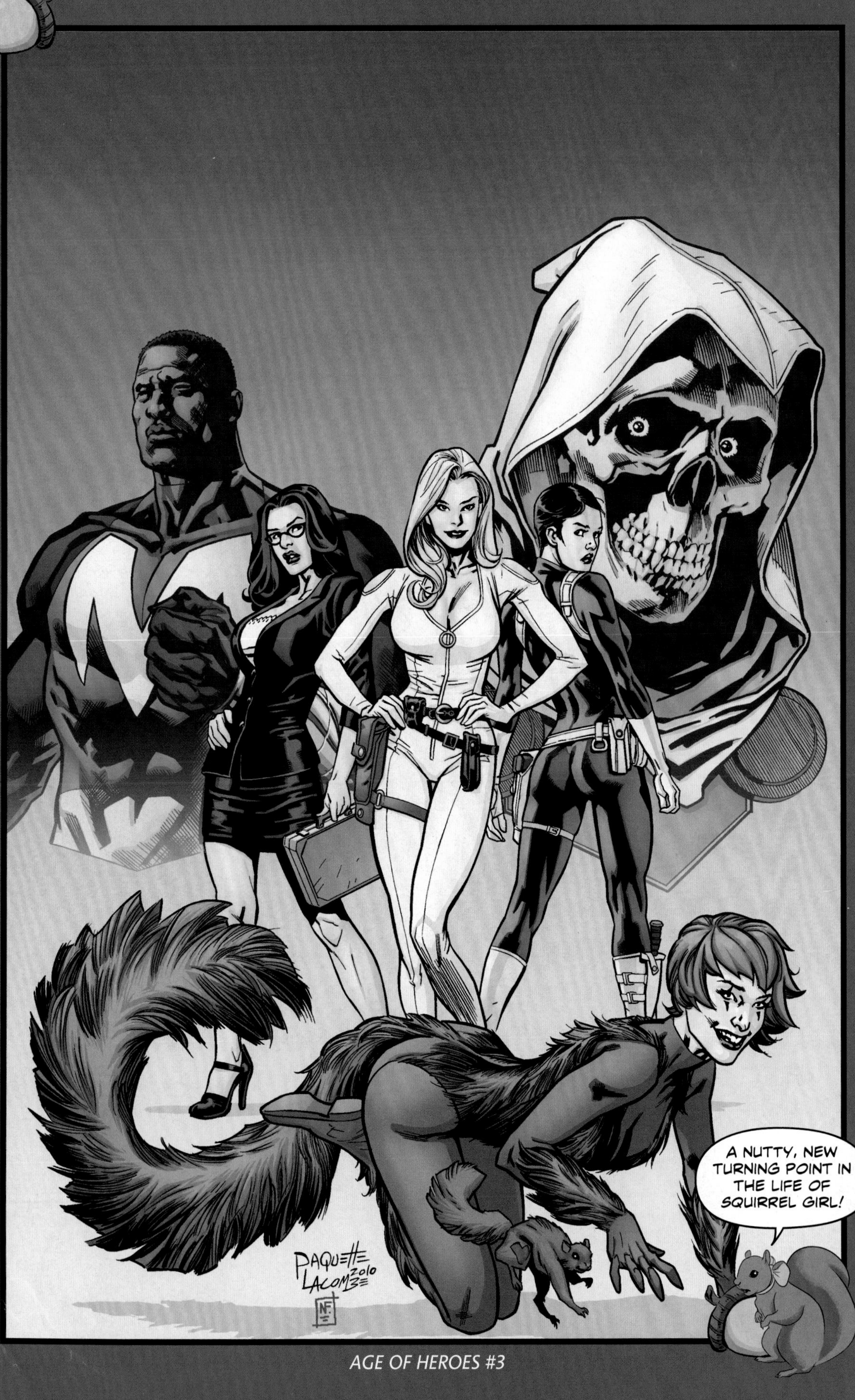
A NUTTY, NEW TURNING POINT IN THE LIFE OF SQUIRREL GIRL!

AGE OF HEROES #3

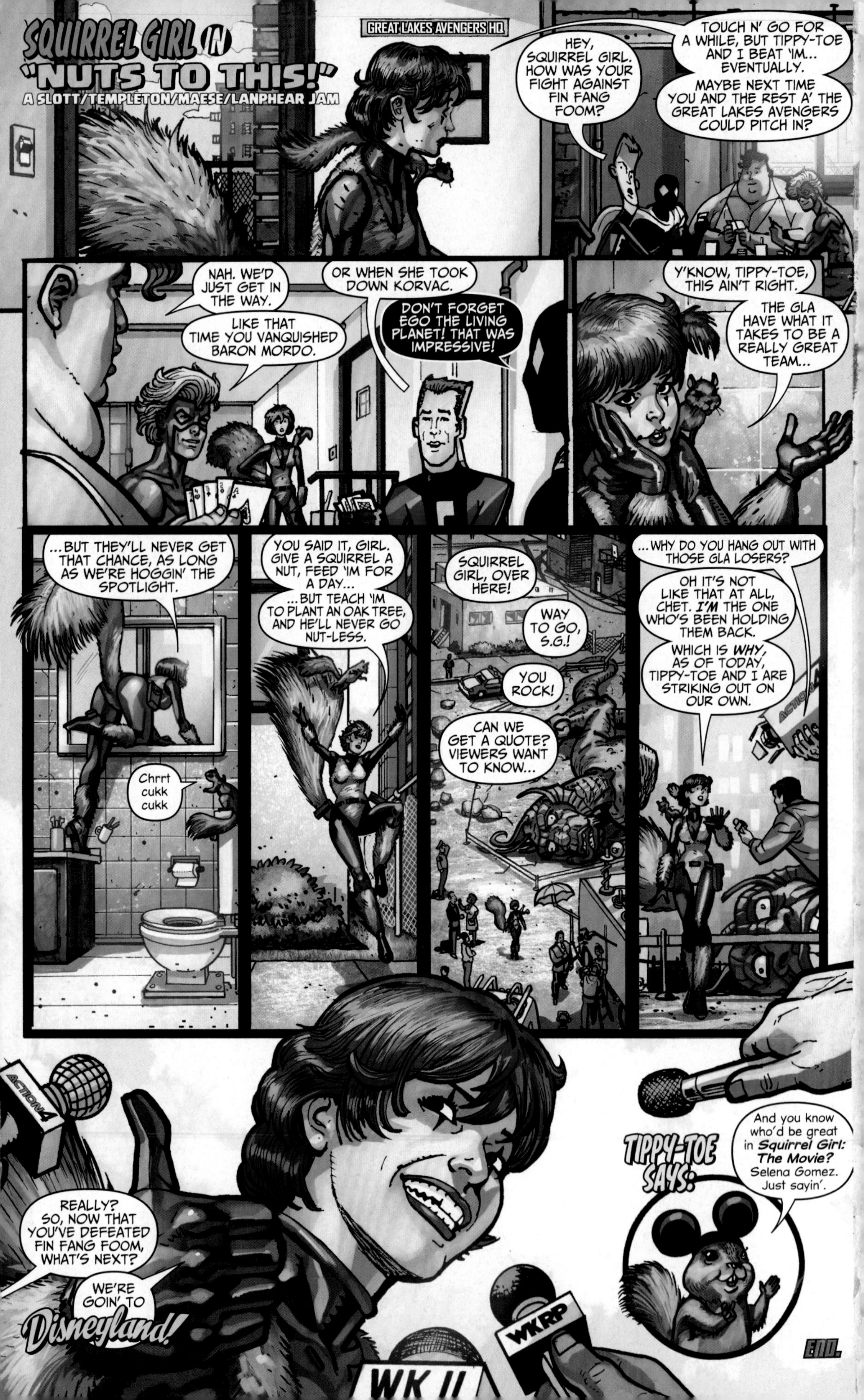

SQUIRREL GIRL IN
"NUTS TO THIS!"
A SLOTT/TEMPLETON/MAESE/LANPHEAR JAM
GREAT LAKES AVENGERS HQ
HEY, SQUIRREL GIRL. HOW WAS YOUR FIGHT AGAINST FIN FANG FOOM?
TOUCH N' GO FOR A WHILE, BUT TIPPY-TOE AND I BEAT 'IM... EVENTUALLY.
MAYBE NEXT TIME YOU AND THE REST A' THE GREAT LAKES AVENGERS COULD PITCH IN?
NAH. WE'D JUST GET IN THE WAY.
LIKE THAT TIME YOU VANQUISHED BARON MORDO.
OR WHEN SHE TOOK DOWN KORVAC.
DON'T FORGET EGO THE LIVING PLANET! THAT WAS IMPRESSIVE!
Y'KNOW, TIPPY-TOE, THIS AIN'T RIGHT.
THE GLA HAVE WHAT IT TAKES TO BE A REALLY GREAT TEAM...
...BUT THEY'LL NEVER GET THAT CHANCE, AS LONG AS WE'RE HOGGIN' THE SPOTLIGHT.
Chrrt cukk cukk
YOU SAID IT, GIRL. GIVE A SQUIRREL A NUT, FEED 'IM FOR A DAY...
...BUT TEACH 'IM TO PLANT AN OAK TREE, AND HE'LL NEVER GO NUT-LESS.
SQUIRREL GIRL, OVER HERE!
WAY TO GO, S.G.!
YOU ROCK!
CAN WE GET A QUOTE? VIEWERS WANT TO KNOW...
...WHY DO YOU HANG OUT WITH THOSE GLA LOSERS?
OH IT'S NOT LIKE THAT AT ALL, CHET. *I'M* THE ONE WHO'S BEEN HOLDING THEM BACK.
WHICH IS *WHY*, AS OF TODAY, TIPPY-TOE AND I ARE STRIKING OUT ON OUR OWN.
ACTION 4
REALLY? SO, NOW THAT YOU'VE DEFEATED FIN FANG FOOM, WHAT'S NEXT?
WE'RE GOIN' TO
Disneyland!
TIPPY-TOE SAYS:
And you know who'd be great in **Squirrel Girl: The Movie?** Selena Gomez. Just sayin'.
WKRP
WK II
END.